Karen Jackson Taylor is a widow. She is trained in bereavement counselling and was active, until the death of her husband. She has a DPhil in the management of teams. Her thesis formed the basis of her book, *The Power of Difference*, published in 2008 (Management Books, 2000), which she wrote under her professional name of Karen Jackson. For many years she ran the boutique consultancy, The Deva Partnership Ltd, with her husband, Ian Taylor, working for organisations in the UK, Europe and America, such as the oil majors and the Post Office. She was motivated to write this book because so many of her friends were being bereaved and she realised that what was needed was a reference point for all the questions that invariably need to be answered.

Christine Pearson is a psychotherapist with sixteen years' clinical experience, having worked at London Metropolitan University, Woman's Trust Charity and The Counselling Partnership in Surrey. She is currently in private practice in south-west London. She trained at Regent's University in London in integrative psychotherapy, with an emphasis on psychodynamic psychotherapy. She later trained with Dr Richman in EMDR, and uses this treatment as a first choice for PTSD and emotional traumas arising from early life insecure attachment.

KAREN JACKSON TAYLOR
CHRISTINE PEARSON

HOW TO SURVIVE LOSING A LOVED ONE

Coping with your partner's terminal
illness and death, and building the
next chapter in your life

ROBINSON

ROBINSON

First published in Great Britain in 2020
by Robinson

10 9 8 7 6 5 4 3 2 1

A CIP catalogue record for this book
is available from the British Library.

ISBN: 978-1-47214-525-3

Typeset in Sentinel and Scala Sans
by Ian Hughes

Printed and bound in Great Britain
by Clays Ltd, Elcograf S.p.A.

Papers used by Robinson are from well-
managed forests and other responsible
sources.

Robinson
An imprint of
Little, Brown Book Group
Carmelite House
50 Victoria Embankment
London EC4Y 0DZ

An Hachette UK Company
www.hachette.co.uk

www.littlebrown.co.uk

How To Books are published by
Robinson, an imprint of Little, Brown
Book Group. We welcome proposals
from authors who have first-hand
experience of their subjects. Please set
out the aims of your book, its target
market and its suggested contents in
an email to howto@littlebrown.co.uk.

In loving memory of Ian

To my darling Georgie and Lucas

Contents

Preface

This book has been written as a guide for all those people who are faced with a terminal or life-limiting illness diagnosis or the death of their partner, with whom they are, or were, in a relationship and whose care they are responsible for, whether they are a man or a woman. There is also a section about what it means to lose a partner in a transgender situation. The information contained is intended to support anyone who is losing or has lost a loved one permanently and needs to adapt to the alien world that they now find themselves in. You do not have to be married or in a civil partnership to find this book useful. A basic assumption is that you care about your partner and want to do the best you can for them, whether living or dead, although we also recognise that many people are responsible for the care of a partner for whom their feelings have degenerated. We also recognise that people vary enormously and that to make generalisations about, for example, how the different sexes feel and behave in these situations is to invite criticism; but our experience tells us that men and women do grieve differently and do have different needs and requirements following the death of their partner, and we have tried to reflect those differences in the text where we think they would be helpful.

The book offers advice on what has to be done when a death occurs, where you have little or no choice in what you have to do (legal requirements, for example), and what has to be done where you do have choices (planning the type of funeral you want, deciding on cremation or burial, and so forth). We have also included suggestions for what you might do as the weeks and months go by to restore yourself to some sort of equilibrium and hopefulness for the future. What we will never mention is that we think you will 'get over it', or indeed that you should 'get over it'. You never 'get over' a soul-wounding loss, but you do learn to live with it, the pain becomes less severe and sometimes happiness returns. The purpose of this book is to enable you to prepare for a loss that you know is coming, respond to the immediate after-effects of that loss, and find as much happiness as you are capable of regaining afterwards.

All information in this book refers to the United Kingdom unless specifically stated. However, laws, statutes and regulations can vary between the four kingdoms, i.e. England and Wales (generally the same but not always), Scotland and Northern Ireland. For example, the Burial Laws Amendment Act 1880 has been superseded in Wales by The Welsh Church (Burial Grounds) Act 1945. Scotland, too, has its own laws; for example, there the role of the English coroner has been taken over by the procurator fiscal and the rules pertaining to them are slightly different to those of a coroner in England and Wales. In as many cases as we can where we think it is pertinent, we have made a point of explaining what the differences are, but we have been unable to be comprehensive owing to the sheer weight of the information involved. If you live outside England and Wales, you are encouraged to check on issues relating to officialdom where you live.

When we name organisations, especially commercial ones, we are not necessarily endorsing them but simply signposting where you can get support and advice or purchase particular items. It is entirely up to you whether you decide to avail yourself of their services after doing your due diligence and the appropriate research. It is important to mention that we have no commercial arrangement with any organisation.

We appreciate that not everyone has access to the internet or can use a search engine like Google, so wherever possible we have included phone numbers and the hours that these are available which are correct at the time of writing.

The tone we have tried to adopt is that of a knowledgeable friend at your shoulder who, having gone through all this themselves, is passing on what they have learned. As in a real situation, because everyone's circumstances are different, you must feel free to reject any suggestion we make or advice we give when it doesn't suit you, but hopefully only after you have given the suggestion or advice some consideration and know why you are rejecting it.

Disclaimer: Situations, organisations and laws change over time, and although the information was as correct as we could make it at the time of publication, you are advised to check it yourself before proceeding with anything, particularly of a legal nature. The legal advice has been checked thoroughly, but you are advised to use a solicitor if there is any doubt in your mind, especially if the issue concerns powers of attorney, wills or inheritance tax.

Another source of help to keep you up to date is our blog: www.howtosurvivelosingalovedone.blog, which is designed to reflect updates in the law and other information relevant to the subject.

Introduction

Having a terminal or life-limiting diagnosis or situation and loss

Learning that your partner has a terminal diagnosis, or suddenly losing someone with whom you have been sharing your life, is a traumatic and devastating experience. It takes time to come to terms with it. If the relationship was a happy one, there is the anguish of facing life without that special someone. If the situation was less than happy, many difficult truths may surface that you have to acknowledge and deal with. The situation is further complicated if you have children, stepchildren or adopted children, as besides your own distress you will have to take theirs into account, and sometimes the solutions to the issues causing distress might be in conflict.

Coping with the death of your partner starts for many people with the news that there is no more treatment available or that a chronic illness is gradually becoming more acute and that it is only a question of time before the end, even if some palliative care or life-lengthening treatment is available. As we believe that the interim period before death is as demanding to deal with as the death itself, and needs as much practical support, we have started with the diagnosis. Equally, many of you reading this book will be faced with the death itself, which, if it is sudden – for example, caused by a stroke, heart attack, suicide, accident, murder or manslaughter – will be overwhelming in its complexity and immediacy, as there has been no time at all to plan. In this case, Part Three of the book onwards will be most relevant to you. Most people, however, do have some warning and can spend at least some time getting their affairs in order, with or without the support of their partner.

Loss, bereavement and mourning are shared human experiences, but they are also uniquely individual ones. Although many people will have undergone a similar bereavement, no one will have been in exactly the same situation as you are, with exactly the same set of feelings, family configurations, issues and problems that you have. And although people are in general eager to help, you are the only one who can find your way through the minefield that is family relationships and the maze of untangling your life and your persona from the person who is about to depart, or who has just departed from it.

What this book aims to do

That is where this book comes in. There is plenty of information out there. It is knowing what you want and accessing it that is the difficulty. Nearly everyone nowadays has access to a computer or knows someone who has, and even though not everyone is computer savvy, most people (but we appreciate not all) can use a search engine to find out what they want from official websites.

Most relevant organisations have a helpline and contact phone numbers, and we have made a point of including these as we know that some of you will much prefer using the telephone and may not have access to a computer. Many organisations, such as your local Registry Office of Births, Deaths and Marriages, Age UK, Which? or Citizens Advice, and banks such as the Halifax, are also able to provide you with literature that is helpful. However, what you need as you progress through the difficulties of a terminal diagnosis or a death is something where all the information you will need is in one place, and not only gives you as much information as possible about what you need to do and when, but also tells you about your choices when they are available.

We have tried to offer you advice only when we think it is necessary and helpful, and to warn you of difficulties that you might encounter. Our overall aim is to give you the freedom to choose. A book is portable and always there as a handy reference point that you can easily take with you wherever you need to go. All decisions you have to make are clearly designated. We have tried to be wary about giving you too much advice, but have, hopefully, offered you things to think about that you might try. We have included lists of publications, organisations, websites and other sources of information at the end of every Part, as well as at the end of the book, for you to explore for yourself, so that you can use this book as a source of reference long after the event has occurred.

A reference book like this isn't meant to be read as a novel. The idea is that, although you may want to read one of the Parts right through because it suits your situation, the likelihood is that you will access its contents through the Index (p. 336) or through the Questions (Appendix 6, p. 322) that are listed separately at the end of the book, Part by Part. As a result, you will no doubt see that we have repeated ourselves quite a lot, especially on such issues as inheritance and intestacy (where there is no will) and, more contentiously, on organ donation. Bear with us! Owing to the difficulties of taking in information when one is in a stressed or anxious state, we felt it was better to give the information more than once than not to give it at all, and sometimes the contexts are different.

It may surprise some people to realise that grieving and loss can begin long before a terminal diagnosis is given or a death occurs. One partner can see the other partner change before their eyes in ways that makes it very difficult to cope with and accept. One clear example of this is any kind of dementia, where a partner's personality changes completely to the point that they cannot recognise who their loved one is. A debilitating illness can have the same effect, but it is the announcement that an illness is terminal that requires the surviving partner to acknowledge that the time left is limited and precious. This guide begins, therefore, with the practical steps needed to be taken before the death takes place. It covers what you need to know to survive, how to protect yourself and your family, and tries to ensure that at the very least you are not left destitute or mentally incapacitated.

How the guide is arranged

When your partner is given a terminal diagnosis or you are told that there is nothing more that can be done for them, the most important thing will be for you to ensure that they receive the best palliative care – care that is as pain-free and dignified as possible. You will want to plug in to as much help as you can, either from the National Health Service, the local authority, or, if appropriate, charities, local care homes and carers. You will want to plan ahead. Depending on their condition, your partner will want to make sure that you and any children have the best possible provision after they have gone. They might want to get married, make a will, take out powers of attorney, or plan ahead for what they want to happen with their treatment, and perhaps more importantly, what they do not want to happen. They may want to plan their funeral down to the last note, and may have a list of things that they want to accomplish, from reconciliations with family members to round-the-world trips if that is still a possibility. Parts One and Two of this book suggest what you may want to happen as well as how to bring it about.

After a death there are a thousand and one practical things that have to be seen to. Nearly always (except where there is no body or the body has to be repatriated) the most essential primary task is the funeral, followed by the granting of probate, which officially gives an appropriate person the right to dispose of the dead person's estate. A funeral is a surprisingly complicated thing to arrange, especially when your mind is in a whirlwind. In Parts Three and Four we cut through the obfuscation and tell you what you need to know; for example, the implications of choosing a burial or a cremation, whether you can bury your loved one in the garden, whether you need a coffin, and much more – even whether you would like your loved one to be helping to revive a coral reef after cremation.

Where there has been a chronic illness, death can be sudden and unexpected. Sometimes this is the result of the illness they are suffering from, where the loved one has deteriorated in health surprisingly quickly, or it might be the result of, for example, a stroke, heart attack or brain haemorrhage occurring as a result of the underlying illness. If the person has been receiving treatment, the death might be acceptable to the authorities and a doctor will sign the death certificate, but in other circumstances the death might be considered 'unexplained' and a coroner may need to make an official enquiry. This will always happen in the case of accidents, suicide, murder and manslaughter. A post-mortem may have to be held, followed by an inquest to officially decide the cause of death. All this can be very difficult for the surviving partner and our aim here is to help you understand what to expect.

Part Five is about the grieving process: what you can expect to happen, what might happen and what you can do about it. Grieving is in itself a healthy and natural process and a price we pay for caring. However, your mind and body have to spend much of your energy adjusting to the shock and the world you now find yourself in. This means that you may behave differently to the way you usually do – by being less aware of what is happening to you, being more forgetful, and in extreme cases feeling as if you are going mad. We try to show you that this is very unlikely to be the case.

But sometimes a death can raise issues that may have been under the surface or hidden before the person died and are now exacerbated by the death; for example, the knowledge that you can never say certain things to them. This is sometimes called complex or complicated grief. In this case you may need counselling help. Several specialist organisations exist to give support to the bereaved, including those bereaved by murder or suicide and for children. You may become depressed or unable to sleep or eat, and may need support from your GP. Or you may decide that the issues you have are long-standing and that you want to undertake some form of psychotherapy in order to re-establish your identity. There are also certain therapies that you can undertake in order to overcome trauma such as that which occurs following death in a road accident. All these situations and issues are discussed in great detail in Part Six so that you can decide for yourself which is the right course of action for you to take.

Part Six is primarily about the person you are and the person you will become after the death. You will not believe it for some time, but what has happened to you is an opportunity to take control of your life and be the person you want to be. At first you will be so exhausted you will not want to do anything except survive, but gradually you will feel the odd brief flash of happiness and be again the person you used to be. This Part explains what you can do and what might work for you as life returns. Sometimes, having been in a close partnership, we forget who we really are and the new person needs to be established. This is often a painful process and not without its heartache, but gradually it will happen. We have put in a few exercises here to help you make progress.

The words we use

We had something of a dilemma in what to call the person you have lost. The words 'loved one' or 'partner' cover a lot of different situations. Sometimes, we are actually referring to husbands, wives or civil partners (both same-sex and heterosexual), owing to the legal provisions that pertain to them because you are, or were, married, such as inheritance laws. On other occasions, what we are saying refers to your partner, whether or not you are married or in a civil partnership, and is relevant to such actions as taking out powers of attorney. Where the subject matter is sensitive, we sometimes refer to your loved one, but to do so all the time would be cloying and, indeed, it may not be true, so we have been economical with that phrase.

As the book has been written jointly by two of us, we mostly refer to 'we'. However, there are some anecdotes and specialist information that clearly originate from the experience or knowledge of either one or other of us, and to say 'we' in those circumstances would be rather odd. In those cases we have used 'I' and hope it is not too jarring. This particularly refers to Part Six.

Further material, such as books, articles, websites and organisations that you might find helpful, is listed at the end of each Part for easy reference. These are listed again alphabetically at the end in the Bibliography, which also includes books not mentioned in the text. We asked people we knew what books had been helpful to them and have included these with a few words of description from the person who suggested them.

We have put a series of blank templates in the Appendices section at the end of the book for you to make a start on. Keeping notes is a very good way of discerning what progress you have made.

Lastly, we have tried to be sensitive about when we make reference to the ending of life. We do not particularly like the phrase 'passed over', although it is used by many bereaved people and funeral directors, and we can see that it softens the finality of what has happened. We must apologise if you find our use of the words death and dying insensitive and uncaring. We certainly do not want you to feel that way.

Contact us

Our primary aim has been to give you as much support as possible at a difficult time. If you think we have missed anything out, or that we have got something wrong, or just want to make a comment on your reaction to the book, please do not hesitate to contact us with your experiences: deva.karen@btinternet.com. For up-to-date information on laws or provisions that may have changed since the book was written, please visit our blog: www.howtosurvivelosingyourlovedone.blog.

Part One

A Terminal Diagnosis or Life-Ending Illness – What Can I Do Immediately in Terms of Planning and Care?

1
Introduction

If your partner has just had a frightening diagnosis of an illness that is terminal or they are suddenly totally incapacitated by illness or accident, you will be consumed with shock and probably unable to think clearly. It may be difficult to do anything other than react to the immediate needs of the sick person and gather your relatives around you for support and comfort. The thought of their death may be the last thing you want to think about, and providing for yourself after their death may seem extremely selfish and uncaring. This is all completely understandable.

However, your life will go on after their death, and you will save yourself a great deal of distress and heartache in the future if you can stay calm and start making plans, both for the person who is dying and for yourself, as soon as possible after hearing the news. This is what this Part is all about. It aims to give you as much support as possible concerning what you are able to and should do before your loved one dies. In addition to the two scenarios described above, it will also be helpful for those with a partner with a chronic illness who might be expected to die within twelve months or so, or sooner if some unforeseen medical event occurs such as pneumonia, sepsis or a blood clot.

Clearly, there will be a considerable spectrum of ways in which the person concerned can help you, ranging from not at all – perhaps because they are in a coma or unconscious – at one end, to being perfectly able to make decisions that affect you both, now and after their death, at the other. Some partners will not want to be involved, or will refuse to consider the subject of their demise, perhaps because they are in denial, but others, knowing how much it will help you, or because they are blessed with neat and tidy minds, will be only too willing to get involved. At the other extreme, they may turn this into their last all-consuming project, with an attention to detail that might surprise you and may become somewhat unnerving and overwhelming.

What you will want to prepare for will also depend on the person who is dying and the person who is left behind, and their role in your partnership. It might be useful at this stage to prepare a list of who does what and then think about how you will plug the gaps in your experience or knowledge for after they have gone. There is also the issue of the parenting role and what is involved in bringing up your children if you have some and they are still at the age where they need your support. Some of this might divide into male and female roles, but we have tried to steer away from this contentious issue. Some of the things we suggest, such as gathering computer passwords or checking where the stopcock is, will take a bit of effort when you are probably only wanting to spend time with your loved one. Others are shared things, such as planning the type of funeral your loved one wants; this gives them and you the comfort of knowing that you are doing what they wanted when the time comes.

You will have your own idea of priorities. We have listed them in an order that makes sense to us, but this is not a novel – you will not be reading it from cover to cover – so you can dip in and out as seems appropriate. Before we list the priorities, we just want to say something about the effect that the news might have on you both.

Just to remind you – we are in an age of civil partnerships and living together, as well as of marriage, so the terms your 'spouse', your 'loved one' and your 'partner' have been used in the text interchangeably, as appropriate, in order to avoid just one of them being over used.

2

Receiving the News and Understanding the Diagnosis and Treatment

It may be that the first decision your partner has to make is whether or not to have treatment. That might be an easy decision for some, but as their condition weakens it may be that more and more of the contents of Parts One and Two become relevant. It is only a question of time. However, a diagnosis that no more treatment is available; that treatment is only likely to delay the end, not prevent it; that a chronic illness has become terminal; or that your loved one has been suddenly stricken with a totally incapacitating disease or accident, is always going to be a shock that reduces you to helpless panic in the first instance. Gradually, though, the shock will lessen and you will realise that you have to start functioning in the best interests of your partner and your family.

Your doctor or other healthcare professional should give you and your partner all the information you need about your diagnosis and possible treatments, including your options, the pros and cons of treatments, potential risks and side effects. If your partner doesn't want treatment, your doctor should explain the consequences of them not having it. If you want a second opinion, you should ask for one. You have no legal right to a second opinion on the NHS, although you could pay for one privately. If your partner is totally incapacitated and unable to make decisions and you have power of attorney (see p. 54), you will be able to take decisions for them. If you have an advance decision (living will) (see p. 58) already in place, this will also enable you to make the decisions your partner would have wanted if they cannot decide for themselves. The question to ask your partner if you are able to is this: 'Do you understand the implications of your illness?'

Reacting to the news

Before you start planning and organising, it is useful to think about how your loved one might be reacting to the news and what you can expect in how they behave. Assuming that your partner is not in a coma or otherwise totally incapacitated, you may find that they react to the news in a number of different ways. They may be in the same shocked condition as you are, especially if the news is unexpected.

Fear

They may feel fear: fear concerning how you and/or your children might manage without them, that there will not be enough money to support you, especially if they are the breadwinner; or fear about the dying process, the pain they might suffer and the indignity they may have to undergo.

Anger

They may feel anger that their life is being taken from them before it should be and that they will not see their children growing up – and, depending on their ages, their first steps or going to school or university, or seeing them find love with a partner of their own – or their grandchildren do so. They may be angry that they will not be able to spend their retirement years with you when you have both worked so hard to provide your children with a home and education, and now are in a better position to spend money on yourselves. They may also feel angry about some aspect of their diagnosis and treatment; that something was missed early on and now it is too late. They may feel angry that a certain treatment is not available to them that could prolong their life, especially if you have young children, through cost or age limitations.

They may feel resentment that people who have led less blameless lives than them are not undergoing the suffering and pain that is currently their lot. They may be asking themselves and you, 'Why me?'

Denial

They may be in denial; that is, they simply do not accept the diagnosis. 'There has been a mistake! It's not me!' They may ask you to check again with the medical staff, to tell them that it can't be true, that they have got their results mixed up with someone else's. This can all be very hard on you – for example, when you are put in the difficult position of having to query the diagnosis with medical staff – but rest assured, they have gone through this process a million times and will sympathise with you both.

Another form of denial is to simply not want to get involved in planning for death. In this case there is no point causing disharmony and resentment by insisting. You will just have to get on and do what you can in a way that makes sense to you. Your loved one may feel a sense of helplessness. They simply do not know what to do. Their usual purposefulness and management abilities have leached out of them and they cannot see which way to turn. This is where this Part can be particularly useful, as it gives you both the prompts you need and the practical guidance to do what you can to arrange as much of your affairs as possible before death occurs.

Sadness

On hearing the news of a terminal illness, some people are overwhelmed with sadness – all those things they will never be able to see and places they will never be able to go! There is a real risk here that the sadness becomes depression, and it is something to watch out for, as it may be that your doctor will think it safe and appropriate to prescribe some mood-enhancing medication that might make the time remaining for your loved one easier to bear, and give them the energy and motivation to help you with the tasks that need to be done. This, in turn, may give them a sense of satisfaction that they have done the best they can in the circumstances, and that everything is neat and tidy for you to cope with after they have gone.

Frustration

Some people also feel a sense of frustration, because they feel impotent in the face of what life is throwing at them, when previously they felt that they were in control. This can be particularly difficult for those who are of a controlling nature and like to feel that they are in charge. Sometimes people move to a bargaining stage in which they promise to do something if only they may be saved from what is to come. Religious people, for example, may attempt to bargain with God or perhaps call on the aid of St Jude, the Patron Saint of Lost Causes. However, in cases of terminal illness, this is rather unlikely to happen (though not unheard of), and a person moves on to another stage.

Isolation

Your loved one may also feel isolated, even though you, your family and your friends are around them. This is because every person's experience is unique and no one can quite know or understand what another person is experiencing as they approach the final weeks, days or hours before death. Alternatively, your loved one and even you may feel a sense of relief. This might sound odd, but there is something to be said for the realisation that there is no more fighting to be done, no more painful and distressing treatments to be undergone; just an acceptance that what could be done has been done and that now preparations must be focused on the inevitable end and making it as dignified, pain-free and joyous as possible.

All this can feel very disorientating for you as you see the once strong and decisive person you knew crumple before your eyes. However, this is where you can be particularly supportive, first of all by recognising that the reactions listed above are perfectly normal and are, in fact, to be expected. You should explain this to your loved one. Your awareness of, and acceptance of, these feelings can be of great assistance in helping your partner accept their situation. Of course, on occasion (and perhaps more often than that) you will find it very distressing to witness your loved one suffering these emotional and psychological responses over and above their pain and physical disabilities. You are likely to be feeling the same anguish as part of your pre-bereavement grieving (see Part Five on **Grieving and Mourning**), and will sometimes also run out of the energy required to be positive and forward-looking. Of course you will! But the best support you can be to your partner at this time is to bring light and laughter into their life and ensure that their remaining time with you is as happy as it possibly can be. You will be left with some positive memories at the last, with nothing to feel guilty about, and they will feel reassured that you are left in the best possible position that you can both bring about.

For more information on common responses to the knowledge that one is dying, we recommend Elisabeth Kübler-Ross's book *On Death and Dying*, which was based on the author's experience of working with the dying as a psychiatrist. Kübler-Ross produced a five-stage model. Although many people saw this as a linear model with people progressing through the stages, in fact these stages are not linear; any of them can be experienced at any time and many people do not experience all of them but only one or two. It is now often used as a grief model, but its original purpose concerned those who knew they were dying. You might find it useful reading.

3

Issues of Control

Often the first response of anyone who has been given a terminal diagnosis or news of a life-threatening illness is to feel a lack of control. They can feel that non-negotiable processes are playing out without them. 'Events are taking over from me and I have no autonomy left.' This can lead to complete denial on the part of the sufferer and a refusal to do anything to acknowledge or plan for what is going to happen, sooner or later. Denial is itself a form of regaining control, at least in the mind of the denier, even if, subconsciously, a lack of a sense of control can result in all sorts of behaviours that they would be quite ashamed of in other circumstances. You will need to be very patient and understanding about this.

However, your partner may not be the only one with control issues. You may also be exhibiting behaviour that is not helpful either to them or to other members of the family. You may feel that as time is short you do not want to share your partner with anyone else but want to keep them all to yourself. You may be acting as the gatekeeper for access, which means that you are preventing other people, who may have a quite legitimate need to access your partner, from engaging with them. This can cause people to feel cut off – not only friends and relatives but also children and stepchildren. You may feel that your partner has only so much energy and that you need to harness what they have towards yourself. It's important to ask yourself occasionally whether you are allowing others to spend time with your partner and to build up their own memories before they can have no more.

On the other hand, you may not be exerting enough control. When we are in the GP's or consultant's room it is difficult not to experience that feeling of being completely powerless. Faced with this powerful authority figure, we tend to dissolve into lumps of jelly. We forget to ask the list of questions that we carefully wrote down. We don't want to be a nuisance and waste their time. We realise we are only one of many patients they are seeing, and so on. But we need to have an honest and truthful conversation about symptoms, diagnosis and treatment. We need to assert ourselves for the good of our partner. We have to look the consultant in the eye and ask the difficult questions, especially about whether any more treatment really is going to be beneficial. Eric Byrne's book *Games People Play* is helpful here, especially in explaining how we get 'hooked' by the parent figure – in this case the consultant – into becoming the child figure, and how important it is that we stay in the adult role. Another useful book on this subject of what is right for someone at the end of life is Atul Gawande's *Being Mortal*, a book about the priorities that the end of life confronts us with.

Slightly different to when you, the partner, are not being assertive enough is when power is taken away from you by a conspiracy between medical staff and the person who appears to be the authority figure on your side. Take the example of Susan, a high-powered articulate woman, who ran her own successful business, but whose husband's treatment was discussed with her partner's sons, her stepsons, rather than herself, as they were of a similar age to her and assumptions were made about her relationship. As she pointed out to the medical staff, she had been married for thirty-five years and might be expected to know what her husband wanted. The hospital finally conceded unintentional bias and the situation was resolved, but if she had not articulated her disquiet she may have been overruled on several issues by her stepsons. Marriage is always the decider. Unfortunately, if you are 'just' a partner, without power of attorney or an advance statement or living will (advance decision) (see p. 58 for fuller explanations of what these terms mean), you might find yourself overruled not only as to treatment but also on the question of the funeral, where we have known partners to be completely frozen out. You need to protect yourself as much as possible from this happening.

Your children may try to take control because they see you are suffering and they want to lighten the load for you. However, you should always be clear in your own mind when this starts to happen as to whether you are happy for this to continue, and nip it in the bud if it is not what you want. Other people who might feel they are better able to make decisions include your partner's parents and your own parents, especially if you are not married or in a civil partnership, and if you are still quite young and they feel you need that kind of support. I was once a witness to a brother who assumed control of decision-making in a medical emergency for a couple who were mature adults in a same-sex relationship. He was used to people doing what he said and instinctively began to question the treatment and support being offered. Unfortunately, this alienated everyone else who had been trying to help and support fell away.

If you do not take the necessary decisions or appear to be in control, this leaves a vacuum and someone around you will inevitably fill it for selfish or unselfish reasons. Of course there will be times when you are only too glad for someone to take decisions for you, but it is important to be aware that this is happening and to ask yourself whether it is something you want to keep on doing. Equally, this is a time of uncertainty for everyone. You may not have experienced anything like it before. Do not be surprised if you cannot make decisions quickly. Unless a decision has to be made at once on anything, take your time, ask for advice and listen to your instincts as well as the facts. This is particularly true when it comes to further treatment as opposed to palliative care. What does your partner really want out of their remaining months, days and hours?

Let's go on to discuss those practical steps that will leave you as much in control as you reasonably can be, and that you may need to take to make your loved one's life as comfortable as possible.

4
Making Life Easier

The first thing on your agenda will be ensuring that your loved one gets the best possible treatment and support up to the time of their death. As everyone's situation is unique, it is difficult to provide information to cover all eventualities, but we are going to take the approach that someone has just had a life-limiting diagnosis, but they are still able to travel, for example, and then take you through the different stages that might arise.

The first person to consult is your GP, who may well be the person who gave you the news in the first place. It is important that you know the likely stages that your partner's illness will take, so that you can be prepared. You will probably want some sort of timescale, although of course this is difficult to predict – it might be a few weeks or a few months. You and your partner need to sit down and make a list of all the things that seem important for you to do given the time available, and then perhaps you need to discuss it with the rest of your family, children and stepchildren, both sets of parents if they are alive and able to make decisions, and perhaps your friends too. We are taking the approach that any further treatment will be a decision you take based on many factors, but that the treatment will enhance your partner's current quality of life and/or lengthen it, but not prevent the inevitable.

Everyone will have different priorities and different timescales related to what is important to them, especially as the time left will vary in length. The list of things to consider is not meant to be sequential and each item is explored in greater detail later in the book. But it might look something like this:

Plan palliative care: Most people are not afraid of death per se, but of dying. That is because we associate it with pain, indignity and distress. It does not have to be like this. In this section we look at the options on palliative care and what you can do. As this is probably the first thing on everyone's mind, we start with that.

Prepare your children: You may have children for whom the shock will be just as great as for the pair of you. The age of your children will be a big factor here. If they are not really old enough to be able to remember their father or mother very clearly, you will want to remedy that. If your children are older, you may want to give some thought not only to the death but also to the actual dying process and how much of it you want them to witness.

Think about power of attorney, advance care planning, advance decision and advance statement: This is all about talking through with each other how your loved one wants to be treated as their condition deteriorates and they become less able to make their own choices. They will have the peace of mind of knowing that you are doing exactly what they want. Bear in mind that many of these documents cannot be completed unless your partner is able to take decisions both mentally and physically, and you should consider the timescale ahead of you before deciding which ones to choose.

Make a will: This subject is dealt with in some detail in Part Two.

Make your home a safer place to be: As your partner's illness becomes worse and they become more incapacitated, you will find that things they used to do easily, like walking upstairs, become much more difficult. Additionally, your partner might be discharged from hospital and want to be at home, at least in the first instance, so you may have to plan this before they leave hospital. This section considers the changes you can make to your house to make it easier for your partner to move around in or for carers to help you in.

Organise home carers or a nursing home: Your loved one may be at home at the beginning of their diagnosis and want to stay there as long as possible. In that case you may need carers to assist you in looking after them and take some of the burden off you. This section explains how to go about this and what provision the state makes to help you, and is explored in End of Life Care and Palliative Care on p. 26. Alternatively, you may opt for palliative care in a nursing home and need to find a suitable one.

Get married! This might seem a bit odd given that if you are not married or in a civil partnership you probably feel that you have very good reasons why you aren't. However, it may surprise you to learn that getting married or entering a civil partnership can solve a lot of your potential problems at a stroke. These will become obvious as you go through the text, but they mainly have to do with inheritance laws. Planning a wedding does not really come under our remit, but you could have a lot of enjoyment making this into a great celebration of your life! If the thought of arranging and/or paying for this is daunting, there is a charity called The Wedding Wishing Well Foundation that may contribute to the cost and make all the arrangements for you at very short notice, if necessary. You can find out more about the difference between marriage, civil partnership and a cohabitation agreement in Appendix 1.

Plan the funeral: This could be a source of comfort to you both, and will also help you to be more aware of what it is likely to cost. There is information on this in Part Two and a more detailed section on the topic in Part Three.

Decide about organ donation: Max and Keira's Law, which means consent to donate suitable organs will be presumed, with people having to opt out if they wish not to be a donor, came into force in May 2020. One or other of you may feel strongly about this decision and there is information on this topic in Part Two and Part Three.

Stabilise your financial situation: Having an understanding of your financial situation both now and after your partner's death is vitally important. We give you some suggestions as to how you might go about this in Part Two.

Love your computer: If you are a whizz on the computer, you may not need any help here. This will depend mainly on your age group, what your employment involves, how you previously divided up tasks with your partner and your interest in the subject. However, many of the suggestions recorded in this book do need access to a computer search engine, and you may find that you need the internet more than ever before. So, for some of you, here is an opportunity to learn a new skill and join the rest of the world!

Look after your own health: You are no good to anyone, least of all to your partner, if you are not strong and fit enough to cope with all the things that you are going to have to deal with during this very demanding period leading up to the death of your partner. This section suggests some simple ways you can look after yourself. They are augmented in Part Six.

Have a big party: This might be the opportunity for your partner to see people whom they have not seen for a long time and want to say goodbye to, enjoy a celebration, and in some ways have their wake before they die. In fact, there is such a thing as a 'living funeral' that you can organise, where your friends and family can say the things they want to tell your partner before they die, and there are people who can organise this for you. Your partner may find this a tad embarrassing!

Have a bucket list: If your loved one is relatively well, they may want to use the time to write a book or put their family tree in order or do something else that they have always set their heart on. If so, now is the time to get going on it.

Travel: Go somewhere that you both have always wanted to go to or take a holiday, perhaps a cruise, provided your partner is likely to be well enough to enjoy it. There might be difficulties with travel insurance and you might have to be prepared to pay for medical services if your partner's condition deteriorates while you are away or you need repatriation. You may also have to face the fact that your loved one might die abroad, with all the trouble that might cause. However, if you have done your homework and know what to expect, why not? It is best to think carefully about this. In order to help you decide, you may like to acquire a Foreign, Commonwealth and Development Office (FOCD) bereavement pack, which gives guidance on what to do in most countries worldwide.

Achieve peace of mind: This may seem rather an odd thing to put last on this list, but all the preceding things will contribute to you feeling that you have done the best you can in the circumstances. However, there are some other issues that are pertinent to your loved one's spiritual needs. Clearly, these are not for everyone – many people have no faith at all, or rely on their own religion to support them. In this section we detail some different ways of approaching this that might be helpful.

We now go into much more detail on the items above that we think you might need help with.

5

End of Life Care and Palliative Care

One of your very first considerations will be ensuring that your loved one has the best possible care and particularly that they are pain-free and have access to as much support as possible. Your first step is to talk to your GP or to call the telephone number your healthcare professionals have given you.

Palliative care may be a new term to you, but what it means is an inter-disciplinary approach to specialised medical and nursing care for people with life-limiting or terminal illnesses. It focuses on providing relief from the symptoms of pain, physical stress and mental stress at any stage of illness. It has generally come to mean the care that is given when the patient is no longer on any active treatment, and instead involves a concentration on pain management and making the dying person feel comfortable. It can take place in hospital, in a hospice or nursing home, or at home.

The National Institute for Health and Care Excellence (NICE) has published guidance, quality statements and measures in 'End of life care for adults: service delivery', which explain what the universal standards are and what you can expect. These include, 'Quality Statement 10 – Specialist Palliative Care, the care of dying adults in the last days of life', which covers how to manage common symptoms, as well as guidance on maintaining the dignity of the dying person and for all involved. You can use these as a source of reference for the type of care you should expect. You should get information on how to access people who can help you from your healthcare professional, including access to a Community Matron Team who will make onward referrals to all appropriate Community Services.

There are a number of books you can read on palliative care and some of them are mentioned at the end of this Part. The Sue Ryder charity has a guide you can download from the internet called 'A Better Death', which covers many aspects of this topic, as does the charity Compassion in Dying. *With the End in Mind* is a book by Kathryn Mannix, a palliative care doctor, which gives you some idea of what to expect when your partner is dying, although it is controversial in that some in the palliative care profession feel it paints too rosy a picture of the reality. There is more on how to recognise the signs of dying at the end of Part Two.

The GP responsible for your partner's care or any of the healthcare professionals assigned to you will let you know what end of life care is available. Below, we detail some of what is available generally and offer some leads for you to follow in your area.

Having more treatment

When your partner is given a life-limiting diagnosis, it is possible that they will be offered a series of interventions, some of which will prolong life but only for a limited period and that may require some harrowing treatment when your partner is at their frailest. If you have young children or for other reasons – such as hoping for a miracle to happen – you may jointly decide not to have any more treatment.

Some treatments can be very debilitating and make the last few weeks of life, which really should be peaceful and contemplative, a living nightmare. For example, a person with a brain tumour could conceivably be offered surgery or chemotherapy or radiotherapy, none of which will have a curative effect. On the other hand, to some people, just a few weeks of extra life will seem very precious and will enable you as the surviving partner to get everything sorted out, with your partner making a contribution. If your children are quite small, it may enable your partner to make careful provision for their well-being after they have gone. The worst of all worlds is if your partner wants the treatment but you have a more realistic view of the effect. You are in a difficult position, for who wants to deny their dying loved one the possibility of a cure or relief?

Here is a thought-provoking comment from Atul Gawande's book, *Being Mortal*. He says that the American Coping with Cancer Project published a study in 2008 showing that the terminally ill cancer patients who were put on a mechanical ventilator, given electrical defibrillation or chest compressions, or admitted, near death, to intensive care had a substantially worse quality of life in their last week than those who received no such interventions. In these circumstances you, their partner, would have very little access to them, and if you have not said what you wanted to say to them by this time, it is likely that you have missed the window of opportunity. A similar situation arises if your partner is in isolation and being 'barrier nursed', perhaps as a result of Covid-19. You will not have access and will be unable to say your last goodbye. Gawande also notes the finding that six months after the death of a terminally ill person who received medical intervention near the end, their care givers were three times as likely to suffer major depression.

People with serious illness have priorities besides simply prolonging their lives. Surveys found that their top concerns include avoiding suffering, strengthening relationships with family and friends, being mentally aware, not being a burden on others and achieving a sense that their life is complete.

This is something that you and your partner will need to discuss at some length, as it is a very personal decision. The sections on 'Advance planning' (p. 56) might be helpful here.

Transport issues

As those who have chronic illnesses will know, your life can revolve around getting to and from hospitals, clinics and surgeries. The fewer and simpler you make the arrangements for these, the better. This is where your friends can help. They may, for example, be able to drive you to these appointments and pick you up again. Even though you may have your own transport, parking might become an issue and an extra pressure. Friends can drive somewhere nearby for the duration or wait to park. If you are having long-term treatment, you are likely to be able to get a token that exempts you from parking charges at the hospital you attend.

Another alternative is to use hospital transport, volunteer drivers, community transport or GP-organised transport. Who to contact should be printed on your appointment letters, or your healthcare professional should have a number you can call.

Medication

If your partner has been ill for some time, you probably have experience in helping them with their medication. Sometimes a patient has to take many tablets or capsules at different times of the day. Medication may also include the delivery of oxygen or bulk supplies of particular items. Trying to rationalise the timings when the repeat prescriptions are ordered so that you make fewer visits to the pharmacy can be helpful, although it is not always possible. Once agreed by a GP, most prescriptions can be sent electronically to your local pharmacy. It may be that there is a delivery service organised by the pharmacy, which would make life easier for you, as you would not have to go and collect drugs, especially if the pharmacy is out of your way. Your GP can authorise a delivery for you.

One of the problems with prescribed medication is that people do not always take them as directed or can forget to take them entirely. Although you are there to help your partner, you cannot be there all the time. In order to help with this issue, you can buy a dispenser or wallet. This is sometimes called a dosette. They range from the simple to the sophisticated; you can even get decorative ones made, for example, out of glass. At one end you can make up a week's supply of drugs separated out into the times of day they should be taken. At the other end of the scale is a dispenser with alarms that warn the patient or carer that the drugs in a certain compartment need to be taken immediately. These are often also tamper-proof so that the patient cannot take any medication at a time that is not programmed into the dispenser. Such a system is particularly useful if you have to leave your partner with a carer, as it also relieves the carer of the responsibility of having to remember the times that medication should be taken. You can purchase dosettes at your chemist or online.

Leaving hospital

If there is nothing more that can be done for your partner and any future treatment will be administered as an outpatient, it is likely that the medical profession will want them to leave hospital, assuming that is where they are when the prognosis is received.

You have to decide on where the most beneficial place is for your loved one to be, and what is best for you, too. The choice may be between coming home or going temporarily or permanently into a care home, nursing home or hospice. (Whichever home you choose, your partner is likely to need nursing care, so from now on we will simply refer to nursing homes, as care homes generally do not provide the level of nursing care you are likely to need.)

The thought of your partner coming home might be quite daunting, as you may not know whether you have the right environment to be able to support them. Do not feel that you have to have them at home if you do not think it is the right thing to do, but you have not yet arranged for a nursing home. Tell the hospital staff you are not prepared to have your partner leave hospital yet. They will provide you with the help and advice you need, or put you in touch with someone who will. There are two important things to be aware of here: your loved one should not be discharged from hospital until there is a care plan in place; and your GP has overall responsibility for the care that your partner receives.

There are three quite separate types of assistance that you will probably need for this next stage. They are nursing care, social care and home help. We explain the differences between them and how you might get help with funding in the next sections. Of particular importance is a DS1500 medical condition report, which enables terminally ill people to be fast-tracked for special and higher welfare benefits from the government. Your GP or consultant should have copies of this form and will be able to fill one out for you before sending it to you or directly to the relevant government department. Marie Curie has a helpful section on their website.

In April 2019, Which? published a supplement called 'Solutions for Living Independently', which contains useful information and more detail about financial support schemes, including those for carers like you. We deal with this in more detail in the chapter, 'Stabilising Your Financial Affairs Prior to Death'.

The most recent research conducted in 2015 by the Office for National Statistics concluded that 80 per cent of people would prefer to be cared for in their own home at the end of their lives, so that is where we will begin.

6

Coming Home

Having your partner at home and preparing for their arrival can be demanding, not only in terms of finding what is necessary in terms of physical assistance, but also in researching what is available to you in terms of financial support. To make it more complicated, the money comes from two different sources, explained below. Terminal patients are treated as a special category and are routinely fast-tracked or given higher welfare benefit payments if they have only a short time to live. We will try to guide you through this maze, but the most helpful, detailed and authoritative explanation can be found in the Which? information on 'Later Life Care'.

This section comprises information concerning obtaining actual physical support for the nursing care and the ongoing needs of your partner at home, and where to get funding for paying for these. Generally speaking, 'nursing' care is paid for by the NHS (called Continuing Healthcare) and is free at the point of delivery by carers in your home, although not all terminal patients are reckoned to be eligible. It depends on the nature of their needs.

'Social care' is paid for by the local authority or council and is means-tested. (Means testing is described in more detail below.) When it comes to finding the help you need, you can choose between a care agency and other providers. Support in the form of help in the home is rarely paid for by any agency, although a charity or trade union may be able to help you. Which? provides a list of care agencies searchable by postcode, together with details on employing private individuals. In Northern Ireland, domiciliary care is free to all who have been assessed by their local authority as needing it, regardless of their personal circumstances, so there is no financial assessment. In Scotland, personal care is free to those over sixty-five who are assessed by their local authority as needing it. Again, this is regardless of personal circumstances, so no financial assessment is required. However, charges still apply to non-personal care services.

Nursing care

The NHS may fund home nursing care costs under certain circumstances. Under the Continuing Healthcare scheme, the NHS may pay for carers to help you in your own home. This funding is not means-tested, but the eligibility criteria are high and having a terminal diagnosis isn't necessarily enough to receive funding. You must have 'a complex medical condition with substantial, ongoing care needs'. If this is not the case, you are likely to have to pay for some or all of these costs yourself. In your area there will be an NHS Continuing Healthcare office. You can contact them for further information or obtain it via your healthcare professional.

Social care needs

If your partner is confined to bed or is relatively immobile, you will almost certainly need help looking after them, especially if they need support during the night. This is known as home care or domiciliary care, but is more often now referred to as 'social care needs'. Social care usually involves personal care such as washing and dressing, while 'home help' usually involves cleaning, laundry and gardening. You might want both. You can talk to your GP about applying for this, or to any care professional you are in contact with. Most local authorities have dedicated teams who will help you organise this.

If your partner is deteriorating with a chronic illness over a longer period of time rather than within a few weeks, you may need to apply for a needs assessment, which assesses what help you need and determines eligibility for help with payment. If you are eligible, the council will arrange the home care in consultation with you. If you are not eligible, the council must still give you free advice about where you can get help in your community. Even if you are intending to make arrangements yourself with an agency or private carer, it is still a good idea to have a needs assessment, as it will help you to explain in more accurate detail to the agency or carer you employ what kind of help you need. Obviously, you will want to have a say in what the care package contains, even if the local authority is funding the care you are receiving, as there may be some things that you think are important for you, rather than a stranger, to do for your loved one.

If the needs assessment recommends social care, you may get some help with the cost from the council. The amount you will contribute depends on your income and savings. The council will work this out by carrying out a financial assessment or means test. Generally, the council helps to pay for social care costs for someone with savings of less than £23,250 (at the time of writing, though Age UK, which produces some very helpful factsheets, warns that the figure can sometimes change during the year). A Financial Assessment Officer from the council will visit you at home to ask about such things as your earnings, pensions, benefits savings and property. If you go down this route, it helps to prepare by having all the information to hand, including disability-related expenses. The value of your home won't be included in the financial assessment. Remember, the savings relate to your partner, not to you.

Private home care

If you are paying for home social care yourself, you will need to find people to provide it. The best course of action here is through word of mouth. Friends and neighbours may be able to tell you the relative merits of various agencies. Failing that, your best source is the Which? 'Later Life Care' postcode search, as mentioned above, Citizens Advice, Age UK, the internet, or adverts in your local newspapers, and your local GP surgery. Interview several agencies or individuals and be absolutely sure before you start what care you want. When you select one, do so as far as possible with your partner and ask that care provider to be on a trial or probation period to begin with, so that you can see how they all get on. Questions to ask an agency include whether or not their policy is to send the same person to provide care every day or will you get someone different? It can be very disorientating for a sick person to have to deal with a different person day after day. If the carer is going to be full time or 'live-in', you will want to be scrupulous about taking up references.

Help in the home

You may also want to consider help for yourself. If you are devoting yourself to the time that is left to your partner, do you really want to do the housework as well? Providing support in this way can be an exhausting business, especially if you have a job to do or family to maintain. You may have to pay for someone else to do your housework, and this expenditure is another consideration in what might either be a very open-ended situation or one that is very specific in its time-scales.

While you may get financial help with social care, most local authorities do not support home help, and you will have to pay for this privately or tap into friends and relatives who can help you. Alternatively, you might approach a charity or trade union, which may be able to support you.

Home security

If you are working or need to be away from home sometimes, and if your partner is unable to answer the door, you may want to invest in a keypad. This is a small box fitted to the wall of your house, which contains your house key. You distribute the code that opens the box only to those who need to know. In the interests of security, you might decide not to put the key in there all the time, although this does severely test your efficiency in putting it there when needed. You will have to think about your options here. It is worth having a safety net, such as letting a trusted neighbour or two keep a spare key for you. Carers can be informed who these neighbours are in the event that there is a failure of the system. It is not a good idea to be reliant on neighbours for keys all the time, as this puts a strain on them and their freedom of movement, but most people are happy to help in an extremity, especially if you have a neighbour who works from home.

Assessing your home

If you want your partner to be at home, one of your first tasks is to get an assessment of your home in terms of their safety. The hospital should help you to provide a plan for returning home. If your partner is in an acute hospital, a hospital occupational therapist will talk to you before discharge and will arrange for the community occupational therapist to come and see you at home and assess what needs to be done.

If your partner has been in a care or nursing home and is returning home, it is likely an occupational therapist from there will come and assess your home and tell you what needs to be done, sometimes for a fee. Otherwise, talk to your GP about contacting one locally.

If you are in contact with a social worker, nurse or other healthcare professional, they can also help you to reach an occupational therapist via health or social services, or they may be able to make an assessment themselves. Don't have your partner home until you have agreement from healthcare professionals that your home is safe, you have the right equipment and your partner's care needs have been sorted out. The following section suggests some of the things that should be covered in such an assessment. A service called 'Hospital at Home' can also be a great help in getting your partner home with the maximum of care. They operate as a care team, co-ordinating what is required, but at home rather than in hospital. Contact them through your GP, or other healthcare professionals.

Showering and toileting

If your partner is still mobile, i.e. walking about and not confined to bed, you will want to ensure that they do not come to any harm at home and that the basics of life can still be maintained such as toileting, showering or bathing. You will need to ensure that the lavatory seat is at the correct height – it may need an attachment, which can be obtained from a specialised unit. If your partner cannot reach the bathroom, especially at night, you may need a commode. These can be obtained, along with other equipment, from specialised shops. You may find yourself having to empty a commode as part of your tasks in caring for your partner. This is probably one of the least attractive tasks one might have to do, but it is inevitable and best carried out with a glad heart knowing that your partner is still with you.

Another thing to think about is your shower provision. Having a walk-in shower, one that either enables your partner to shower on their own or with a carer, is very useful. If you do not have one, most plumbers will be happy to install a walk-in shower and remove a bath, or you may decide that it makes more sense to create an en suite off one of your bedrooms. Obviously, all this is dependent on the time that is left, the speed with which you can find a plumber and get organised, and whether you have the space, not to mention whether you can afford to pay for it. Such a shower would need handrails and a stool to sit on.

Supporting mobility

Balance is one of the things that people often lose when they are not well, and therefore moving about the house and particularly going up and down stairs can become hazardous. You might like to think about having more handrails or 'grab rails' fitted on your stairs or along the passages. Many organisations supply items like this, including, for example, Complete Care Shop and Middletons. Such organisations often advertise on daytime television. Some offer services to pick you up and take you back home, or they will come to you.

You may also need a wheelchair, which can be supplied by the Red Cross, as can some of the other pieces of equipment already mentioned, depending on your area. Another consideration if you can afford one is a stair lift. They can be adapted to fit most homes. You will have to decide whether installing one is worth the trouble and expense for the extra mobility they provide.

Besides internal mobility there is also the question of external mobility. Your partner may be at an early stage where they can still get around with a bit of help from others. You may want to hire or purchase a wheelchair or a mobility scooter. Another thing you might consider if you are a driver, or your partner is able to drive, is a Blue Badge. The Blue Badge scheme helps disabled people and those with a health condition that affects their mobility to park closer to their destinations. 'Disabled' is a wide term in this instance and in August 2019 it was extended to include people with hidden disabilities such as Parkinson's disease, learning disabilities, autism and mental health conditions. The Blue Badge is linked to the person, not to the vehicle, so you can use it with any car. This also includes taxis and hire cars that your partner is travelling in as a passenger. The scheme is administered by county councils and you should apply to your local county council in the first instance. More information can be obtained from Citizens Advice, your local library or the gov.uk website.

One last point about mobility involves looking after your partner's feet. This may seem a somewhat odd thing to focus on, but in terms of mobility it is crucial. If feet are not looked after they may cause your partner to stumble and fall. This could potentially lead to a broken hip. The outcomes from broken hip surgery do not make for happy reading. You do not want to add this distress for you and your loved one to the other issues that you are facing. If they are able, regular trips to the chiropodist are in order, or, if that is not possible, pay that little bit extra for them to come to you. You might get attention for yourself at the same time. It is worth the investment.

Upstairs or downstairs?

One of your first considerations might be where you want your partner to be in your home. For various reasons, such as safety and accessibility, assuming you do not live in a flat or bungalow, the ground floor may be the best option, but this might not be feasible. If there is a downstairs toilet facility and shower, you might want to move a bed downstairs and make a bedroom out of your living area. This could also be useful for you, as you may have more peace of mind knowing that your partner can be seen and heard by you. They may feel less cut off if you are nearby and easy to talk to, rather than them being isolated upstairs in a bedroom, although, alternatively, peace and quiet for them may be more acceptable.

For social services, living downstairs is considered preferable. If there is no toilet and shower facility downstairs, you may have to make a substantial adaptation to your home in which social services might be involved. A financial assessment would have to be undertaken for a 'Disabled Facilities Grant' application. This can take some time, but may be fast-tracked depending on circumstances. If time enables you to do it, you might think of moving to a bungalow, perhaps renting this while you rent out your own house, although this would be a lot of work to accomplish.

If you wish your partner to live upstairs, a risk assessment would need to be done by whoever is co-ordinating the care, but in theory this would not be automatically ruled out. If your partner has to be upstairs, is there a working smoke alarm? There is a scheme that many fire brigades run relating to fire safety for the incapacitated. In Oxfordshire, for example, it is called '365 Alive'.

If you are in a bungalow or a flat, or at least on the same floor, you should consider how isolated or protected your partner is in their bedroom. You may also need a bedroom for yourself and possibly a daybed or couch for a carer who is staying overnight.

The correct bed

The correct bed is a very important piece of equipment. Normal beds are not really suitable, as your partner needs to be able to get in and out of bed safely. If possible, you should get hold of a hospital bed, ideally one that undulates, so as to prevent bedsores. You should also obtain a skin health test to enable you to estimate how likely pressure sores might be. This is often done by the nurses in the hospital or nursing home.

If your partner is incontinent, you will have a lot of washing to do or you may want to have a laundry service. Another alternative would be incontinence pads, which you can buy over the internet or ask your local pharmacy for. You will need to have a waterproof cover on the bed or else you might be dealing with a wet or dirty mattress. Added to the effect of limited movement, this can also cause bedsores. The community occupational therapist or the district nurse will support you by providing the specialist equipment you require. As with all of these suggestions, how your home is organised will vary from place to place and it is difficult to be prescriptive.

A home alarm system

If you think your partner will be on their own for periods of the day and are worried something might happen to them, you can invest in an alarm system that alerts a call centre that help is urgently required at your home. These usually come with a pendant to be worn around the neck or a wristband. Of course, there is no provision against someone not wearing the appropriate equipment, but you cannot cover every contingency. Payments for these services vary, depending on what you choose to have, but your partner may be eligible for your local authority to pay for this and it is worth enquiring whether or not this is the case.

7
Going into a Nursing Home

There is an important distinction between what comprises a care home and a nursing home. Care homes provide living accommodation and meals, and help with personal care. Nursing homes provide this too, but also provide medical care from a qualified nurse who is available twenty-four hours a day. We are making the assumption that, owing to the terminal illness of your partner where palliative care may be required, they will need a nursing home and we proceed on that basis.

Paying for a nursing home

If you decide that a nursing home is the best option for your loved one, your next thought will probably be concerned with how you are going to pay for it. Fees for homes vary depending on the type of care and accommodation you are looking for. They can range from £700 to over £1,700 per week at the time of writing.

The two components to nursing home fees that you could get help with are nursing and bed and board. There are two different funding schemes available from the NHS: NHS Continuing Healthcare and NHS-funded Nursing Care. Owing to the terminal nature of your partner's diagnosis and the likelihood that they may have complex or unpredictable medical care needs, they may be eligible for Continuing Healthcare from the NHS. This means that the full cost of the nursing home fees is covered, not just the nursing component, which is the normal situation for non-terminal patients. The rules are strict and complex and you may not be eligible, but it is always worth pursuing.

As part of NHS-funded Nursing Care, the NHS provides some financial help, but either your partner will be expected to pay the remaining nursing home fees or you will need to get some support from the local authority towards the cost. Remember that the basic rule is that because the NHS is free to all at the point of delivery, Continuing Healthcare funding is available to all who are assessed as needing it, whether in their own home or in a nursing home. Bed and board social care in a nursing home can be paid for either out of NHS Continuing Healthcare (in exceptional circumstances, which yours might very well be), or on a self-funded basis (by you), or by the local authority, or somewhere in between, with you paying some of the cost and the council paying some, depending on your savings, as it is means-tested. The website www.whentheygetolder.co.uk on ageing is a useful one, and includes such issues as debunking the myths associated with Continuing Healthcare funding.

You may be entitled to free nursing care (FNC) if your partner needs nursing care, as they almost certainly will. This sum is usually deducted from the nursing home fees. At the time of writing it is £158.16 per week, with a modest increase at the beginning of each financial year. It is the same amount you would receive if your partner was at home. Often, your chosen nursing home will apply for this on your behalf to the NHS centre applicable to them. If your partner is completely self-funding and over sixty-five, they may also be eligible for Attendance Allowance, just as they would if they were at home [the information is below]. You usually have to apply for this yourself on your partner's behalf. Download the Attendance Allowance claim form, which comes with notes telling you how to fill it in, on www.gov.uk/benefits/carersanddisablitybenefits/attendanceallowance or phone 0800 731 0122. Return the form to: Attendance Allowance Unit, Mail Handing Site A, Wolverhampton, WV98 2AD.

If your partner has savings and you apply to your local authority for assistance towards payment of a nursing home, because all other channels are closed to you, the savings are means-tested. The rules are complex and are applied on an individual basis, so you are advised to check with a body like Age UK, which has a useful guide, or contact your own local authority for advice. At the time of writing, and speaking in simplified, general terms, if your partner has capital of £23,250, full fees must be paid by them (known as being self-funding). If their savings are between £14,250 and £23,250, it is likely but not guaranteed that your local authority will contribute towards some of the fees and you'll fund the rest. Below £14,250 the local authority will pay for all fees. However, they will still take any eligible income into account. If a local authority is paying, then your preferred choice of home is covered by the Government Choice of Accommodation Regulations. You can find this document online by searching for 'The Care and Support and After-care (Choice of Accommodation) Regulations 2014'. The NHS website has more details.

Depending on the length of the prognosis for your partner, you may worry that you will run out of money to pay the fees for a residential home, and that your savings and even your home will be used to fund the shortfall. Rest assured – your savings are not included in your partner's assessment. If you are over sixty, your home is not included in the assessment, even though it is jointly owned. If you are under sixty, different rules apply. You should check with the council or the relevant nursing home as to what happens if your money runs out. Alternatively, you could consider an immediate-needs annuity. In exchange for a lump sum, an insurance company will cover the difference between someone's income and their cost of care. There are pros and cons in these annuities and they are most useful in dementia cases where time of death is difficult to calculate. These products are offered only through authorised financial advisors with a specialist care qualification. You would have to pay a fee for the help required to guide you through the process. The Society of Later Life Advisers has a directory of accredited advisors to contact.

Our experience is that the administration staff of nursing homes are very helpful in assisting you to understand what your partner is entitled to and applying for it on your behalf. They have usually had years of experience in dealing with what is a byzantine situation and can use their knowledge in your service. If you are thinking of this option, it would be useful to raise the issue of what help is obtainable with the staff of the nursing home on your first contact or when you visit.

Choosing the right nursing home for your partner

You may decide that a nursing home is the best option either for a respite period or for the longer term. How do you choose which one? Some counties have care home associations that publish guides to local care and nursing homes. The best place to start is the Which? Later Life Care Services Directory, on the internet; your local Citizens Advice office; Age UK; local social services; or the NHS. Your local offices can be found online, in the phone book or through directory enquiries. Citizens Advice usually have offices in the centres of most large towns if you want to go in person, although you may have to make an appointment. Age UK also often list the nursing homes in their area and a list can be sent to you if you contact them.

If you have a list of homes, telephone and ask them to send you a brochure and arrange a visit to look around. It is a good idea to look at a number of homes to get an appreciation of what is available and what you like. It is also helpful to take someone with you so that you can talk over the pros and cons with another person. They may have spotted things that you have not. Homes vary a lot in what they focus on. Some have very much a 'home from home' atmosphere with a bar and the carers are non-uniformed, while others have more of a hospital feel to them with uniformed nursing staff. Some care homes specialise in dementia care or have special dementia floors if that is a consideration for you. One friend and I thought first impressions of a home were very favourable until we realised that the bedroom shown to us was on a corridor with two others and the only exit downstairs was via a door with a combination lock on it. We could see this would have been ideal for a dementia patient, but it was not what was wanted in this case.

8

Using a Hospice

You may imagine that hospices care for people in the last weeks or days of their life on an in-house basis, and of course they do this, but they also care for people at home, in their day centre and on the wards of surrounding hospitals, as well as in their own inpatient unit. Their care is centred on the patient's needs in the here and now in order to make the present as good as it can be for the patient. The care provided takes many forms, from pain management, pastoral care and advice with accessing financial help, to help with maintaining independence. As a patient's condition changes, the staff adapt the care provided to suit the patient and their family.

As hospices vary round the country, you are advised to contact your nearest one to check what services they provide, even if you do not feel that you want one just at the moment. If you do not know where your nearest hospice is, your own GP or surgery will help you. A friend of mine told me that the most professional of all the help she received came from her local hospice community team member. This person was able to give advice about what to expect and how to make her home safe for her husband to leave hospital. The community team often includes specialist nurses and doctors, as well as physiotherapists, occupational therapists, a pharmacist and a benefits advisor.

Many people with a life-limiting illness do not need the involvement of a hospice, as GPs and district nurses are able to provide the care and support necessary. Referral to a hospice can be made by your GP, district nurse, consultant or other healthcare professional. Your partner can be seen either at an outpatient clinic or in your home, depending on what is the most convenient. An Advanced Nurse Practitioner (ANP), a specialist nurse in palliative care, can visit your partner at home or in a nursing home to give what advice is possible, be it on medication, therapies, counselling or information. The ANP might suggest your partner visit the hospice day centre or be admitted as an inpatient. Many nursing homes have relationships with local hospices so that the care is seamless.

One of the many good things about hospices is that they are always on call for telephone advice and referrals seven days a week and often have access to a specialist palliative care doctor if needed. As your partner's condition worsens, you may feel that you would like to have them admitted to a hospice for the additional support that it provides or for some needed respite from care for you.

It has recently been acknowledged that there are certain cultures that rarely use hospices because they see them as places where you go to die. Actions are now being taken to change this image. Hospices can be a source of great support at the end of life in many ways.

9
Other Organisations That Can Help

If your partner is suffering from cancer, there are several organisations that can help. One such example is Macmillan Cancer Support. This provides physical, emotional and financial support to help sufferers to live as fully as they can. From diagnosis onwards, Macmillan nurses can provide information, experience and a listening ear to you and your partner. There is also the Marie Curie charity, which provides support for terminally ill patients in their own homes.

Maggie's Centres are centres situated at many hospitals to provide support to cancer patients and their families. They also have an online centre, available through their website, which is available twenty-four hours a day, all year round. It is staffed Monday to Friday, 9 a.m. to 5 p.m.

Many specific illnesses have a charity that is there to raise awareness about the illness, raise money for research and give help and support to those afflicted. You are probably aware of the one relevant to your own situation. One little-known cancer charity is UCARE, which exists to improve outcomes for people with urological cancers such as prostate cancer, bladder cancer, kidney cancer and testicular cancer. They have their own tulip named for the charity, which you can purchase.

10

Preparing Your Children

Telling children, especially young children, that their parent is about to leave them puts you in a quandary, as you would like their childhood to be as normal as possible, but on the other hand what is happening to them is not normal, and they do need to be prepared for it. Children in their teens have probably had some previous experience of loss, either in their own lives or in those of friends, but this is less likely for small children. They, nevertheless, may have been acquainted with loss through the death of a pet, or having a grandparent die. In this case you have something to build on. However, although such previous experiences are helpful, they do not compare to the loss of a parent.

The website www.kidshealth.org has a very helpful list under the heading 'Helping Your Child Deal with Death'. The list is for after a death has occurred, but it is just as useful for a pre-bereavement situation. Here it is:

> When talking about death, use simple clear words.
> Listen and comfort.
> Put emotions into words.
> Tell your child what to expect.
> Talk about funerals and rituals.
> Give your child a role.
> Help your child remember the person.
> Respond to emotions with comfort and reassurance.

If your partner has been ill for some time before the terminal diagnosis or before their situation deteriorates significantly, your children will already know something of what is happening and may already be fearful of the consequences. Sometimes, knowing exactly what is going to happen can relieve this anxiety, but they will still wonder what is going to happen to them. Will you still be in the same house? Will you have to move? Will they remain at the same school? And will they lose their friends? Some of this will be unspoken, perhaps because they do not want to upset you or cannot voice their fears. You may not be able to answer these questions with definite answers at this stage, but you can reassure them that you will do your best to keep things as normal as possible.

As a child I was farmed out to friends of my parents when my mother's illness became particularly acute, and kind though these friends were, I absolutely loathed the experience. Anything would have been better than leaving home. Sometimes this is absolutely necessary, but do try to choose people who your child or children are comfortable with and who have roughly the same attitude to child-rearing as you have in terms of boundaries and rules. It was the changes to these latter that I found baffling. Things that my mother allowed me to do were now forbidden and this seemed to add insult to injury.

Try to make sure that any time you spend with your children is of the highest quality in terms of your involvement and attention. Ask friends to replace your partner and yourself in the activities that they might normally have had with you, but warn them in advance that the child might resent this and find it an intrusion. Rope in family and friends to keep things as normal and regular as possible in terms of their activities. Ask other parents to take on some of the burden of transporting your children to shared regular activities. Your friends will be glad of something specific they can do to help you.

If you and your partner spend time in planning their funeral (see p. 104), make sure that you involve your children in this activity, even though it might be difficult for them. Would they like to read a poem or play an instrument? Let your children decide if they want to take part, and how. Make it as fun as possible. How would they like to remember their parent, step-parent or adoptive parent? Would they like to help you make a video, put photographs together or act out an incident that meant a lot to them? Much of this depends on how able the dying parent is to be involved, but the effort will be well worth it afterwards, as your child is likely to adapt more quickly to the loss than if it had not been discussed or acted upon. If you think your children might need professional help, try Jigsaw or Winston's Wish.

You will also have to decide how much you want your children to see of their dying parent. Physical changes can be very difficult for young children and also the not so young, who may have had no experience of the physical changes that illness can bring. I can still remember waking up in a hotel bedroom aged about five to find my father had got sunstroke – his face was very swollen and his eyes invisible – and being absolutely traumatised. Such illnesses as cancer or motor neurone disease, which leave their inimitable marks on the face and body, or seeing a parent wired up to a life-support system, can be very distressing and stressful to witness for children, who do not really understand what is going on. This is a very difficult decision to have to make on your part, but you know your children best and as long as you have thought through the implications, you will make the right choices.

11
Being in Control of What Happens in Your Partner's Treatment and Care

The following is a short list of all the different ways that you can safeguard what happens to your partner should they become mentally and physically incapable of saying what treatment they want or don't want. Of course, no matter how carefully you plan ahead, it is impossible to cover all contingencies. However, if your loved one has had one stroke or heart attack and survives, for example, it is useful to be able to declare what they want to happen in the event of another one. The text below briefly explains the differences between the various systems available. They are then described in much more detail, so that you are aware how to go about getting them done.

Next of kin

Whatever you do, and especially if you are not married or in a civil partnership, do make sure that you are registered as your partner's 'next of kin' on all their records wherever they receive treatment. Otherwise you risk being frozen out of decision-making pertaining to them. There are numerous instances of decisions being taken over by parents and siblings, when in fact you are the best person to say what should happen. Ensure that it is in writing and that your partner has signed it.

Advance care planning

Advance care planning is the process of discussing your partner's preferences and wishes about future treatment and care with those close to them and their healthcare team. Your partner's care planning can involve the lasting power of attorney, the advance statement, the advance decision and the Unified Do Not Attempt Cardiopulmonary Resuscitation (uDNACR), or any combination of these.

Lasting power of attorney

Lasting power of attorney (LPA) is probably the most well known of legal instruments when it comes to giving one person the right to say what should happen to another should that person lose either the physical ability or mental capacity to do so for themselves. There is a Health and Welfare LPA and a Property and Financial Affairs LPA. It costs £82 for each one (at the time of writing) unless you use a solicitor, which will cost you much more. You can complete these yourself either in the form version or online.

Advance statement

An advance statement allows your partner to record their wishes, feelings and values in case they need care or medical treatment. It often forms part of advance care planning. For example, if your partner would strongly prefer to die at home, this would be in their advance statement. It can be seen as a positive declaration. It is not as legally binding as an advance decision.

Advance decision to refuse treatment (living will, also known as an advance decision)

An advance decision enables your partner to record what medical treatments they do not want. It can be seen as a more negative declaration. For example, if they were to suffer a heart attack, they can declare in advance that they do not want to be put in an induced coma, or given nutrition through a feeding method, or, indeed, do not want any treatment at all. The Mental Capacity Act 2005 provides the legal framework for advance decisions. Advance decisions are legally binding if they are valid and applicable. This is a particularly useful instrument if your partner has had experience of some incapacitating health situation, such as a stroke, and now knows what it feels like and what they do not want.

Unified Do Not Attempt Cardiopulmonary Resuscitation (uDNACPR)

In the event of a cardiac or respiratory arrest, no attempts at CPR will be made on your partner. All other appropriate treatment and care will be provided.

We now describe this list in more detail, giving you as much information as possible about each one.

Advance care planning

Now is the time for you and your partner to think long and hard about advance care planning. Your partner may currently have capacity – meaning the ability to make a decision for themselves – but what if the illness they have means that they may no longer have the means to do so in the future? For example, they may develop an impairment or disturbance of the mind or brain owing to the fact that they lose consciousness, suffer worsening dementia or mental health, or a brain injury or stroke. Because of that impairment they may not be able to understand information relating to the decision on their care in the future. They may not be able to retain that information for long enough to make a decision, take the information into account when making the decision or be able to communicate the decision. These are all issues that relate to capacity. Although the law in England and Wales states that people must be assumed to have capacity unless it is proven otherwise, a healthcare professional who has reason to doubt capacity may make decisions on your partner's behalf that you know your partner would not have agreed to, but which you now have no way of proving. You will be powerless to stop this happening unless your partner has made an LPA (Health and Welfare), which covers this eventuality, or unless they have made an advance decision. The laws in Scotland and Northern Ireland describe capacity slightly differently and you should check these if you live there.

Healthcare professionals have to give an individual all the information they need to make a decision about whether or not to consent to a particular medical examination or treatment. This includes what the examination or treatment involves, any benefits or risks, whether there are reasonable alternatives and what will happen if they don't have the treatment. The advance decision form has a space for your partner to write this information and what is involved, thus making clear that they know what they are refusing. Consent must be voluntary, and to give consent an individual must have capacity. If they do not have capacity, the healthcare professional will make what they think is the best decision for them.

Bear in mind that this is a process, and it will take some time to decide upon. It cannot be done in one session or at speed, unless this is an absolute necessity.

Lasting power of attorney

Lasting power of attorney replaced enduring power of attorney (EPA) in 2007. EPAs signed prior to this date are still valid and can be registered, but the LPA is far more flexible and there is the option of taking out either a property and financial affairs LPA or a health and welfare LPA, or both. EPAs were restricted to money and property. As long as a person is eighteen or over and has mental capacity – the ability to make their own decisions – they can make an LPA. Be aware that there is a different process in Scotland and Northern Ireland, although a person does not need to live in the UK or be a British citizen to make one.

The health and welfare LPA covers daily routines such as washing, dressing, eating, medical care, moving into a care home and life-sustaining treatment. It enables the nominated attorney to make decisions on these issues on behalf of someone else if they are incapacitated.

The property and financial affairs LPA gives your nominated attorney the power to make decisions for you concerning managing bank or building society accounts, paying bills, collecting benefits or a pension and selling your home. Only LPAs enable one person to make decisions on behalf of another.

All LPAs have to be registered with the Office of the Public Guardian. It takes eight to ten weeks to register an LPA if there are no mistakes. This might be a consideration for you and your partner in taking the decision to make one or not, depending on the prognosis.

It is likely that you and your partner will choose you to be their attorney, but depending on your age and health you may decide to have more than one attorney to spread the load a little. Perhaps you might choose one or more of your children, another relative, or a friend. You cannot choose someone who is subject to a Debt Relief Order or has been declared bankrupt. If you appoint more than one attorney, you must decide whether they will make decisions severally (separately) or jointly (together). The more attorneys you have, the more they might differ about what your partner would want if they have to make joint decisions, unless your partner has made their wishes clear in all eventualities. You can let them make some decisions 'jointly' and others 'jointly and severally', depending on what makes sense to you both. You can also choose your solicitor, but they would charge you if they were called in to make decisions on your partner's behalf. You can also pay non-professional attorneys and there is a section about this on the form. However, if you do not record any such agreement on the form, they will only be able to recover out-of-pocket expenses.

It is important that the attorneys you choose are able to look after their own affairs and make decisions as you would do, so it is important that they do not have beliefs that differ from yours when it comes to medical matters. It is also important that the attorneys you appoint are happy to take on this task for you and your partner, as in a few weeks or months it may be a very real possibility that they will be taking life-and-death decisions with you and for your partner as their illness worsens. You can nominate replacement attorneys to cover in case your original attorneys cannot act on your behalf at some point, such as because they move abroad or travel a lot.

You can use the online service to process your LPAs on the gov.uk site or you can use paper forms. You need people to sign the paper forms whichever route you choose. The value of an online account to prepare your LPA is that you can obtain help and guidance at every step, you do not need to complete it in one attempt and you can fix any mistakes very easily.

Other ways to be in control of your partner's care

You may or may not have decided to complete either, or both – health and welfare, or property and financial affairs – lasting powers of attorney, depending on your timescales and the cost. Even if you decide to complete LPAs, you and your partner may still feel that neither of you have sufficient control over what treatments they may be given as their illness progresses. You may be resigned to the fact that the illness will just take its course, with the doctors and other medical professionals making decisions for you at every turn. In addition, you may worry that should your partner deteriorate mentally and physically, there is no way that you can convince medical staff what your partner's wishes would have been, if they still had the power to be able to tell them.

In fact, there are ways that your partner can have their say about what happens to them, what treatment they receive and when they can ask for treatment to cease or not be administered. Bear in mind that all these documents depend on your partner having the mental capacity to make decisions now, and they cannot be completed if your partner is in a coma, unconscious or on a life-support system. This is also true if their mental capacity deteriorates to the point that they cannot make decisions – for example, owing to dementia – so you need to think about these things now. Fifty-three per cent of people wrongly believe that they have the automatic right to make decisions for a loved one who is seriously ill, when in fact they can be overridden by a healthcare professional.

All the different forms you can complete and decisions you can make in advance are somewhat confusing, but well worth the effort in sorting them out if you both want complete peace of mind. The following is a list of what is currently available. The organisation Compassion in Dying provides the paperwork you will need, as well as guidance and support to enable you to complete the forms. Or you can register with an organisation called My Decisions to make an advance decision and/or an advance statement.

Advance statement

It is important to realise that if your partner is unable to make a decision about their medical treatment, care or welfare then a health or social care professional, such as a doctor or social worker, will make a decision on their behalf. An advance statement will help to make sure that their wishes, feelings and beliefs are taken into account when these decisions are made.

Writing an advance statement can help to start a conversation between the two of you of the kind that can sometimes be difficult to talk about. Some people are much more inclined to talk about this subject than others. What is important to your partner? How have they communicated this? Writing it down makes it into a permanent record of their wishes and is less likely to be challenged at a later date. Because it is voluntary, your partner can change it at any time.

What sort of things might it contain? Do they want to die at home? If they do, you should discuss what that means for you and for their care. How easy is it to adapt your home? Are they able to have a specialist bed that will make them more comfortable? How long might it be before they get specialist help such as pain relief or relief from nausea, especially at a weekend or on a Bank Holiday? Would they be better in a nursing home with specialist care to hand at the touch of a bell? When do they want to be admitted to hospital or a hospice?

The form supplied by Compassion in Dying permits your partner to write an advance statement as section 6 of their advance decision. In summary it explains why your partner is making the advance decision and what is important to them in relation to their health, care and quality of life.

Always discuss the outcomes with your partner's healthcare professionals to see just how feasible they are. They are not bound by your partner's wishes and the statement is not legally binding in the same way as an advance decision, but they must consider the wishes your partner expresses when making a decision on your behalf.

Advance decision to refuse treatment (living will), also known as an advance statement

If your partner has wishes about how they would or would not want to be treated in the future, making an advance decision (as it is shortened to) will help to ensure those wishes are respected if at some later date they cannot make decisions. It allows them to record any medical treatments that they do not want to be given in the future. This was previously known as a living will and is still often referred to as such. An advance decision cannot be used to ask for life to be ended or to nominate someone else to decide about treatment on your partner's behalf. The only way to do the latter is through the lasting power of attorney.

In England and Wales an advance decision is legally binding under the Mental Capacity Act 2005, as long as it is valid and applicable. If a healthcare professional knows that an advance decision has been made, they have to follow it. If they ignore it, they could be taken to court. In Scotland, advance decisions are known as advance directives and are not recognised in legislation, but they are still widely acknowledged and used by healthcare professionals. In Northern Ireland, the Mental Capacity Act (Northern Ireland) was passed in 2016 and some of its provisions have yet to come into force. If you live in Northern Ireland, you are advised to check with the organisation Compassion in Dying for an up-to-date assessment of what is in force.

It is important to know what makes an advance decision valid and applicable. There are several conditions that make for a valid decision, but one of the most important is that you must not, after making your advance decision, have made a lasting power of attorney for health and welfare, which gives your attorney power to make the same treatment decisions described in your advance decision. If you are considering making both an LPA and an advance decision, it is important to know that the more recent document takes precedence. This means that if you appoint an attorney after you made your advance decision, your attorney can override your advance decision (as long as you have given them power over the same issue). If you do not want this to happen, you can include an instruction in the LPA form that says your attorney must follow your advance decision. Enduring power of attorney does not cover health and personal care; therefore, if you only have an EPA, you have not given your attorney power to make those decisions for you.

Another important issue is that if your partner wants to refuse life-sustaining treatment, they need to clearly state that their advance decision applies even if their life is at risk. If your partner wishes to refuse life-sustaining treatment, they need to sign and date their advance decision in the presence of a witness.

For the advanced decision to be applicable, your partner must lack the capacity to make the decision and their advance decision must include details of the specific circumstances they are in. It must also refuse the treatments that a doctor has proposed for them and there must also be no reason to believe that something has happened since making their advance decision that would have affected the decisions they made. For example, if there had been developments in medical treatments that they did not expect or were not aware of.

What might be put in an advance decision? It can include the following. When would your partner not want to be resuscitated? How does your partner feel about invasive treatments, blood transfusions, chemotherapy or radiotherapy, a ventilator or life support? At what point will they feel that enough treatment is enough? Another example might be if your loved one suffered severe brain damage as the result of a heart attack or stroke and was unlikely to regain consciousness. You both might feel that it would be in their best interests to withdraw the clinically assisted nutrition and hydration (CANH) that keeps them alive but in a persistent vegetative or minimally conscious state. In a 2018 High Court case, the judge ruled that in cases where there was no dispute between the family and the doctors supervising the case, families and doctors would not have to apply to the courts to have CANH removed from a patient. You cannot bank on this happening and it is always better to have what you want to happen written down in your advance decision. Happily, many of these treatments are actually listed on the form, which makes it easier to decide, as most of us have little or no experience of what might await us and therefore are unable to say what we don't want. Section 3 of the form, 'In respect of a known illness', allows your partner to say what they do or do not want. Hopefully, you both will have been told what lies in store for your partner and will be more informed about that aspect of the treatment, so will be more confident about being specific.

Unified Do Not Attempt Cardiopulmonary Resuscitation (uDNACPR)

Everyone has a right to refuse to be resuscitated in the event that medical professionals deem this to be the correct procedure for the life-threatening situation a person might find themselves in. As you are not able, for obvious reasons, to express your wishes at the time, you have to make the decision in advance and have signed paperwork available to demonstrate to the medical professionals that this is indeed the case.

A scheme run by the charity The Lions (or another similar charity in some places) provides the forms, labels and plastic tubes to GPs for distribution to those who ask for them. As can be seen from the title, it only covers resuscitation, but if you feel strongly about this it is a useful stopgap until you have all the other forms in place. You or your partner need to make an appointment with your GP or ask them to provide you with the relevant form and sign all the paperwork. They attach their copy to the notes at the surgery. Sometimes at the bottom of the form there is a tear-off portion, or there is a copy, which goes in the plastic tube, that directs the searcher to where it is kept. The tube is kept in your fridge. There are a couple of stickers with crosses, which you can put on your fridge door and behind your front door. Ambulance crews are trained to look out for these stickers and having them in these two places means they are easily observable and stops them having to waste time looking for them. You must make sure that your partner (or more probably you) is very specific about where your form is kept and that it is accessible. The form will be taken by the ambulance crew and will follow your partner around. This is not as foolproof a method as the other methods of determining treatment outlined above, and it is only legally binding in the sense that your partner could bring a case against the ambulance authority or the NHS if they failed to follow the instructions, but it will make you both feel that you have done something, while you get on with making the more detailed decisions.

Making people aware of your partner's wishes

As you can see, making an advance decision takes care and thought and you need to discuss it at length with your partner. You should also make sure your partner discusses it with their GP and gives them a copy to be put with their notes at the surgery. You don't need your GP's consent to make an advance decision, but your partner can ask them to witness their mental capacity by signing the declaration on the form. It should also be discussed with your specialist doctor and they should be asked to witness the form. They should also be given a copy to put with your hospital notes. You might want to write on the copies where the original is kept. You, the partner, need to keep the original in a safe place.

The advance decision form comes with a notice of advance decision card. Your partner should fill this in and carry it at all times.

Additionally, you can register with MedicAlert. MedicAlert provides medical identification jewellery for people who need to convey information in an emergency; for example, that they have made an advance decision. If you join MedicAlert, 'Advance Decision' will be engraved on your jewellery to alert healthcare professionals that you have made an advance decision. MedicAlert will also create a detailed medical record for you, which is held securely and can be accessed at any time, including in an emergency. A copy of your advance decision will be held on the record and be transferred to the hospital immediately if they request it. MedicAlert charge a monthly fee.

Lastly, you should check whether or not your local Ambulance Trust holds copies of people's advance decisions. Generally speaking, they only do this for people with terminal conditions or those approaching the end of life.

Put any paperwork in a safe and accessible place. You cannot always be sure that you will be to hand if anything happens to your partner. Any carers that you have hired should also be informed of what decisions have been taken and should know where the paperwork is, together with a friend or neighbour you can trust. Make sure they have a key!

12

Pain Management

The things that everyone fears about the end of life and dying are the possible pain and indignity. With some illnesses the latter is an inescapable fact, as an individual is less and less able to do things for themselves, but they are conscious of what is happening to them. Pain is another issue. Most but not all pain can be relieved. The exceptions, such as bone cancer for example, require morphine drips and in some cases self-administered morphine.

Pain management should be discussed at an early stage so that you and your loved one know what to expect and how it can be relieved. Everyone in the caring professions is anxious to make sure that a patient is as pain-free as possible and will try to ensure this happens, whether in a hospice, hospital, nursing home or in your own home.

Pain and stress can be alleviated in other ways. If your partner is well enough, they might like regular massages to relieve tension or visits to a health club where facilities such as a Jacuzzi could provide them with some relief. One relatively new idea is a sound bath, where people lie fully clothed and allow sounds from gongs and bells to wash over them. Some hospices have virtual reality suites or goggles that are sufficiently distracting to allow pain sufferers some relief. You can ask your healthcare professionals what alternatives there are to medication in your area.

13
The Limits to Palliative Care

In 2015 *The Economist* ranked the UK as the number one in the world in a comprehensive study on the quality and availability of palliative care. However, palliative care is not capable of relieving all suffering all of the time. It is a great torment to see a loved one suffer and feel incapable of doing anything more to alleviate their distress. Simple things like having done your homework on what to do if your partner's pain level suddenly increases, or being up to date with the necessary analgesics, so that you do not run out, can be very important.

You may feel that you would do anything to help your loved one. However, it is worth remembering that it is currently illegal in the UK to assist someone to die, even if they self-administer whatever it is they are using. The Campaign for Dignity in Dying in the UK is intent on changing the law to make it legal for individuals with a terminal illness with about six months left to live, and who are capable of making their own choices, to self-administer, with certain safeguards, medication that will end their life. You may feel that this is against your values or principles; that the method of your dying is part of life; or you may feel that it is a cause you heartily endorse and would like to help.

14
Conclusion

In this Part we have looked at the immediate aftermath of a diagnosis of life-terminating illness or a life-ending situation, providing you with a comprehensive list of considerations so that you have the best possible opportunity to make the end of your partner's life as life-enhancing and happy as possible. We have covered the most important issues, including where your partner wants to be during this period, adjusting your family to this new reality, how you can get the best possible treatment for them, and how to cover future contingencies when their condition deteriorates.

In the next Part we will discuss issues that are important to your future and the peace of mind of your partner and yourself, including stabilising your financial affairs, making a will, looking after your own health and preparing for being on your own.

Organisations

Age UK, a charity that supports older people, www.ageuk.org.uk. Advice line: 0800 678 1602, open every day from 8 a.m. to 7 p.m.

Attendance Allowance, www.gov.uk/benefits/carersanddisablity benefits/attendanceallowance, 0800 731 0122.

The Benefit Agency, www.gov.uk, benefit enquiry line: 0800 882 200.

British Association for Counselling and Psychotherapy, www.bacp.co.uk, 01455 883 300.

Compassion in Dying, www.compassionindying.org.uk, 0800 999 2434.

Complete Care Shop, for mobility issues, www.completecareshop.co.uk.

Cruse Bereavement Care, www.cruse.org.uk. National helpline open Monday and Friday, 9.30 a.m. to 5 p.m., 0808 808 1677, or use a search engine to find your local Cruse centre.

Dignity in Dying, www.dignityindying.org.uk, 020 7479 7730.

End-of-Life Rights information line: 0800 999 2434.

Equity Release Council, www.equityreleasecouncil.com.

Foreign, Commonwealth and Development Office (FOCD), www.uk.gov/government/organisations, 020 7008 1500.

HM Inspector of Anatomy, www.organdonation.nhs.uk, for information on organ donation, 020 7972 4551.

Jigsaw, www.jigsaw4u.org.uk, 020 8687 1384.

KidsHealth Foundation, an American charity providing advice and support on children's health, www.kidshealth.org, 'Helping Your Child Deal with Death'.

Lifeline 24, home alarm systems, www.lifeline24.co.uk.

Macmillan Cancer Support, www.macmillan.org.uk. Helpline open seven days a week 8 a.m. to 8 p.m., 0808 808 00 00.

Maggie's Centres for cancer patients, www.maggiescentres.org, and at your local main hospital.

Marie Curie, www.mariecurie.org.uk, or call free on 0800 090 2309.

The MedicAlert Foundation, www.medicalert.org.uk, 01908 951 045.

Middletons, 0800 999 4164.

My Decisions for Advance Statements, www.mydecisions.org.uk.

National Counselling Society, www.nationalcounsellingsociety.org, 01903 200 666.

National Health Service, www.nhs.uk.

Office of the Public Guardian, customerservices@publicguardian.gov.uk, 0300 456 0300.

Red Cross, www.redcross.org.uk, 0344 871 11 11.

Royal College of Occupational Therapists, www.rcot.org.uk.

The Society of Later Life Advisers (SOLLA), admin@societyoflaterlifeadvisers.co.uk, 0333 2020 454.

Telecare 24, home alarm systems, www.telecare24.co.uk.

Urology Cancer Research and Education (UCARE), an Oxford-based charity committed to improving the treatment and care of cancer patients nationally through research and education, ucare@ucare-oxford.org.uk or 01865 767 777 during office hours.

The Wedding Wishing Well Foundation, www.weddingwishingwell.co.uk, info@weddingwishingwell.org.uk, 07875 030 393 (leave a message).

Which?, consumer advice organisation, www.which.co.uk. Phone line open Monday to Friday 8.30 a.m. to 6 p.m., Saturday 9 a.m. to 1 p.m., 029 2267 0000.

Winston's Wish, a charity supporting children and young people after the death of a parent or sibling, www.winstonswish.org, helpline open Monday to Friday 9 a.m. to 5 p.m., 08088 020 021.

Books and publications

Byrne, Eric, *Games People Play*, Grove Press, 1964.

Colvin, H., 'National Survey of Bereaved People (VOICES): England, 2015', Office for National Statistics, https://www.ons.gov.uk/peoplepopulationandcommunity/healthand socialcare/healthcaresystem/bulletins/nationalsurveyofbereavedpeo plevoices/england2015.

Compassion in Dying, *A Guide to Your Rights at the End of Life*, 2011.

Doyle, Derek, *Oxford Textbook of Palliative Medicine*, 4th edition, Oxford University Press, 2017.

Gawande, Atul, *Being Mortal*, Profile Books, 2015.

Gov.uk, 'The Care and Support and After-care (Choice of Accommodation) Regulations 2014', https://www.legislation.gov.uk/uksi/2014/2670/made.

Kübler-Ross, Elisabeth, *On Death and Dying*, Macmillan, 1969.

Mannix, Kathryn, *With the End in Mind*, William Collins, 2018.

National Institute for Health and Care Excellence: 'End of Life Care for Adults: Service Delivery' (NG142).

Which?, 'Solutions for Living Independently', 2019.

Websites

www.gov.uk/powerofattorney: Lasting Power of Attorney.

www.legislation.gov.uk: Paying for a Care Home – 'The Care and Support and After-care (Choice of Accommodation) Regulations 2014'.

www.nice.org.uk: The National Institute for Health and Care Excellence (NICE) has published guidance, and quality statements and measures on End of Life Care for Adults, or phone 0300 323 0140.

www.whentheygetolder.co.uk: Useful information on all matters to do with the elderly.

www.which.co.uk: Later Life Care information

Part Two

A Terminal Diagnosis or Life-Ending Illness – What Can I Do to Plan for the Future?

15

Introduction

Apart from Part Six this was probably the most difficult Part of the book to write in terms of gender neutrality. We were anxious not to make assumptions about the different skills that partners bring to a relationship. Most partners divide up the tasks they have to do in some shape or form so as to prevent duplication and to play to the skills of each partner. This does not mean to say that the partner who doesn't do most of the cooking can't cook; simply that it makes sense for one partner to take it on most of the time. Perhaps the other partner cooks on special occasions or at weekends, or, if they were anything like mine, never if they could possibly avoid it. We are using this as an example to demonstrate how very thin the ice is here when trying to be helpful and suggesting what skills the surviving partner might need to develop. The best advice we can give in reading this Part is to take from it what makes sense to you and pass over what seems obvious.

We are also aware that we may be addressing both of you or just one of you depending on the circumstances and that this might change in the text according to the issue under discussion. For example, it will be the person who is dying who will be making the will and the person left behind who is inheriting. Generally, we have taken the line that it will be the person left behind who is doing most of the things we suggest, but occasionally, with a subject such as 'Writing Your Biography', we will be addressing both of you.

We have already discussed how to come to terms with the shock of a terminal diagnosis or life-ending illness. You will have a sense of how to start to plan and organise your affairs so that the remainder of your partner's life can be as pain-free and joyous as possible, and so that you can feel confident that you are doing all you can for your partner's treatment and care.

Now we look to the future, considering issues such as financial stability that are as important now, when your loved one is here, as they will be after their death. Opening joint accounts so that you have access to some money during your partner's illness and afterwards (unless there is some other reason that it would be detrimental), is a relatively simple thing to do. As is checking what benefits are available to you either from your partner's place of work, your place of work or the state. If you yourself are working, you may have to consider changing your hours or perhaps leaving in order to devote yourself to the time that your partner has left. You may need to cut back on spending or raise some cash, perhaps by remortgaging if you own your house.

Making a will is somewhat more complicated, especially if the estate is large or you have stepchildren, adopted children or previous spouses who are being supported, and myriad other issues to think through. However, making a will is one of the most important things you can do to safeguard everyone's future and it must be done while your partner is of sound mind, otherwise it may be challenged.

If your partner is in the frame of mind to be able to do so, you may want to start thinking about their funeral, although this subject is written about in much more detail in Part Three. You may both have jobs that involve computers on a day-to-day basis or you may be in retirement and use your computer regularly for a hobby or role in your community. If neither, getting up to speed on the computer so that you can use a search engine and perhaps internet banking if you do not already use it is an important skill for the person left behind to acquire.

Depending on who has been the DIY person in your household, getting to understand more about how your home works, replacing worn-out or broken items, and buying services are going to be crucial skills for the future. One of the easiest and best things you can do is buy a subscription to *Which?* magazine. This consumer organisation tests all sorts of products and services, and gives advice on what to buy. Not only could it save you from making expensive mistakes on such items as household appliances, but it is also helpful on many other issues that you might have to sort out, such as energy costs and insurance. We have had cause to quote from it and recommend it already in this text. You can also find it in your local library and online.

Lastly, but not at all the least important, is how are you going to look after yourself? Everyone is likely to be looking to you for support and guidance, so you have to stay strong and be able to cope. You may not think of yourself as a carer, but as a spouse or partner who is looking after their loved one. But you are indeed a carer and there is support in the wider community for people just like you, which is explained below. Don't miss out on the support available.

Being able to accomplish at least some of these things will give you more peace of mind when the time comes.

16

Stabilising Your Financial Affairs Prior to Death

If your partner's illness has affected their earnings, you will already be aware that you are paying the same bills with less money. Alternatively, if this is a sudden occurrence you will be faced with this situation now. Getting a grip on your finances may not be your number-one priority but it soon needs to be addressed.

As it is not helpful to make generalisations about financial competence and who has responsibility for it within your relationship, we begin with the basics of budgeting; you can skip over this if you want to, but it is there if you need it. If you use a computer all the time at your work, are the one who organises your family finances, sees to direct debits and does the internet banking for yourself or both of you, then the likelihood is that you do not need to read the next section, as you will continue to do these things after your partner has gone. However, if you do not, or if you are at sea as to where to start with all this, then read on.

Budgeting is an essential part of stabilising your finances. Simply put, this is 'money in' compared with 'money out'. The first thing you need to do, in conjunction with your partner, depending on how well they are able to do this, is to make a list of your bills. If you use internet banking, you will find a list of your standing orders and direct debits on your account. Or you can ask your bank or building society for one or refer to your last statement, bearing in mind that some bills may not appear on your statement depending on how regularly they are paid. Your standing orders and direct debits will probably range from monthly to annual payments. A standing order is an instruction to a bank by an account holder to make regular fixed payments to a particular person or organisation. A direct debit is an arrangement made with a bank that allows a third party to transfer money from a person's account on agreed dates in order to pay bills. The amount can vary depending on your usage, such as utilities, or on your spending, such as credit cards. If you can build up a spreadsheet, even using pencil and paper rather than a computer, it will be helpful.

Go back over at least the last year when it comes to mortgage or rent payments, internet and telephone bills, utilities, etc. and a few months for groceries, petrol, clothes, etc. You can calculate a figure for such things as entertainment, which might be severely curtailed from now on, anyway. There may be some subscriptions of your partner's that you want to close as they are no longer practicable. You can see annual membership fees on their bank account files and you may want to make a note in your diary as to when to close them if you do not want to use them yourself. There are rarely any rebates to be had on membership fees, so unless some of them are due soon you can relax about them. The next thing to do is make a list of your income and savings. The important thing is to look at the dates the money comes in and the dates it has to go out to pay bills, and see if there is any shortfall. If there is, you may be able to use your savings or look for other sources of income.

It may be that your partner was the main breadwinner and you will need to know from their employers if any continuing support will be forthcoming from them. Ask your partner to contact their employer and/or trade union official or professional body representative, if they are able to do so, to check what ill-health retirement provision there might be or insurance money. If your partner cannot do this, you must do it yourself. Your partner may have been self-employed or in a professional partnership. There may be some support coming from the latter, but in the case of the former, if your partner cannot work your income will be turned off like a tap, unless there are people or businesses who owe your partner money.

You may be the main breadwinner but want to give up your job to devote yourself to your partner while they are still alive. There is no statutory right for you to have paid compassionate leave from work.

Some employers will be sympathetic to you taking unpaid time off or to holding your job open, and some will not. Some will allow indefinite unpaid time off, while others will specify a time at which you must return. If you cannot get compassionate leave for as long as you want, you may have to resign, which means that you will probably lose your accumulated rights if you choose to return to the same place of work afterwards. Leaving your job might be out of the question financially for various reasons and, indeed, you may feel that you do not want to do so until your partner's condition becomes extreme. In this case there will be ramifications for the type of issues discussed in Part One concerning nursing and social care. See if you can get an interview with someone from the human resources department or equivalent in a small firm, and/or your trade union official as soon as possible to discuss your options. It is often useful to take a friend with you so that you can discuss it afterwards and check that you have heard everything correctly.

If either of you are self-employed, you may have bought some insurance scheme that pays out in cases of sickness. If your income dries up completely, you may have to apply for state benefits, such as statutory sick pay or a carer's allowance.

Some further suggestions and amplification are described in more detail below.

Joint accounts

In conjunction with your partner and with their agreement, you are advised to make as many of your bank accounts as you can into joint accounts so that you can have access to them now and after your partner's death. If an account is held jointly, you automatically inherit it after your partner's death. They are easy to access as they do not normally have to pass through probate. However, the tax situation will vary depending on whether or not you were married or in a civil partnership. (There is much more information on this in Parts Three and Four.)

Clearly, it depends on your relationship as to how comfortable your partner feels about you having access to their bank accounts and turning them into joint accounts. You will need passwords and PIN numbers too. In fact, passwords and PIN numbers are the one thing that everyone forgets to find out before their loss, as a friend of mine found to her distress as she had considerable difficulty in accessing some of her late husband's information.

Protecting your home

The sole aim of this book is to give you as much support as possible in what is a very difficult time in your life. Ensuring that you have a home for you and your children, after the death of your partner, has to be one of your top priorities. There are some fundamental issues that you should be aware of, no matter whether you are in a private property with a mortgage or in private or local authority rented accommodation. It is all too easy to find yourself in a position where you have no rights to live in a property after the death of a partner, whether you are financially independent from them or not. What follows is a very brief summary of what issues you should be aware of. Citizens Advice has a comprehensive website on this topic and you can always go and see them. If you are in any doubt about your rights, you should consult a solicitor. More details about this topic can be found under Wills and Probate.

It may also make sense to change bills such as utilities, telephone and digital services, and council tax into both your names if not done already. You can subsequently change them into your own name, but in the interim it makes for a smoother transition if you do not have to shut everything down. This, though, will all depend on the time available to you.

Title deeds and mortgages

Title deeds are legal documents that show who officially owns and holds title to a property or land. Most but not all titles to a property are registered with HM Land Registry. Where there is no mortgage on the property, the document registered is known as a Land Certificate. If there is a mortgage, the document is known as a Charge Certificate. If the title to the property is not registered with HM Land Registry there will instead be a set of title deeds, the most recent of which, known as a Conveyance, will show ownership.

If you own your home outright it is likely that either you or your solicitor has the deed(s). If you and your partner are buying a home together on a mortgage, the title deeds are kept by the lender until the mortgage has been repaid. If you are married or in a civil partnership, it is likely (but not always the case) that both your names are on both the mortgage and the deed, and you own the property as beneficial joint tenants, i.e. you own the property jointly. However, if, for example, either of you has moved into a property that the other was buying, you may not have amended either the mortgage – because it continued to be paid by one of you and the other partner paid for other things – or the deed, to show that you had any title to the property and you will not be beneficial joint tenants. This is unlikely to be a problem if you are married, because normally the spouse automatically inherits, or if there is a will leaving you the property. However, if you are not named on the mortgage and there is money outstanding, you would need to renegotiate repayments with the lender, as you are not named as a mortgagee, unless your partner had taken out some form of mortgage protection insurance, which is quite possible. In this case the debt will be paid by the insurance.

If you are unmarried or not in a civil partnership and your name is not on the title deed, you have no claim to the property after your partner's death, unless your partner has made a will bequeathing the property to you. If there is no will, the property will form part of your partner's estate and will be inherited by their next of kin, perhaps children by a previous marriage or their parents and siblings, who may not wish to include you in their plans.

If you think you are in a vulnerable position with regard to the property you are living in, it is important that you discuss the situation with your partner. You will also need to have a conversation with your lender as soon as possible. They will be able to clarify the situation for you. Be aware that some mortgage lenders demand repayment of the mortgage if there is any significant change made to the deed.

You are in a difficult position if your partner is not able to help you with this because they are incapacitated either mentally or physically. Additionally, if they have not made a will, they will no longer be able to write one, which might otherwise have rectified the situation. You may need to consult a solicitor to understand completely your position in this situation.

Protecting mortgage payments

If you have a mortgage, you may have bought some sort of mortgage protection scheme when you took it out. But if you cannot remember and your partner is not available to ask, making an appointment to see an advisor at the bank or building society where your mortgage comes from is essential. They will be able to tell you the situation.

You will also need to know if you have a repayment mortgage – one in which you repay capital and interest together – or an endowment mortgage – in which you pay off the interest and the capital is repaid at the end of the term by an endowment policy (that is, an insurance policy).

Your bank or building society may also be able to advise on you taking money out of your house if you have owned it for some time. At the very least, you will know that you can fall back on that if necessary. You may decide that you do not have enough money to manage and, if you own your own home, even though you are still paying a mortgage, you may consider taking some money out of your house, which is known as equity release. However, many schemes have an age at which such schemes begin, such as fifty-five. Do not do this without a lot of thought and advice from financial professionals. It used to be that these schemes were weighted on the side of the finance companies, but more organisations have now entered the market and competition has meant that these schemes are more equitable. Even so, you will need an equity release specialist to help you. Citizens Advice might be able to assist you here or the Equity Release Council, which is the industry body for the equity release sector.

Rental agreements

You could be renting accommodation privately or through a local authority or housing association. Whose name is the rental agreement in and does it safeguard the surviving partner? When it comes to private landlords, they are more likely to have discretion and be happy to carry on as before, as long as you can pay the rent, but with a council tenancy, often strict rules apply and you need to know what these are and act accordingly if they do not safeguard the surviving partner. This is particularly important if you have children.

Life insurance and assurance

Life insurance is designed to pay out a tax-free lump sum if you die during the term of the policy. It is a fixed-term policy. A decreasing basis type is often taken out with a repayment mortgage so that the amount the dependants receive on death is equal to the amount outstanding.

Life assurance typically covers you for your entire life and so is often known as 'whole life' cover. Unfortunately, once you have had a terminal diagnosis you are not going to be able to take out insurance or assurance for obvious reasons, so if your partner has none it is too late to take it out now. However, it is not too late for you and this is one way that you can protect your dependants. What you decide to do and what it will entail depends on your age. You can also take out insurance against being unable to work. The payments from this are now tax-free. However, such insurance does not come cheaply. You are advised to shop around or consult a financial advisor if you are thinking of doing either of these, so that you get cover that suits both your circumstances and your pocket.

State benefits

Every individual's circumstances are different and there is no way that we can predict what you might be entitled to before or after the death of your partner. The best thing you can do is find out for yourself by contacting the Benefits Agency and making an appointment with your local Citizens Advice, who will advise you on what you are entitled to.

You could also talk to your health professional. You may, for example, be entitled to some benefits by virtue of being a full-time carer for your partner, especially if you have had to give up working. Usually (but not always) these benefits are means-tested, so be prepared for that if you have some savings.

The Which? Guides 'Solutions for Living Independently' and 'Later Life Care' give details of the benefits and support schemes, other than local authority and NHS funding, that could help you and your partner, such as a Personal Independence Payment (PIP), an Attendance Allowance, or a Constant Attendance Allowance (CAA). In addition, you may be entitled to help with energy bills or reduced council tax. Carers and disability benefits information and how to apply can be found on the gov.uk website. There are special benefit rules for people with a terminal illness so that the payments can be increased and/or fast-tracked. You will need a DS1500 report, which you can obtain from your GP or consultant.

Benefits from work

If your partner is employed by someone else, you will both need to sit down with a member of the human resources department to talk about their benefits, pension, pay during sick leave and other considerations, assuming your partner is still capable of doing that. Otherwise you will have to do it on your own. Some companies do not have a human resources department, but you will still need to speak to someone with the authority to deal with these kinds of matters. The terms and conditions under which people are employed vary from organisation to organisation, and a lot will depend on your partner's contract of employment. They might have a statement of terms and conditions that you have access to, which will explain the main provisions. For example, some pension schemes allow you to receive a one-off lump sum if your life expectancy is less than twelve months, or to retire early and receive your pension. Do not be fobbed off by vague promises from someone who is clearly out of their depth. You have every right to get the most you can obtain in this difficult situation. The employer should be insured for just this contingency and the insurer will have statistically worked out how many employees this will happen to. On the other hand, it is up to you to keep the employer informed about your partner's condition. They will have to find someone to do your partner's job and in some instances this will be difficult for them.

If your partner is a member of a trade union, you should immediately let their representative know what has happened. Some unions have funds available for just such a situation and can offer assistance in other ways. At the very least, here is someone who can fight your corner when your energy for doing so is at a low ebb. Again, you need to keep them informed.

If your loved one is a partner in a business or professional firm, you will have to contact a representative of the partnership, who should have similar contingencies in place. Here the difference is that your partner probably knows all the members of the partnership and the discussions are more likely to be amicable.

If your partner is self-employed, for example as a builder or consultant, there are more complications. They may have taken out insurance to cover sickness and they may pay into a pension scheme. You will have to sort out what they are entitled to – perhaps they are eligible for early retirement provision – or ask someone else to do it for you. You may also find that your partner has contractual obligations that are legally binding. Some organisations might demand financial compensation for unfinished contracts. You need to be able to see the contract if one exists. If the agreement was verbal, you might never know what the agreement was as it is one person's word against another. If you think you are going to have problems, you are advised to have a session with a solicitor who is conversant with the law of contract and employment law, who will be able to advise you. It is worth paying someone with experience in these matters. Sometimes a single solicitor's letter will show people that you are to be taken seriously.

Leaving work

Having money coming into the house on a regular basis is critical to how you manage your financial affairs. If your partner is incapacitated or too ill to work, then the question of when they leave work simply does not arise. However, it may be that in some cases they can carry on working for a while, albeit at a reduced capacity. Indeed, their employer might be very grateful to have a handover period, which means that the break in continuity is not too abrupt. You can come to an agreement about how this will work, perhaps tapering down to a few hours a week, as long as it does not exhaust your partner, exacerbate their illness or steal time from the two of you wanting to be together. The other side of the coin is that it would probably be good for your partner's morale to still be valued at work, so that they do not feel completely useless, which is a feeling that many terminally ill people are prey to. Of course, there will come a time sooner or later when work becomes too much, but your partner can leave with dignity knowing that they have done what they can to keep your finances going.

If you work and contribute to the family pot, then deciding when you should stop, if at all, is also very important. If you have a demanding job that involves long hours and travel, you may find that this is impossible to maintain together with your concerns for your partner. You may already have found that hospital appointments begin to rule your life after a while. Your employer might be sympathetic and help make your role less demanding.

Alternatively, if you know roughly how long your partner might have left to live, you may feel that you want to spend as much time as possible with them and your children so that in effect you become a full-time carer. Be aware that not everyone is cut out for this. Looking at it dispassionately, you may decide that it would be better for them to be cared for by professional carers, and that to care for them yourself would do more harm than good to your relationship. Continuing to work might be a lifeline for you in terms of your morale and will make it easier for you to go back to work afterwards. There are a lot of issues to think about here, so do not be in too much of a hurry to take a decision unless it is absolutely forced upon you.

Saving money

How you economise depends very much on the type of lifestyle that you had before you got the news concerning your partner. No matter what your lifestyle was before the illness, you are advised to draw up a budget to get an accurate picture of what you are spending. If budgeting is completely new to you, then you might ask someone to help you. Two minds are much better than one on this sort of thing. If your partner can help you, then so much the better, but you may not want to trouble them with this.

Clearly, some areas of spending might be curtailed because neither of you are able to benefit any more from them, such as expensive gym memberships, although keeping going to the gym might be important for your health. You can ask for memberships to be stopped and in situations like this it is likely that the organisation will be sympathetic and waive your contractual obligations once given proof that you are sincere. If you are prepared to do so, you might want to explain the reason for your early termination and ask for your special circumstances to be taken into consideration, although you may not want to do this. You can look at other memberships – club memberships, museums, art galleries, cinemas and so on – to see when they expire and decide whether you are going to stop them. It is a good idea to have a diary that you can enter dates in and give yourself adequate warning about notification. Bear in mind that you will have a life afterwards and that some of these memberships might provide you with an opportunity to get out of the house and meet new people. Particularly good in this respect is the U3A, or University of the Third Age, which provides activities for members as well as having specialist speakers at regular meetings.

If one of you has been something of a shopaholic or indulged quite a bit in retail therapy, you may find that curtailing your spending is rather difficult and that you cannot just turn it off like a tap. Your budget will help you to see where you are spending most. If it is on clothes, you might have to declare a moratorium on any new ones for a while or resort to charity shops, although it can be time-consuming spending time going through their racks. You might have a friend who works in one and perhaps you could ask them to keep an eye open for things that they think would suit you. Or you might decide to wait for the sales rather more than you did before.

One thing it is harder to stop spending on is your children. They do not want to have to stand out from the crowd by having less than their peer group. Here you might have to resort to asking your friends and relatives to give them money for birthdays/Christmas so that they can buy the things they need for themselves.

Food is another thing that you should not economise on in terms of quality, although it may be possible for you to economise in other ways and eat better! Good cooking takes time, and if you are at home more than you were, you might find that you can make more of your own food, rather than buy in ready-made meals or takeaways. A good nourishing soup is very easy to make and there are plenty of recipes you can find for all palates. Vegetable-based soups are good for invalids (although you may have to sieve vegetables like celery or asparagus), because they contain roughage, vitamins and trace elements, and are relatively easy to swallow and digest (see 'Cooking for an Invalid' on p. 118 for more information). Be aware that introducing more fruit and vegetables to your partner's diet may have a downside; you are encouraged to read about the FODMAP diet if you find that an increase in some fruits and vegetables causes digestive problems. This book explains about the problems caused by excess sugars introduced into the gut from some fruit and vegetables, gluten and dairy products. Information can be found online or in books like *The Complete FODMAP Diet* by Dr Sue Shepherd and Dr Peter Gibson.

You will probably favour a particular supermarket. If you go in at the end of the day you will find many items marked down as they are close to their sell-by date. As long as you use them on the day or before they expire – you do not want to put anyone's health at risk – and you do not mind being flexible about what you eat every day, you can make substantial savings on a basketful of items. You may decide to go a bit downmarket from your usual supermarket. It is probably a bit late to start growing your own food, but you might think of that for the future. Growing vegetables in your garden or an allotment can be a very therapeutic way of dealing with grief. You may also find that planning meals in advance and then ordering the ingredients via an online supermarket stops all those impulse buys that often end up in the waste bin.

Paying the bills can become a real worry when your partner and/or you can no longer earn money. However, many organisations who you bank with can be very helpful. If your partner has been diagnosed with cancer, and you are one of their customers, the Halifax has a Cancer Support Team (see p. 129) who can help you manage your spending. Other banks and building societies may have similar teams and are worth contacting.

17
Making a Will

If you have a will, are happy with its provisions, it is not significantly out of date and there is nothing you feel you want to change, there is probably no need for you to read this section. However, if this is not the case, this is an important section to understand and act upon.

What follows is not a comprehensive guide to making a will under any and every circumstance. It assumes that your partner will be making the will and wishes to bequeath their estate to you – their spouse, civil partner or unmarried partner – and make provision for any children, be they yours together, theirs or yours, together with any other bequests that they would like to make, say to friends, other relatives, their old school or rugby club. According to a Which? survey in 2019, only four in ten adults have made a will. Having said that, it would make sense for both of you to make your wills at the same time, as this ensures that everything is neatly covered and that your surviving children, if you have any, are provided for.

Making an up-to-date will is one of the simplest things you can do to obtain peace of mind. You can use a solicitor or you can write one yourself. You can buy a kit from a stationer, such as W. H. Smith, or you can obtain the materials from any organisation that would like you to leave them something in your will, such as a charity or an art gallery. Perhaps you or your partner have been supported by an illness-related charity and you would like to support them in kind. The benefit of using a pre-prepared form is that it has all the legal jargon written down and you just have to fill in the blanks, but there are drawbacks to this if your financial affairs are at all complicated or you have a large estate. A middle road would be to draw up the will yourself and then ask a professional to review the one you've written. This can help to keep costs down while giving you some reassurance that there are no glaring mistakes.

You may already have a will, but how long ago was it written? Wills should be reviewed every five years and after a change in your status, such as marriage. A will made before a marriage was contemplated, unless it is made in contemplation of marriage, is in fact null and void in England, although this is not true in Scotland. Think twice about employing a will writer, because they are unregulated and you may not have the same level of consumer protection as you would with a solicitor, unless you have seen evidence of their handiwork or know that the individuals concerned have learned their skills in a solicitor's office. Often, such organisations charge for storing your will and have themselves written in as executors, thereby gaining the fees they might have forfeited by writing your will cheaply. Banks are also in the market for making wills, again with the hopes of handling the estate after death. Unless you have a warm relationship with your bank manager, you should think twice about using your bank.

Philip Kingsley's book *A Straightforward Guide to Producing Your Own Will* shares some truly worrying statistics and facts: 75 per cent of people with dependent children have not made a will. This means that if both parents died at the same time, for example in a car crash, custody of their children may not go to the person they intended. Eighty per cent of couples living together without marrying have not made a will either, which is even more worrying!

Many people believe that if they die without making a will – meaning they are intestate – their husband or wife will inherit everything. Unfortunately, this is not the case. Similarly, almost 90 per cent of parents who are married or in a civil partnership are not aware that if they die without a will, under the laws of intestacy there are very specific rules. If the estate is valued under £270,000, the spouse or civil partner receives the whole estate. It is the same if there are no children. If there are children, the surviving partner will inherit the first £270,000 from the estate, plus personal chattels, plus half of the remainder of the estate. The other half of the estate goes to the children, grandchildren and great-grandchildren if there are any. In addition, the surviving spouse or civil partner inherits a house that was jointly owned automatically, together with any joint accounts.

It is common for families to include children from previous partnerships who have to be cared for. An ex-wife, or civil partner who was legally divorced from the deceased or whose civil partnership with the deceased was dissolved before the date of death, gets nothing from the estate under the rules of intestacy, i.e. where there is no will. However, they may be able to make a claim under the Inheritance (Provision for Family and Dependants) Act 1975.

So the key message here is: **if there is no will, it is possible, indeed likely, that the best provision has not been made for you and your children**. People who are married or registered civil partners do not have to pay any inheritance tax on money or property left to them by their spouse. Anyone can leave up to £325,000 free of inheritance tax. The existing inheritance tax nil-rate band is set to remain at £325,000 until the end of the tax year 2020/21. You can leave an additional £150,000 tax-free if you are passing on your main home to a direct descendant under the 'main residence' band, which became law in the 2019/20 tax year. This gives a total allowance of £475,000 per person. This figure will increase to £175,000 in the tax year 2020/21, thus giving a total allowance of £500,000. For estates valued under this amount the beneficiaries won't pay inheritance tax. Unmarried cohabiting couples have no automatic right of inheritance if their partner dies without a will, although they too may make a claim under the 1975 Act mentioned above.

The text below is addressed to both you and your partner, although it is likely that the surviving partner will be advising the terminal partner. It aims to explain what is involved in making a will and the pitfalls to avoid, even if you use the services of a solicitor. It does not aim to be totally comprehensive. These notes are to give you some ideas of what is needed and how to undertake it. The aforementioned Philip Kingsley book should help fill in the detail, or you can refer to a government website such as www.gov.uk, Citizens Advice or Age UK, all of which give comprehensive advice. What follows appertains to England and Wales. Scotland and Northern Ireland have slightly different laws, which are described later in the text.

The mental health of your partner may present a practical concern. It is important that the person making the will has decided on its provisions without outside interference and has not been unduly influenced. A person who is certified as insane and detained in a mental institution, and who requires guarding against serious exploitation, would not be deemed capable. If you have been living together and have noticed a deterioration in the reasoning powers of your partner, it would be best to use a solicitor, who can give an expert judgement as to the fitness of the will-maker. They generally keep notes on this point, if it seems relevant, just in case a will is contested. On top of everything else, you do not want to have to wait for the will to be released before you can obtain probate or access to the money that you may desperately need for living expenses.

The provisions of a will

The purpose of any will is to ensure that everything that is owned or has been accumulated in life goes to the people the will-maker wants it to go to. There is something of a mystery over why Shakespeare left his 'second best bed' to his wife, but that is what his will said.

What might have been accumulated?

Money: In whatever form. This will include savings accounts, endowments, premium bonds, etc. It is helpful if there is a list kept together with a copy of the will saying exactly what these constitute and how to access them.

Property: If there is a sole owner, then a property can be disposed of as wished by the executor, though always bear in mind that there might be an outstanding mortgage or bank loan that has to be repaid. Sometimes properties are remortgaged so highly that there is very little left to distribute. If the property is jointly held, ownership on death reverts to the other joint owner as long as it is based on a beneficial joint tenancy, which most mortgages between couples are. A 'tenants in common' agreement is ideal for people who want to own property with their partner but wish to leave their share of the property to someone else when they die.

Insurance policies: Insurance policies sometimes have rules about beneficiaries. People named in the policy may benefit – such as a first wife – and there may be no alternative but to allow such people to benefit. The small print needs to be looked at carefully before these are included in the will as things that are bequeathed. However, mention should be made of them for clarity and completeness.

Shares: Shares can be left to any beneficiary except in the case of some private companies, which may have a 'buyback' clause. These should all be checked.

Trust funds: If a trust fund is required, perhaps for your surviving children, you are strongly advised to get specialist help.

Personal effects: Personal effects can be bequeathed to individuals as a remembrance. As this sometimes changes over time, it easier to do this as a Letter of Wishes, but it does not carry the same weight as being mentioned in a will. If death is on the horizon, it would be better to be specific in the will.

Other things that you might want to take into consideration are:

The funeral: Provisions for the funeral are covered in great detail in Part Three (p. 133). It is always recommended that the funeral plans are discussed with those who will be left behind, as it is a comfort to them to know that they are carrying out the last wishes of the deceased. Funeral expenses are paid free of tax.

Donating organs or the use of the body after death: This may not be a subject either of you feel up to sorting out at this stage, but alternatively you both may feel strongly that you want to benefit others by their death. More about this topic can be found on p. 139.

Contentious wills

If you think it is likely that the contents of your partner's will may be challenged after death, you should always seek the advice of a solicitor. Challengers may involve children from previous marriages or former spouses. They can put something called a 'caveat' on the will, which lasts for six months.

Another thing you can do is to write a recital. A recital is a statement at the end of the will that explains how and why the will has been drawn up in the way that it has. It might explain, for example, why someone has been cut out from this or a previous will, or why a certain executor has been chosen. Should the will be challenged, this gives the lawyers (and judge if it comes to court) an understanding of what was in your partner's mind. As long as they are not breaking the law in any way, and the explanation appears to make sense and your partner does not appear to have been unduly coerced, such an explanation is more likely to get the agreement of the courts.

Writing the will

Always bear in mind that a will should be written so that you are not bequeathing more than you actually own. This should take the tax liability into account. It is often easier, apart from small sums that are being left to individuals or organisations such as charities, to divide the residuary of the estate into percentages. Thus x will receive 25 per cent of y, whatever y is, because you won't know exact figures at this stage. Be aware also that the last few weeks and months of life can be very costly in terms of care, whether at home or in a care home or hospice, and this may reduce the amount to be distributed quite considerably.

You need to make a list of beneficiaries and what you want to bequeath to them. Include all their contact details. If a trust is proposed, the trustees should be in agreement before being named. Charities should be contacted. They will supply a legacy clause. Bequests to charities are exempt from inheritance tax.

The simplest of all wills is to leave everything to your spouse or partner. Be aware, however, that if they too die within twenty-eight days the inheritance may pass to others whom you might not have chosen. To prevent this happening another beneficiary or beneficiaries should be named.

Choosing an executor

Being the executor of a will is quite an onerous task, particularly so if the executor is not working in conjunction with a solicitor. The person concerned must be in agreement with undertaking the role. If you do not include a solicitor or the bank, you are recommended to choose two executors. Do not choose any more than this, as they then have to agree everything among themselves, which is onerous and very time-consuming. Your spouse or partner may be an obvious choice, but they may not feel they are up to the task. Your children might seem suitable, but it is always difficult to choose one over another. It is sometimes easier to have a friend, who can adjudicate and see fair play. It doesn't matter whether the executor is or isn't a beneficiary of the will. However, if they are not a beneficiary, it is courteous to leave them something as a thank-you for doing the job. They will have earned every penny!

Witnessing the will

It is critical that your partner's will is valid. Once the will has been written (preferably typed so that it can be easily read), it needs to be witnessed. It is actually the signature that needs to be witnessed, so all the signatures should be done at the same time. The witnesses witness your partner's signing of the will and then sign it themselves. There must be two of them and they must both be over the age of eighteen. Nothing can be left to the witnesses or their married partners. In other words, they cannot be beneficiaries. It is best to choose a neighbour, a health professional you are in contact with or someone completely unknown to your family – even a passing stranger will do if they are willing. Please see p. 98 for the rules in Scotland and Northern Ireland.

Storage

If death is likely in the not-too-distant future, the will needs to be put somewhere safe and accessible, rather than stored with a solicitor or bank. Only an original will can be used for probate purposes. Whatever you do, make sure that you know where the will is when the time comes.

Overseas property

If the estate includes an overseas property, a provision now exists (but for how much longer at the time of writing with Brexit looming?) to allow owners to make one will and have it administered in any country that is party to the convention. You would have to check whether the property you have is in one of those countries. There are certain criteria to be followed, which are:

- The will must be in writing but in any language.

- The person whose will it is must declare in front of a solicitor/notary that the will is really hers/his and this must be witnessed by two people.

The person making the will must then sign it at the end, and sign and number each page, in the presence of a solicitor and witnesses, who must sign at the end. The date must be added by a solicitor.

As this is a new piece of legislation, you are strongly advised to seek professional help. In the past, a separate will was often required that had to be authorised by a notary in the respective country. If the terminal prognosis is weeks rather than months away, getting out to your other home and will-making might prove a problem, especially if your partner is too ill to travel.

If there is time, you might want to think about selling your overseas property and therefore simplifying the whole business. However, it is another problem to deal with when you are already dealing with a lot of problems, unless you can see it will be straightforward or you can delegate it to someone else.

Wills and taxation

Unless you are unusually generous people, you and your partner will want the estate to be left so that as little as possible is paid to the state, so minimising inheritance tax liability is an important consideration. Inheritance tax became law under the 1986 Finance Act to replace Capital Transfer Tax. It is the tax you have to pay on your estate when you die if it is worth more than £325,000. Strictly speaking, inheritance tax is a tax on what is known as 'transfer of value'. This means the tax is levied on transfers made by the person upon death or within seven years of death. You cannot now start giving large amounts away to reduce your tax liability! See 'Gifts' (p. 98) for more information on this. The amount of inheritance tax payable depends on:

- The value of the estate.

- The value of any substantial gifts made within the last seven years.

- Any exemptions from inheritance tax on death such as those on gifts to a surviving spouse, charities, etc.

If a person is domiciled in the UK, the tax applies to all that person's property wherever it may be situated. If a person is domiciled abroad, then the tax is applicable only to property in the UK. The threshold for inheritance tax is 40 per cent on the estate after exemptions and after a tax threshold, which currently stands at £325,000. If your partner has a large estate and is intending to leave it to someone other than their spouse, or spouse and children, you should also get the help of a financial advisor, who will help you with your tax affairs.

The laws on wills in Scotland and Northern Ireland

The laws in these countries are slightly different. Only the ones deemed applicable to the situation in this book are outlined below. There are similar laws relating to the will being voluntary and that the maker of the will is capable, meaning they are of sound mind and aware of what they are doing.

If you do not make a will in Scotland and Northern Ireland (also known as being intestate), the amount that the spouse may have and the amount the children may have are significantly different. In Scotland, marriage does not revoke a will. Scots law says you cannot disinherit your children. Legal rights in Scotland are an automatic entitlement enjoyed by the surviving spouse or civil partner and any children including adopted and illegitimate children.

Elsewhere in the UK the term 'children' applies to illegitimate and adopted children (but not stepchildren), who have the same rights as natural children. In Scotland, the will must be made in writing and signed on every page by the person making the will in front of a witness. If you live in Scotland and there are multiple offspring from different relationships, you are advised to consult a solicitor.

Gifts

There are complex laws concerning gifts, which make them exempt from inheritance tax. If you wish to make any gifts prior to death, you are strongly advised to consult a financial advisor or at least get a book on the subject. You can give away a total of £3,000 each tax year to people other than exempt beneficiaries without paying tax. You can also carry this amount forward for a year. Exempt beneficiaries include your spouse and charities.

Tax-free gifts can also be made, up to certain limits, on the occasion of a marriage or civil partnership. The tax-free limit for wedding gifts is £5,000 where the gift is to a child of yours, £2,500 where it is to a grandchild and £1,000 where the gift is to someone else.

Other small gifts of up to £250 per person per year can be made free from inheritance tax. Such gifts can be made to as many people as you like, as long as the recipient has not benefited from another exemption.

There is also a useful inheritance exemption for 'normal expenditure out of income', which may be used to make tax-free lifetime gifts. It is often used by grandparents to pass money to grandchildren, for example by way of a monthly standing order or to pay for school fees. For the exemption to apply, the gift must satisfy the following conditions:

- It must form part of the donor's regular expenditure.

- The gift must be made out of income (taking one year with the next).

- The donor must retain sufficient income to maintain their normal standard of living.

Gifts made in this way are completely exempt from inheritance tax and they are not subject to the seven-year rules applicable to potentially exempt transfers.

Air miles

If your partner had a job where they travelled a lot, they may have accrued a considerable number of air miles, worth quite a lot of money, before their illness prevented them from taking them. Most airline points schemes' rules state that miles cannot be transferred in the event of death. However, in reality this may not be the case and you are advised to write your partner's air miles into their will. It is likely that the airline will ask to see a certified copy of the death certificate before they transfer the miles.

18

A Lasting Legacy

There are several ways that you can leave a legacy, and we have suggested some of them below. We have on occasion addressed your partner rather more directly, as what follows are all things they might want to think about.

Organ donation

Immediately after death is the time when organs are taken to be donated to others in need and an early decision will be required, so it is helpful to have discussed the possibility with your partner well beforehand.

If your loved one did not have a donor card and you never discussed the matter, this is a very difficult decision to take at such a time. You might feel strongly that you would be happy to think that your loved one's organs had been transplanted into another person to help them live or give them a fuller life. It does not have to be specified in the will but can be done in writing separately or in front of a minimum of two witnesses. If your partner wants to donate their organs, they should acquire a donor card or contact the National Health Service.

Donating their body might help future research into the disease your partner suffered from. If they want to donate their body you should contact the Human Tissue Authority. There is a separate authority for Scotland. A consent form can be obtained from your local medical school and a copy kept with the will. Please note that consent cannot be given by anyone else after your partner's death and that the body might not always be accepted after death.

On the other hand, you might feel it is against your religion or culture to do this or that it is just not right. Or you might feel that you are too distressed to make a decision that you might regret later, when the emphasis is on enjoying what time is left to you both. Different religions have different attitudes to organ transplants. Judaism supports and encourages organ donation in order to save lives. Jewish law requires consultation with a competent rabbinic authority before consent is granted.

A friend of mine whose father developed PCA, a rare type of Alzheimer's disease, in his fifties was able to fulfil his father's wish and successfully donated his brain on his death to Brains for Dementia Research. Such a donation is done in the first twenty-four hours or so following death and does not delay a funeral. Not only was this a valuable gift to help international researchers in their global quest to find a cure, it meant his children also benefited as they were reassured to learn that his disease was not the type that is inherited. In this case the children also volunteered to share medical records and take part in annual interviews in the years before their father died, to give the scientists as full a picture as possible, and found this unexpected source of support very cathartic.

As noted earlier, Max and Keira's Law came into effect in England in May 2020. This reverses the current situation of 'opt in' to 'opt out'. In Wales there is 'deemed consent'. In other words: if you haven't registered an alternative decision you will be considered to have no objection. In Scotland the system is currently 'opt in'. Legislation to introduce a 'deemed authorisation system' will come into force on 26th March 2021. Northern Ireland has an 'opt in' system. A decision was made in 2016 not to proceed with any changes in the foreseeable future. Excluded groups in England and Wales include those under the age of 18 and those who lack mental capacity to understand the new arrangements. There is a website (www.organdonation.nhs.uk) which explains everything in more detail, a fact sheet you can download and a helpline (0300 303 2094), open office hours, to help you decide. You will want to discuss this with your loved one and know what they want to do.

A trust fund

You might want to set up a trust fund for your children or grandchildren, perhaps for their secondary or tertiary education. Another reason for setting up a trust fund might be to inaugurate a series of grants, perhaps to enable students to attend your old school or university or a series of research grants into a topic that you studied yourself or are interested in. All of these will need trustees who are willing to administer it. They need to be chosen with the aim of the trust fund in mind, for example close friends or relatives in the case of your children, or old school and university friends if you have an educational grant in mind, and academics well known in the field for research grants. If you set up a poetry or short story prize, for example, you can set it up in your own name or in the name of someone you want to commemorate. You will need the services of a solicitor to draw a trust fund up.

Setting up a charity

There may have been little or no research into the illness that your partner is suffering from and therefore your partner might decide to set up a charity for research purposes in order that other people benefit and do not suffer as they have. In the case of setting up a charity, you will need to contact the Charities Commission. At the time of writing, charities with an income of more than £5,000 need to register with them. Whether or not your proposed charity is subject to the £5,000 income rule, you will need a method of accounting for the fund: www.resourcecentre.org.uk is a useful source of information on charity registration.

Donations to good causes

You may wish to have something set up in your name after your death. There are the Rhodes Scholarships at one end of the scale and a brick in the wall of a new building with your name on it, at your old school, college or university, at the other, depending on your wealth. Perhaps your local cinema or theatre where you have had hours of enjoyment is refurbishing and is putting names on the new seats. My husband was a reader at the Bodleian Library in Oxford and spent many happy hours there. When they wanted new chairs for their reading rooms, I was able to buy and inscribe one with his name and a comment. This seemed to me to be a very fitting memorial for him, but there is no reason why you cannot do this for yourself.

Your written legacy

If you are an academic or writing is your main source of income, you need to ensure that you have someone who is prepared to continue your work as you would have done, deal with editors and publishers when it comes to republishing and copyright, and safeguard your reputation when it comes to plays or films made out of your books. Often this is your partner, although not all partners either want to do this or are capable of doing so. T. S. Eliot's wife comes to mind here. She rigorously defended her husband's reputation. Sometimes you need a literary executor. If that is the case, how will they be paid for this time-consuming labour? Sometimes royalties are quite extensive and need to be included in the will.

Writing an autobiography

Something more personal might be getting someone to help your partner write their autobiography. If you have children or grandchildren to whom they have not been able to talk about their life, and if there is time available, this is a way to make your partner better known to them. Various organisations will help you do this, such as Life Book.

19
Planning Your Partner's Funeral

If the death of your partner is imminent, you may wonder what is the point of a funeral plan with a funeral director, as one of the main reasons for having a plan is to save money. In normal circumstances you would be hoping that death might not occur for some time. In that case you decide what you want, the funeral director tells you how much it will cost and you pay, either in a lump sum, or in instalments over a period of time at today's prices. As funeral costs are always going up, the hope is that you will be paying now for something that will happen to you in the future and that would cost more if you were to wait until death. This gives you peace of mind, as it takes the burden off your children or beneficiaries, and if you live long enough, comprises a bargain.

One in four of a large funeral conglomerate's funerals are now pre-planned. SunLife produce a 'Cost of Dying Report' every year. In July 2020 they posted that the average cost of a basic funeral in 2019 was £4,417. They also showed that the total cost of dying in 2019 was £9,493, which includes the funeral, plus extras such as the send-off and professional fees. Where you live has an enormous bearing on what you pay, with London being the most expensive and the north-west the cheapest.

The other big benefit of pre-planning a funeral is that your partner gets the opportunity to decide how they want their funeral to be. So now you both have choices. Your partner can ignore their funeral altogether and trust you to do the right thing when the times comes, or you can plan it together and you, the surviving partner, can make notes and use them when the time comes. You can prepay and use the services of a funeral director to help you both plan the whole process. In the latter scenario, you won't be getting the normal benefit of paying well ahead of time.

There are obvious pros and cons to all three choices. Planning a funeral might not be what your partner wants to do at the moment when every minute is precious. On the other hand, if you talk about it, you will know what your loved one wants, such as whether they want to be cremated or buried, where they want to be buried or have their ashes buried or scattered, and the type of service they want plus the music they would like to be played. The pros of pre-planning are that you will be able to get a sense of the costs and will be able to include more things in your choices, such as the type of coffin, the number of limousines and the flowers you want. There is nothing to stop you doing price comparisons with a number of funeral directors in your area and getting a rough idea of what is available and how much it will cost. You, the surviving partner, will also know that, come what may, even if for some reason you are frozen out of the arrangements, your loved one is getting the funeral they wanted.

Other benefits of pre-planning include the fact that you and your partner receive a résumé of what has been planned, and the person who will be arranging the funeral – in this case you, the widow or widower, civil partner or partner – gets a support pack. There is also a professionally prepared will form included in some plans, which is helpful if your partner has not already made one.

Just to give you an idea, one group of funeral directors offers three distinct types of funeral. One for those who prefer a traditional funeral service; one for environmentally conscious people with responsibly sourced coffins that are fully carbon neutral certified; and another that includes a distinctive range of choices for those who want a unique celebration of their life and passions. Each of these can be as bespoke as you both want, with any added extras you may require.

We do not want you to feel that we are advocating a pre-planned funeral – far from it – but it is one way of ensuring that some of the burden is taken off you when the time comes. Having said that, planning the funeral can be a great distraction from grief and gets the surviving partner through the first days after the death, as there is usually so much to think about that it can delay the shock they are actually feeling until their body has got used to the idea.

20

Get Computer Savvy

If you have a job where you use a computer a lot, or do the bill paying and computer banking for the family and consider yourself proficient, there is no need to read on. What follows is for those who rarely touch a computer and have certainly never used it to pay household bills or for internet banking.

You may not think of what is on your computer as a legacy, but if you or your partner have internet banking; use your computer to access, say, your utilities accounts; or have been involved in social media, you will need to know the passwords for all the accounts your partner holds in order to have access to them. You have no right to photographs, for example, if you cannot unlock your partner's accounts. Of course, if you do not know the passwords already, your ability to do this will depend on how ill or incapacitated your partner is. It is therefore something to get organised as soon as you possibly can if you wish to avoid hours of frustration while you try to work out how you are going to get into their accounts. We know partners to whom this has happened. If your spouse is still able to do so, get them to help you unlock their various accounts. You may not think of yourself as computer savvy and perhaps all this sort of thing was done by the person who is now no longer able to do it, but unless you want to appear very needy to your family and friends, this is something you simply have to come to terms with.

In addition, it is both something that your dying partner will feel better about – knowing that you are not completely helpless, and if they are not too unwell, it can be a project for you to do together. It can also be something that you decide you are going to get better at. You can put yourself on a course at your local college or continuing education facility

– your local library will also help and may even hold courses or offer one-to-one help. This may have been something you were just lazy about or never felt interested in, but it is essential that in today's world you get to grips with it. Your local bank or building society will help you get started with internet banking if you do not already have it. As you get older, this ability will become far more useful.

If you have family miles away, it is wonderful to know how to use Skype or Zoom, or upload photographs and videos to your computer. After the funeral and things settle down, your family and friends cannot be on the doorstep all the time. Here is a wonderful opportunity to learn a skill that has positive ramifications for your health and well-being.

It may be that your partner had someone who they called upon if a computer problem was too difficult for them to solve. This may have been one of your children, or someone they paid. Getting help from children and grandchildren is great if they are local and/or willing to drop everything to come to your aid, but more problematical if solving your computer problems has to wait for their two-monthly visit. Find someone local who you can pay in either cash or kind and do not be afraid to call on them. A kind friend might be able to help you, but make sure they have lots of patience!

Our local library offers one-to-one computer lessons and problem-solving sessions that are free. Why not enquire whether or not your local library does the same? A website that might be helpful is www.learnmyway.com. This offers courses in all sorts of topics, including using a computer, and aims to develop digital skills for people to make the most of the online world. If you have an iPad you may find that you can get a lesson from your local Apple Store or another computer outlet that sells computers. People will be happy to help, especially when they know your circumstances. Don't be too proud to ask for help.

A website called www.mywishes.co.uk enables someone to record their wishes in terms of their will, funeral, bucket list and advance care planning. Once you register you can follow their video tutorials, which will guide you through each of their features, as above. You can also safeguard your online accounts.

21
Looking After Your Own Health and Well-being

You will be so busy looking after the needs of your partner and your children that it can be tempting to neglect your own needs. Everyone will look to you for support, but if you collapse who can they turn to? Obviously, if time is very short you can afford to do what you have to do and recover after the death has occurred, as every minute is precious. However, if you are in for the long haul, there are things you can do to ensure that you manage the energy you have productively.

We all have psychological, spiritual and physical needs. It may be helpful at the outset to recognise that you could experience problems here and discuss it openly with a close friend. Ask them to keep an eye on you and make you do things that you know will be helpful.

Looking after yourself is explored much more deeply in Parts Five and Six, and you may wish to read the chapters there in conjunction with the paragraphs below.

Psychological needs

Caring for a terminally ill or dying partner and any children you may have is very demanding psychologically, as you may be the font of support to many people. Who is caring for you, the carer? How do you keep your strength up? Seeing your partner terminally ill or dying may raise issues that you thought were long buried, either concerning your partner or other people, perhaps your parents. Do not be frightened by this. It is common but often goes unacknowledged. Some charities such as Cruse Bereavement Care offer a pre-bereavement service that you can use. Their waiting lists are sometimes lengthy, but they will often respond very quickly to a pre-bereavement situation, as clearly you cannot wait for support in this circumstance. If you think your needs go deeper and it is affecting how you function, in fact you are becoming dysfunctional, you might consider counselling or therapy (described in more depth in Part Six).

You may have a partner who wishes to keep their illness secret for various reasons, and you have the task of having to cover up for their absences or weakness. You might find this very difficult to handle, as you may feel that it denies the people that should know the opportunity to say their goodbyes as well as your partner. It is difficult to know what to do about this. Only you will know if you want to go against your partner's wishes and tell people on your own account. This does add to the psychological burden.

Your local GP might have a counselling service or could point you in the direction of somewhere else you could seek help. There are several national counselling and psychotherapy organisations in the United Kingdom. Use a search engine to find out by searching for 'counselling or psychotherapy near me'.

If your loved one is disappearing before your eyes owing to dementia or one of its associated illnesses, Nicci Gerard's book, *What Dementia Teaches Us About Love*, may be very helpful.

Spiritual needs

Even if you have a strong faith, it may have been sorely tested by what is happening to you. You may feel that it is all very unfair. 'Why is this happening to me and my loved one?' In this case it may be beneficial to seek out your own spiritual advisor – a vicar, priest, rabbi or imam, for example – and discuss your misgivings with them. They will not be surprised by your distress, as they will have seen it many times before. It may be that your faith in a just and loving God is wavering. You may need to put what is happening into perspective and they will help you do that. The hospital, hospice or care home chaplain may also be able to offer you solace.

If you have no particular mainstream faith, you may find that meditating is helpful. This can be difficult if your mind is whizzing with thoughts, but just trying to quieten your mind for twenty minutes and focusing on an object, a sentence or a completely blank wall can leave you feeling more refreshed. A local course might help you. Try your local library or online.

Physical needs

One of the first things that goes out of the window in a situation like this is sleep. You lie awake worrying about what is going to happen and how you are going to cope. However, we all need sleep to enable us to keep going and if you find you are consistently lying awake into the small hours, finally falling asleep through sheer exhaustion and waking up groggy, you must do something about it. You may not like to take medication, but in these circumstances, you might want to ask your GP for some sleeping pills. Get into a routine – read a few pages of a book or magazine, have a hot milky drink, do not use your computer, tablet or laptop just before bedtime. Restraining yourself from using such technological gadgets last thing at night is difficult, but necessary. Conversely, you may be so exhausted that you fall asleep instantly but wake up as though you have not slept at all. There is a lot of literature available about sleep, which you may find helpful.

During times of immense stress, many people stop eating proper meals and eat snacks, sandwiches and sugary treats such as chocolate, cake and biscuits instead. This is absolutely understandable in the short term, but after a while not fulfilling the prescription of 'five fruit and vegetables a day' will begin to have an effect. Try to have a breakfast that includes at least two fruit – perhaps by putting strawberries, banana and blackcurrants on your morning cereal. Perhaps your friends could supply you with smoothies that you can keep in the fridge? Obviously, you need roughage too, so make sure you have a supply of fruit and veg to take to the hospital, nursing home or hospice with you. Carrots make good snacks and are full of roughage and essential vitamins and minerals.

Either you or your partner may have been the person who did the cooking in your household. Both of you will now face challenges. If it was the person who is terminally ill who did the cooking, it is unlikely that they will want to carry on with this for much longer and there will come a time when they cannot. If you are the carer, you either will have a lot less time in which to think about meals, shop and cook, or you never did it in the first place and it is all new to you. This is not a skill you can pick up immediately and you may have to rely on friends to put things in your freezer or give you basic lessons. See also, 'Cooking for an Invalid' on p. 118.

Next comes exercise. How do you do that? You will probably be sitting quite a lot. Get up and move around frequently. Do you do Pilates or yoga? Do some stretching exercises. Try standing on one leg with your foot on top of the standing leg and with your eyes open. This is good for balance and the flexibility of ankle and foot. Try to get at least one walk in every day out in the fresh air. Whatever exercise you have done in the past – line dancing, ballet, running, badminton – try to keep it up. Are you a gardener? Gardening is one of those activities where time and stress seem to disappear for long stretches of time. Whatever you do, try to make sure that you have some physical 'me' time. It may seem selfish to be thinking of yourself. In the long run, it is not!

If you have a pet, such as a dog, it can be very helpful in making sure you get the exercise you need. Pets have needs too, which you cannot ignore! Research shows that stroking can be very therapeutic and calming and reduces blood pressure in some people. If your children have pets, it is important that these continue to be cared for, as the death of an animal at this time is just what you don't want! Your child could find their gerbil, rabbit, mouse or other furry friend a great source of comfort right now.

Last but not least comes sex. You and your partner might have had a very satisfying sex life before they became ill or were incapacitated, and you are going to miss the physical intimacy that comes from sleeping with another person. On the other hand, it might have tailed off recently and you have got used to it or were never that interested in the first place. If the former is the situation, there is no easy way of saying that difficult times lie ahead for you. You may find yourself suffering from the dull ache of longing and it might seriously impair your ability to cope. Your frustration will make itself felt on those around you, just when you least want to cause friction and disharmony. If you feel you can, talk to your GP about this. There are specialist sex physiotherapists, psychotherapists and counsellors who will be able to help you.

22
Being a Carer

You probably do not think of yourself as being a 'carer' and this term may have a rather odd ring to it in your ears. You will see yourself as looking after someone you love and for whom you are only too happy to perform this service. However, you are also a 'carer', and in the eyes of the community you have special rights. Indeed, if you are spending most of your time in caring for your partner or spouse, actually over thirty-five hours a week, you may be eligible for a carer's allowance. You will have to check this out for yourself. You can do this through any medical professional you are in contact with, your local authority or a charity such as Marie Curie or Macmillan.

However, this section is not really about material benefits but about the help that is available to you in other ways. You can tap into a lot of support by finding out what is organised for carers like you in your neighbourhood, town or county. Access this through your GP's surgery, social services support worker or by contacting your county council, all of whom can redirect you to such organisations as Action for Carers. You can meet people in similar circumstances to yourself, you can learn about respite care for your loved one and yourself, and you can generally obtain information and advice that helps you feel that you are not alone because of the interaction and information you obtain. Jane Matthews has written a great no-nonsense book, *The Carer's Handbook*, which you might find helpful. She covers all the practical and emotional aspects of the role from both her own experience and that of other carers.

We are assuming that in most cases you will want to be the person who looks after your partner. However, for various reasons, such as your own incapacity, this may not be practical or possible. You may then want to obtain the services of an end of life doula. This is a relatively new role in the UK. End of life doulas are a specialist personal service that aims to support an individual through the last period of their lives. Many have been trained to do this and there is a qualification for the role. The qualified doulas require payment. Those in training often offer their services for free as part of their development. If you think you would like to know more, contact either End of Life Doula UK on eol-doula.uk or Living Well Dying Well on lwdwtraining.uk or 01273 474 278.

23
Parenting

Domestic parenting

You may have children living at home who are still very much dependent on you for their care and will continue to be so for some time to come, depending on their ages. In today's world, parenting is shared much more than it ever used to be, but even so it might be that up to now you have divided the parenting role with your partner in fairly distinct ways so that one of you does the 'taxi' duties and the other makes sure that your children go out of the door properly dressed for school and with the right books and gym kit, at least until they are of an age to be responsible for this themselves. Conversely, one of you might have been working shifts or long hours and the other did everything around the home. If the partner who is dying was the one who did most of the hands-on parenting, you will have another set of tasks to add to working, attending hospital appointments or having your partner at home: that of parenting your children. This could present a steep learning curve and one that will continue long after your partner has died.

First of all, you may have to be responsible for meals. It is understandable if you rely on takeaways or buy ready meals in the short term, but over the long term this is not sustainable, both owing to the cost and also because processed foods are full of chemicals, fat and sugar, which it would be better for your children's sake to avoid. If this is all a closed book to you, get someone you know, who has children and cooks every night, to talk through with you how you might tackle this. Ask them, if you need to, to teach you some basic recipes. Have a rota of meals: a variety of pasta one night, a curry with rice another, perhaps a roast chicken big enough to do several meals, including sandwiches for you, at the weekend, and so on. This also makes the shopping list a lot easier. Of great help can be 'one pot' meals like those of Rukmini Ayer, where you get the ingredients, put them together and the meal pretty well cooks itself. Could one of your children help you? Could you delegate some of it to them? Above all, try to make it a fun thing that you all share.

When my mother died, washing was a big thing for my father and me. Luckily, we had a Chinese laundry up the street for bed linen, but we had to devote whole Sundays to 'the wash'. Nowadays, washing machines and dryers make this a lot easier, but someone has to be responsible for collecting it and making sure it gets done. Again, one of your children might be able to help with this. Do not expect to have the same standards as previously. And it is likely some ironing will not get done, even if it was before, unless you pay someone to do it for you; this all depends on how much money there is to spend on these items. Some parents might be able to pay a housekeeper, but we are assuming this is a rarity. It is more likely that you and your children will be responsible for the clothes you turn out in to go to work and school.

Relationships with schools

Some or all of your children may still be at school. You may have had little or no dealings with their schools, except for the odd parents' evening. Now you will find that there is quite a lot of correspondence between families and schools, covering all sorts of topics, such as term dates, exams, concerts, holidays and school uniform, which your partner may have dealt with on a day-to-day basis.

Unfortunately, we have all heard stories of bereaved children being sent home from school on one pretext or another – incorrect school uniform, wrong length of hair or not following instructions correctly. My whole class was penalised by my teacher because I had failed to return to school in the afternoon after sitting an entrance exam in another town in the morning. A group of us had been taken by someone else's mother and I had no control over what happened. The injustice that I felt rankled for a very long time!

How humiliated I felt. How lacking in feeling was the teacher?

First you lose your mother and then you are publicly humiliated. How can you avoid this situation? Many schools now have people assigned to pastoral care. Arrange to see this person. Ask them to let you know, preferably in advance, what you should be doing and if you are breaking any of the school's rules and regulations. Usually, a person in that role will be a caring individual and will be glad that you have taken the initiative, if they have not approached you first, which we hope they would have done.

There may be lots of other issues on which you think you need help, especially if you have girls who are reaching puberty. Turn to other female members of your family or women you can trust, perhaps from your faith or work, and discuss frankly with them what issues you might expect. Children's charities such as Jigsaw might be able to help you if none of these are to hand.

24
Cooking for an Invalid

Before the diagnosis or trauma occurred, cooking and eating may have been a very enjoyable part of your life together for you and your partner. Dining out with friends, holding dinner parties, trying out new recipes – all of this will have to be reassessed in the light of what has happened. Of course, it rather depends who has been the main protagonist in this and which one of you did most of the meal planning, shopping and cooking. One or several of the following might occur.

The diagnosis does not affect any of the above and you go on as before as much as you can, perhaps a little less than previously but generally business as usual, with a gradual falling off of activity.

Your partner may be left with the inability to enjoy any of the above. This can take several forms. They may be in a coma or on a life-support system and their food and drink intake is entirely in the hands of the hospital or hospice. They may have had a stroke, which makes swallowing difficult, or they may be gradually unable to swallow for other reasons. In this case you may want to cook very light and easily swallowed food supplemented by blended drinks that provide the nutrients the body needs. Before ordering it would be best to consult a dietitian or your GP for the best type of supplement to get. There are lots of different brands. Your partner may need to have an intravenous feeding tube introduced and you will be cooking for yourself and your family and eating without your partner.

They may have lost their sense of taste or have a very partial one, which means that eating is no longer a pleasure. If this is the case, you might want to rely more on savoury dishes that contain tomatoes, anchovies, soy sauce and fish sauce. Such foodstuffs are rich in umami, one of the five basic tastes, as well as in glutamates. Try looking up recipes using these ingredients.

You yourself may find that you have no time to plan, shop and cook in the way that you used to, in which case you may want to have all your food delivered. If you are dealing with your local shop, you may be able to phone in an order and have it delivered. You can order online if dealing with a big supermarket. You may want to support special organic suppliers such as Riverford, or an organic scheme that is local to your own district. Do not hesitate to ask friends to shop for you, although it is best to give them a list and be very specific, leaving no room for choice on their part!

Lastly, you may decide that you have so little time – or feel that cooking is simply not one of your skills and that now is not the right moment to learn them – that it suits you to buy in ready-made meals from an organisation like Cook!, or those that deliver frozen meals that you can put in the freezer such as Wiltshire Farm Foods, or even your local supermarket.

Alternatively, if you have never cooked before, you may decide that now is the time to learn both for the present and for the future. We know of one widower who grasped this nettle and whose meringues became much admired and sought after for parties. He was so busy cooking and finding himself the centre of attention that he wondered why he had never had a go before.

It is entirely up to you how you decide to tackle this issue, but it is best sorted as soon as possible as it is likely that things will deteriorate and you will have less time to spend on it. However, make absolutely sure that you eat properly. If you suffer from poor nutrition, you are going to be no help at all to your partner. And do not indulge too much either. It is true that you deserve some treats, but don't go mad and put on pounds of weight, which may have negative physical and emotional effects later on.

25

Around the House

It is likely that one of you is the person who has in the past taken on responsibility for repairs and the renewal of appliances, unless you live in a rented property where this is done for you by the landlord. Even then, one of you would have to have contacted the landlord or council. The following is written on the assumption that it is the partner who did not normally have responsibility who now needs to learn new skills.

Unfortunately, it is unlikely, as a result of your partner's diagnosis, that the place where you live, either rented or owned, is going to declare a moratorium on household appliance problems, leaks or other incidents that plague us when we live in a property. If you rent a place, then it is likely that your landlord will be responsible for fixing things, but do you know where to find their telephone number if you were not the one to usually call them when necessary? If your partner is severely incapacitated, it may prove difficult to find this, but if your partner is able to communicate, you might start a list or a booklet that contains all these important contact details.

Other contact details might include an electrician, a plumber, a carpenter, a tiler, and even a painter and decorator, if you are not going to do this yourself. If your partner did all these sorts of jobs, you may have to start from scratch. A good place to begin is to ask someone who is a landlord to share their list of contacts with you. They normally have good lists in case they need to contact someone in a hurry on behalf of their tenants. Otherwise, ask friends and neighbours who they use.

Do you know where the stopcock is to turn off the supply of water should you spring a leak somewhere? Do you know what might go wrong with the boiler, say if it suddenly switches off? How long is it since you had the boiler serviced? You don't want it breaking down in the middle of winter. Are there other things that need servicing? Do you know how a smoke alarm works and what signal it gives when the battery needs changing? The same applies to a carbon monoxide alarm. If you came home to find you had no lights, would you know to go to the fuse box to check that something had not triggered it to cut out? Do you have service contracts for your household appliances? Are they still under manufacturer's guarantees or did that cease some time ago? Where would you turn if your washing machine broke down or your fridge-freezer? All these things become more important if you have a sick person in the house that you are looking after. Equally important is the simple point of having a torch, or several torches, to hand – one by the front door, one in the kitchen and one in your bedroom.

What are you going to do about your car? Do you drive and will you want to drive the car you have? Is it just going to be a nuisance? Should you sell it?

You will not be able to do all this at once. Indeed, you may not have time to do it at all. Have you a friend you can delegate this task to? Can they build you a dossier of things with some direction from you? You will have your own ideas of what needs doing. Friends like specific things to do, to feel that they are helping you.

If you have been unused to buying goods and services for your household, you might consider a subscription to *Which?* magazine. Every month it contains 'Best Buys' – which have been found on testing to be the best value for money – and articles on all sorts of other issues, such as retirement, ISAs, energy costs and so on. If your finances cannot stretch to the purchase of membership, you can find copies in your local library and some information is online.

26
Achieving Peace of Mind

This section refers to both of you, but specifically to the dying needs of your loved one. If you have managed to achieve at least some of the things listed in this Part, you will be well on your way to knowing that you have done as much as you possibly can to give both of you peace of mind.

As your partner's condition deteriorates and death becomes more likely, you will want to be with them as much as possible. However, it may be that they have things they wish to discuss or unburden themselves from that they do not want to talk to you about, difficult though this might be for you to contemplate, as you have probably grown closer over the time since the diagnosis. In that case you may want to contact the chaplain at the hospital, hospice or nursing home that they are in, if they are in one, or your local religious representative on their behalf.

Or you both may feel that some sort of counselling is in order. There are pre-bereavement services available, such as the one mentioned earlier offered by Cruse Bereavement Care, which enable you to talk about those things that you cannot and would not wish to talk about with your children, friends and relatives. The service is completely confidential unless there is a possibility that you might harm yourself or others.

27
The Dying Process

Witnessing the dying process would have been commonplace to our forebears, but nowadays not many of us will have witnessed a death. For some people, Kathryn Mannix's book, *With the End in Mind*, will be helpful and she has also made a short video that you can find on YouTube. Our feeling is that being prepared for what might happen is always helpful, difficult though that might be. So, below, we have indicated what is likely to happen to your loved one as they reach the end. If you are not ready to read this then skip it for now and come back to it when you feel stronger or feel the need to know.

As we've said, very few people nowadays have witnessed someone dying and most people are not aware of the deterioration that takes place and the telltale signs that indicate a person is reaching the end of their life. What follows is not only a description of those signs but also some suggestions as to what will give the most comfort to the dying person. Although everyone is unique and their death is unique, there are some generalisations we can make that are universal to all. Everyone wants a peaceful death for their loved ones, and we hope that the following will contribute to that happening for you.

Increased sleepiness or coma
The dying person might spend a lot of time sleeping. They are likely to feel very tired. Too many visitors can be disturbing and unhelpful. Try to regulate these visits. Also try to be a loving presence near the person by sending them loving thoughts, holding their hand and generally indicating that they are in a safe and secure space.

Loss of appetite

The fact that your loved one is no longer interested in food, especially if they previously had a robust appetite, can come as something of a shock. However, as the body breaks down it no longer needs the nourishment it once did and sometimes food can become a discomfort. Even their favourite food no longer tempts them.

You should not press food upon the dying, as this might make them feel guilty, especially if they think you have gone to a lot of trouble to produce something 'appetising'. The person approaching death needs to know that it is OK not to eat. Sometimes they have difficulty swallowing. This makes it frightening for the person to attempt to eat or drink. Watch carefully to make sure that swallowing is taking place using just a teaspoon or less of liquid or food at a time. It is safer to feed a person who is sitting up. Medications can be broken open and crushed and mixed with jam, jelly or yoghurt. Do not crush time-release or long-acting medications. You may have to discuss with medical staff methods of giving medication, especially painkillers.

Confusion

The dying person may have periods of confusion in which they may not recognise familiar people or know what day it is. They may hear voices or see visions. If this is clearly a happy experience, do not contradict or argue with them, but go along with whatever seems to be their reality. If, however, the experience is disturbing, remind them of who they and you are, hold their hand and be reassuring.

Restlessness

A person may become restless and make repetitive motions like picking at the bedclothes. This could be a sign of a lack of oxygen, or of pain, nausea, constipation or a full bladder. Make sure the person will not hurt themselves and attend to whatever you think the restlessness is caused by. It might be a sign of anxiety caused by a desire to unburden themselves or possibly speak about something that is on their mind.

Calm reassurance and holding their hand might help to relieve their distress even though they may be unconscious.

Incontinence

As the dying person's muscles get weaker, involuntary loss of urine or faeces may happen. If the person is conscious, this can cause embarrassment and it is important to ensure that your loved one's dignity is maintained, for example by not exposing them to others. The skin needs to be kept clean and dry in case a rash develops. It is best to use plastic gloves, soap and water or disposable wipes. Incontinence pads may be helpful but not as an excuse to increase the time between changes. Bowel movements will become fewer as less food is taken in.

As the kidneys begin to shut down, the skin takes on more elimination work and your loved one can experience itching. Some people like warm bed baths, others tepid sponging. Various aromatherapy products like lavender oils or calendula can give some relief. Change the bed linen as often as necessary and think about a back massage or putting the person into a more comfortable position.

Body colour and temperature

As the heart begins to fail, circulation lessens and the nails may become bluish, while the arms and legs may become mottled or pinkish/purplish. Extremities become cool to the touch.

Breathing

A change in breathing pattern is significant when a person is dying. First of all, the exhalation is longer than the inhalation. This is a sign that the dying process has begun. The breathing then becomes irregular. Closer to death the whole rib cage is involved; breathing speeds up and then may pause for some time before the next breath. This pattern is called Cheyne-Stokes breathing and can continue for a few days, hours or minutes before death. There may be a rattling noise at the back of the throat, which is caused by the accumulation of saliva because the person can no longer swallow. This does not seem to bother the dying person. However, both these occurrences can be very distressing to observers.

Unexpected alertness and increased energy

A day or two or even a few hours before death, the dying person sometimes has a surge of energy in which they can eat and talk and spend quality time with their loved ones. It rarely lasts long and most people become unconscious hours or days before they stop breathing.

Signs of imminent death

The eyes have a glassy fixed look with large pupils. Extremities are cold and they and the lips become grey or bluish. The jaw is open and breathing is through the mouth, either very slow or very rapid with long pauses. The dying person is unresponsive to voice or to pain. A calm, peaceful atmosphere is helpful.

Clinical death

After death there is no breathing or heartbeat and pulse, and the pupils remain large. There may be release from the bladder or bowel. Beginning with the face muscles, rigor mortis sets in for between three and thirty-six hours and then wanes. This is when the body is washed and prepared.

The above text is adapted from a handout from the 'Living Well Dying Well' End of Life Doula Training Foundation Course.

28
Conclusion

In this Part of the book we have started to look to the future while your partner is still alive. Mostly, though, it is about what you can do to prepare yourself for the inevitable, especially where you have your partner to help you. If your partner is already in a coma or very near death, it is much more difficult. It is unlikely that you will be able to do everything. This book is intended to cover as much as possible that might be helpful to anybody in this situation, but only you will know what your priorities are. Each person reading the book will take different things from it. We are hopeful that it will smooth the transition from life with your partner to life without them.

Organisations

Age UK, a charity that supports older people, www.ageuk.org.uk. Advice line: 0800 678 1602, open every day from 8 a.m. to 7 p.m.

Benefit Enquiry line, 0800 882 200.

British Association for Counselling and Psychotherapy, www.bacp.co.uk, 01455 883 300.

Citizens Advice, a network of independent charities that give free, confidential information and advice to assist people with a variety of problems, www.citizensadvice.org.uk. Advice line open Monday to Friday 9 a.m. to 5 p.m., 03444 111 444. Specialist debt chat line open Monday to Friday 8 a.m. to 7 p.m. Be aware that the advice will vary depending on which part of the United Kingdom you live in. Either phone or use a search engine to contact your nearest branch.

Compassion in Dying, www.compassionindying.org.uk, 0800 999 2434.

Cruse Bereavement Care, www.cruse.org.uk. National helpline open Monday and Friday, 9.30 a.m. to 5 p.m. 0808 808 1677, or use a search engine to find your local Cruse centre.

Dignity in Dying, www.dignityindying.org.uk, 020 7479 7730.

End of Life Doula UK, www.eol-doula.uk in order to complete a form. In an emergency call 07825 795 808 or 07887 840 663

End-of-Life Rights Information Line, 0800 999 2434.

Equity Release Council, industry body for the UK equity release sector, representing qualified financial advisors, solicitors and others, www.equityreleasecouncil.com, 0300 012 0239.

Halifax, Cancer Support Team, helpline open 8 a.m. to 8 p.m., seven days a week: 0800 028 2692.

HM Inspector of Anatomy, information on organ donation, www.organdonation.nhs.uk, 020 7972 4551.

Human Tissue Authority, www.hta.gov.uk, helpline open Monday to Friday 9 a.m. to 5 p.m., 020 7269 1900.

Jigsaw, www.jigsaw4u.org.uk, 020 8687 1384.

Life Book, for creating your own autobiography, www.lifebookuk.com, 0800 160 1118 or 020 3813 9423.

Living Well Dying Well, www.lwdwtraining.uk, 01273 474 278.

The MedicAlert Foundation, home alarm systems, www.medicalert.org.uk, 01908 951 045.

National Counselling Society, www.nationalcounsellingsociety.org, 01903 200 666.

National Health Service, www.nhs.uk.

Office of the Public Guardian, customerservices@publicguardian.gov.uk, 0300 456 0300.

Organ Donation, www.organdonation.nhs.uk.

Royal College of Occupational Therapists, www.rcot.co.uk.

The Society of Later Life Advisers (SOLLA), admin@societyoflaterlifeadvisers.co.uk, 0333 2020 454.

University of the Third Age, www.u3a.org.uk, phone line open Monday to Friday 9.30 a.m. to 4.30 p.m., 020 8466 6139.

Which?, consumer advice organisation, www.which.co.uk. Phone line open Monday to Friday 8.30 a.m. to 6 p.m., Saturday 9 a.m. to 1 p.m., 029 2267 0000.

Books and publications
Dignity in Dying, *The True Cost: How the UK Outsources Death to Dignitas*, 2018.

Doyle, Derek, *Oxford Textbook of Palliative Medicine*, 4th edition, OUP, 2011.

'Information for Patients, Carers and Families', *A Guide to Your Rights at the End of Life*, Compassion in Dying, 2011.

Iyer, Rukmini, *The Quick Roasting Tin*, Square Peg, 2019.

Kingsley, Philip, *A Straightforward Guide to Producing Your Own Will*, Straightforward Guides, 2020.

Kübler-Ross, Elisabeth, *On Death and Dying*, Macmillan, 1969.

Lyness, D., 'Helping Your Child Deal with Death', KidsHealth, 2016, https://kidshealth.org/en/parents/death.html.

Matthews, Jane, *The Carer's Handbook*, 3rd edition, Robinson, 2019.

Shepherd, Sue, and Gibson, Peter, *The Complete Low FODMAP Diet*, Vermilion, 2014.

SunLife, *Cost of Dying Report 2019*, www.sunlife.co.uk/funeral-costs/.

Which?, 'Making a Will: What to watch out for when reviewing yours', Which? Publications, www.which.co.uk.

Which? 'Solutions for living independently', *Which? Supplement*, www.which.co.uk., 2019

Websites

www.bdr.alzheimersresearchuk.org: Brains for Dementia Research.

www.gov.org.ukmake-will: Advice on Wills.

www.gov.uk/browse/benefits/disability: Carers and disability benefits information and how to apply for these can be found here.

Part Three

After Death Has Occurred – the Funeral and Immediate Decisions

29
Introduction

No matter how much you think you are prepared for the inevitable, death when it comes is a shock, and nothing really prepares you for that moment, after which life will never be the same again. This is even more so when it comes as a bolt out of the blue, the death is totally unexpected – an accident, a fatal trauma such as a heart attack or stroke, a suicide or a murder. Your mind becomes a whirlwind of questions or an absolute blank as your body attempts to shield you from the shock. Either way, you may feel that you are in a nightmare from which there is no end.

But life does go on, and you have certain tasks that you have to complete, such as the funeral, the registration of the death (unless this is done by the coroner), the distribution of the dead person's estate if you are an executor, and making an attempt to restore some sort of order back into your life. All this needs doing, besides keeping your family together and supporting them.

This Part aims to give you the best possible support, help and advice. The assumption throughout this Part is that you have given very little thought to this aspect of your loss and are coming to it with all the decisions yet to be made. If you have read Parts One and Two or have already taken some decisions, you may be familiar with some of the things you have to do and the options available to you.

How you might feel, and what might be happening to you physically and emotionally, is covered in Part Five: 'Grief and Mourning'. You may want to read that first.

The assumption throughout the text is that the death occurs in England or Wales. Slightly different laws are in force in Scotland and Northern Ireland. Where the law differs from England or Wales, this is pointed out, but for details you should get advice from the government websites in Scotland and Northern Ireland or a solicitor. There is also information on what happens if someone dies abroad.

30
The Immediate Aftermath

It is more than likely that you will have passed this stage by the time you get to be reading this book, but we cover this topic a) for completeness, especially where there has been a sudden and tragic death; and b) so that those of you to whom this is yet to happen can look ahead and can read it prior to the death of your loved one and therefore be a little prepared.

Laying out and identification of the body

If death was expected, it is likely that you were there with your loved one when it happened. Perhaps you and your relatives were in attendance, holding a vigil, when your partner died. It may have been at home, in hospital or in a residential home. Kathryn Mannix's book, *With the End in Mind*, explains clearly and compassionately what you might expect to happen to your loved one as they die, and she has prepared a three-minute video on YouTube, which you might find helpful. Most bodies are laid out where the death occurred, if it was in hospital or a residential home. If this is the case, there will be no requirement for you to identify the body.

If the death was sudden and unnatural, for example the result of an accident or a murder, where you were not present, you can request to see the body, or may be asked to identify it, at the place where it has been taken. Once again, that may be at the local hospital if death was pronounced there, or it might be at the local mortuary, which is often located at the nearest large hospital. Hospitals have a special suite where the body is placed in a bed. You will be accompanied by police officers, who will ask you to sign papers identifying the body. We suggest that if this is what happens to you, take a friend with you for support, as the experience can be disturbing. Dead bodies have a waxy look and a person does not look the same as they did in life. Those overseeing your viewing of the body are very understanding and will try to make the whole process as easy as possible for you as the circumstances permit. Even so, this is a difficult experience.

The body will remain where it has been taken until you choose a funeral director, who will take the body away. In certain cases, the coroner becomes involved. Those in charge will know when this is necessary and arrange this for you (see p. 194). In some instances, there may need to be a post-mortem or autopsy. This can be very distressing to come to terms with, but it happens so that everyone can be assured that the death was natural; if not, an inquiry will be launched into the cause of death. The post-mortem has to take place before the undertakers can collect the body.

You do not have a choice concerning any of the above situations unless you wish to delegate the identification of the body to someone else and not view it at all.

31
Organ Donation

Information on this issue has already been raised in Parts One and Two in more detail, as it may be something that partners wish to talk about prior to death. If your partner has died from an accident, manslaughter, murder or suicide, you are unlikely to have discussed with them the issue of organ donation and, depending on your relationship with them, may be asked to take a decision on it now. All the information you need should be obtainable in Parts One and Two.

What you certainly have to do now is choose a funeral director if you have not already done so, and start the process of arranging the funeral. This takes us to the next section of the book.

32
The Funeral Arrangements

For most people, in the immediate aftermath of a death, the most important thing looming on the horizon, unless there is no body, is the funeral. What follows is a step-by-step account of all the things that you will need to think about. The most important advice we can give here is not to rush things and not to be rushed by others. Depending on the time of year and where you live, a burial will take two to three weeks to arrange unless it has to be done immediately (as in some particular cultures). A cremation takes a little less time to organise. But there are no hard-and-fast rules if your culture does not determine it. The funeral is an important part of the grieving process and you should take your time, listen to what people you care about have to say and then make up your mind. You will have to find a funeral director to take your loved one to their premises – you can delegate this to a friend or family member if you are overwhelmed – but after that is arranged you can draw breath and take your time over the details. If you have previously taken out a funeral plan, some of the decisions will already have been made for you.

There are 220 different Christian denominations in the UK and what follows mostly relates to Christian and secular burials, as those are the prevailing type. However, it is important to mention the ways that other religions manage the process of death. For certain religions, much of the uncertainty surrounding what you do after a death does not apply, as there are strict laws concerning what happens to bodies. A brief résumé of non-Christian practices can be found on p. 149.

Choosing a funeral director
A funeral director is someone who interacts with the public concerning

the funeral arrangements. The term is often used interchangeably with 'undertaker', although strictly speaking the latter may be only concerned with the preparation of the body for burial. A funeral director has usually studied for a qualification to belong to one or other of the recognised institutes or associations, such as the British Institute of Funeral Directors (BIFD), the National Society of Independent Funeral Directors (SAIF) or the National Association of Funeral Directors (NAFD). Ensure that they are a member of one of these.

Unless you were prepared for the death, and have already identified an undertaker, the chances are you will not have given much thought to the choice of undertaker prior to the death, as it is not the sort of thing you generally think about until you obviously need one. The Co-operative Society has the largest number of businesses under its wing; note that the business may have retained its original name in its promotional and marketing literature in order to maintain local links. Many undertakers were family businesses handed down from one generation to the next. Dignity is another large grouping. Small, independent businesses are becoming relatively rare.

We found that most undertakers offer a good if expensive service, with some exceptional ones here and there. The best advice we can give is to ask around and see what experiences friends and family have had in your area. If this is not possible, the internet will supply local names. Different undertakers tend to have their own strengths and weaknesses. One thing they usually have in common is that they can offer you an appointment very quickly, usually within a day or two of the death. Try www.funeralzone.co.uk if you really do not know where to start. This is a useful website for all matters to do with funerals.

Typically, most people in these circumstances do not shop around for an undertaker. You can, if you wish, enquire about the different costs of various undertakers, but there is usually no handy price-comparison guide available and most people who are grieving would find this a somewhat harrowing process. Prices are often very similar. What is different and what makes the cost mount up is how much you avail yourself of their different services, for example choosing a coffin or booking limousines for mourners.

Meeting the funeral director for the first time – making decisions and solving problems

What you will find when you sit down with the funeral director is that you have numerous decisions to make and problems to solve. In some circumstances, the funeral director comes to you, but normally you will need to go to their offices.

Many funeral directors group their services into types of funeral, listing what services you get and what the costs are for them. For example, one might offer a 'simple' funeral, a 'limited service' funeral and a 'full service' funeral. If you choose a simple funeral, you will be provided with a limited choice of time and day for the service, a specific coffin, and the service will be at the place of committal. The limited service is less restrictive, but you do not get limousines nor any help with the printing of service stationery such as the order of service and a form for attendees to write their name and addresses on so that you know who has attended. Both of these omissions require a certain amount of organisation on your part. The full-service funeral includes all those things that the funeral director has control over, including helping you with stationery, providing limousines and so on, but not the provision of a coffin, which would be extra. A good rule of thumb is that any service or item that the funeral director has to 'buy in', such as the coffin or funeral flowers, is extra.

Most people want a bespoke funeral for their loved one. If this is what you want, then there are a number of decisions you need to make in order to give your loved one the best funeral you can within the confines of your budget. How you do so will depend very much on your family circumstances. One of us was recently involved in the planning of two funerals within a very short space of time. One meeting with the undertaker took three hours because all the decision-makers were present and we came away with nearly all decisions taken, including the date, the place and how it would be done. The second meeting lasted one and a half hours and the widow came away with a list of decisions that had to be taken after conferring with her children and stepchildren, all of whom were entitled to a say in what took place. Scenarios such as the latter can be a long, drawn-out process if those consulted are not easily accessible, but it is important to make all close dependants, particularly children, feel as involved as possible.

On your first visit to the undertaker's, you will usually be greeted by the person who will be taking you through the whole decision-making process and who, metaphorically, will hold your hand right up until the last moment. This person is the funeral director and they are assigned to you from beginning to end. You will be offered refreshment, given condolences and then the actual business begins, usually with the decision concerning burial or cremation. If the order of items below seems rather strange, that is because in many cases it is the order in which you will be asked to take decisions. Bear in mind that **you do not have to make decisions immediately**. There may be the need for copious consultation and discussion with your children or stepchildren, parents, other relatives and friends, and this can be done in the days following your first visit to the funeral director.

33
Choosing Burial or Cremation

The first, and probably the most important, decision from which all the rest stem is whether you want your loved one to be buried or cremated. You may already have some idea of what your partner wanted and have discussed it with them, such that the decision is already made. However, you may not have been able to do this, in which case you will find yourself having to take the decision now. People tend to feel very strongly about what they choose, but the reasons for their choice typically vary. There are pros and cons to both.

The pros and cons of cremation

Cremation only became popular after the Second World War and is now chosen by 72 per cent of the British population. Some people feel that crematoria are rather cold, impersonal places, although efforts have been made recently to improve the amenities they offer, including having somewhere to hold the reception afterwards and places for people to sit while they wait for the service to commence. Others object to the fact that there is only a certain amount of time allotted to each service, that the people from the previous service are filing out as you are filing in, and that those waiting for the service after yours are anxious to take their places as you leave.

Conversely, some people think that crematoria are much more ecologically friendly: recently designed ones use the energy given off to heat homes and businesses locally. Others cannot bear the thought of what happens to bodily remains after burial and prefer to have these dealt with by burning. Many people believe that returning people to ash is a much more satisfying prospect, especially as that ash can be made into jewellery such as rings, or artefacts such as paperweights, so that your loved one is always with you.

A new method of organising a funeral involving a cremation has recently become more popular. This is called a 'direct cremation'. It does not provide for a funeral service. You can use the internet to find several organisations that provide direct cremations. All of the funeral arrangements can be made over the telephone with help from a team of professionals. The cremation does not involve funeral directors, hearses, limousines or pallbearers. Nor does anyone have to attend the crematorium, if that is what you prefer; you can hold a ceremony later with the ashes. Packages and plans are based on the number of people you'd like in attendance. The cost is considerably less than for a conventional cremation. There are extra costs for services such as non-hospital collection of the body or return of the ashes. Be aware of such extras, as this is where the costs mount up.

Please note that whatever service you plan and wherever you hold it, the body does not need to be present and you can send it to the crematorium accompanied only by undertakers. Though we suspect you will want to accompany the body of your partner, we felt, for completeness, that we should include information on the above.

The following religions normally forbid cremation: Greek Orthodox, Islam, Orthodox Jews, Russian Orthodox, Zoroastrianism.

The pros and cons of burial

Some religious groups have a preference for burial over cremation. Although the Pope lifted the ban on cremation for Catholics in 1963, and in 1966 allowed Catholic priests to officiate at cremation ceremonies, the Roman Catholic Church still officially prefers the traditional interment of the deceased, and if you are a practising Catholic this may determine your views.

You may be someone who feels that a burial is much more natural. The most accessible place for you to bury your loved one is likely to be the local cemetery. Many cemeteries have a special Jewish or Muslim area. The vicars of most churches, and the managers of local cemeteries in their area, are all known to funeral directors and liaison is a matter of course between them. Some small 'woodland' sites are attached to existing cemeteries, such as at Wolvercote, in Oxford, where a far-sighted cemetery manager saw the benefit of using an unallocated piece of land at the rear of the cemetery for just this purpose, after attending a conference in the 1990s. Here you get the best of both worlds: an easily accessible site with some of the hallmarks of a woodland site.

You may be fortunate enough to live in a place where burials still take place in the local churchyard. If your loved one was a regular church attendant, this might seem the obvious spot for them. Burial here does depend on the discretion of the vicar and/or church council.

Be aware that buying a burial plot is often considerably more costly than a cremation. You will receive a certificate to the effect of where exactly the plot is in the cemetery, although for a woodland funeral this varies. Some 'woodland' burial places attached to cemeteries have a hybrid system whereby after burial the grave is marked with a simple ground-level plaque, but once this disintegrates no other distinguishing marks are allowed.

Other places of burial
Woodland sites

If you are ecologically minded, you may feel that burial in a properly organised natural or woodland site is most at one with nature. You can ask friends and relatives about their experience or use the internet to locate woodland burial sites in your area. *The Natural Death Handbook* also has a list of sites. There are now a lot more to choose from and their number is growing, so there is likely to be one near you. They are usually always open and someone should be available during the week to help you choose the exact place you want your loved one to be buried. You are likely to be able to choose a tree or may have the opportunity to pay for a nesting box. At some, local woodcarvers can craft something unique for you. You can also pay for printed material to be sent to your guests, which includes a map, directions and what to expect. The people on site can also liaise with your funeral director. A point to note is that woodland sites are sometimes a long way from bus routes and are only accessible by car. This adds to the cost of transport for the burial and also raises considerations of visits by you afterwards. If you feel you will want to go to the burial site frequently after the ceremony, a real woodland burial might not be the most practical of options, especially as you get older.

If you do have the opportunity to choose a tree to be planted near the grave, it may be that the choice is limited to those trees that are indigenous to the UK, so you may find that your preferred choice of a Canadian redwood (*Sequoia*) might not find favour with the authorities. However, you are often at liberty to plant bulbs of your choice, such as daffodils and snowdrops. Sometimes, mourners are requested to bring a stone to help build a cairn over the buried body, with a message they have written on the stone.

Burial on private land

Some people feel that they would like their loved one buried in their own garden or on someone else's land. Generally, this choice requires some effort to arrange, but it is not impossible. The rules can be found in the Burial Laws Amendment Act 1880. You have to be very careful about water contamination and you may need to contact the Environment Agency or the local authority's environmental health department to obtain their authorisation for the burial. You would also have to check that there are no covenants against burial in existence.

The person responsible for the burial must obtain a Certificate of Authority for Burial. This will be issued by the local authority's registrar of births, deaths and marriages (or if a coroner is appointed to investigate the death, it will be issued by the coroner). It must be obtained before the burial takes place, and a notice must be returned to the local authority's registrar after the burial.

Since the Land Registration Act (2002) it is no longer possible for details of burial to be 'noted' on the documents of a property, where the title to that property has been registered at the Land Registry. Instead, the owner of the freehold land on which the burial has taken place must prepare and keep a 'burial register' pursuant to the Registration of Burials Act 1864. This burial register must be kept in a safe place so that it can be passed on to future owners of the land. A burial register is a document that records details of the deceased and of the burial, including an accompanying plan showing the grave's location. Although a small number of burials would generally be unlikely to require planning permission from the local authority, the exemption from planning permission only applies to the burial itself. A gravestone, memorial or other erection may require planning permission and you are advised to check this out. All of the above permissions might make you feel that you want to use a funeral director, who can oversee it all for you.

One point to mention if you plan to bury your loved one in the garden is that you will not be living there for ever and you will not necessarily have access after you move, so it might be helpful to bury someone near a boundary wall or fence so that at least you can place flowers near the grave with no problems of permission. Burying a body in the garden may affect the resale value of the property and if there are no covenants concerning the body on resale there is nothing to stop the new owners reinterring the body elsewhere. Consult the Natural Death Centre for more detailed information.

Burial at sea

If you wish to bury a body at sea you need a free licence from the Department for Environment, Food and Rural Affairs (DEFRA). However, it is a minefield of bureaucratic guidelines designed to discourage you from doing so. For instance, your boat has to be skippered by a captain with a Yacht Master's Certificate. It can be costly and you are rather limited regarding the number of mourners. There are three places around the English coastline where you are allowed to do this and two around Scotland. Presumably, this is to limit the possibility of the body being washed ashore again or being raised by fishing boats. Look up the Food and Environment Protection Act 1985, under 'burial at sea'.

A third alternative?

As of writing, there is no choice in the UK other than cremation or burial. However, in May 2019 the state of New York passed a bill to legalise the composting of human remains. A body can be turned into soil within four to seven weeks. It is considerably cheaper than cremation and burial. With the gathering momentum for green issues everywhere in the world, who knows whether buying human compost at your local garden centre might not be a possibility for the future?

Being buried with your loved one

One drawback to a woodland-type burial as opposed to a cemetery one is that if you plan to be buried with your loved one, most woodland burial sites allow only one body per plot. The only way around this is for you to be cremated and your ashes buried in the same plot. If you have chosen burial as a principled preference to cremation for your loved one, this might prove something of an obstacle for you. However, you would still be able to be buried in the same area, provided there is space.

Non-Christian practices

Jewish

For practising Jews, the body should be buried as soon as possible, for 'as long as the body is outside the grave the soul suffers' (Jamie Oliver, quoted in *Get Dead*, 2006). Where Jewish people are strongly represented, there are groups of people called Jewish Burial Societies who take over the task of organising the funeral so that the families do not have to. After the death, there is then a period of seven days of compulsory mourning called shivah, which takes place in the house where the person lived; it enables the relatives and friends of the deceased to concentrate their thoughts on the person they have lost and not have to worry about other things besides arranging the funeral, such as what they are going to eat. Jews are nearly always buried; cremation is not allowed, mainly because bodily resurrection is expected to take place at some time in the future when the Messiah comes. This is thought to be in Jerusalem, hence why so many people wish to be buried there. A Jewish cemetery is called a House of Life. Many local municipal cemeteries have a portion set aside for Jewish burials. They look particularly austere as practising Jews do not put flowers or other ornaments on graves. As in Christian belief and practice, how far the prescribed codes of practice are followed depends on the level of religious adherence of the family concerned.

Buddhist

Buddhists generally favour cremation, but embalming is allowed. Buddhist funeral rites are conducted on the morning of the cremation or burial ceremony. Verses are chanted and monks may be invited to the ceremony according to Buddhist funeral traditions. Buddhists believe that reincarnation of the soul occurs after death.

Muslim

Muslims are never cremated. It is considered disrespectful. That is because the deference that is shown to a dead body is the same as you would show to a living person. Believing in an afterlife is a cardinal feature of Islam. The body should be buried as soon as practicably possible after death. A post-mortem required by the law is allowed and Muslims can donate organs.

Hindu

In Hinduism the oldest son traditionally organises the funeral of a parent, but that might not always be entirely practicable. People occasionally want to fly the bodies back to India to be burnt, but 50 per cent of ashes go to India to be scattered in the Ganges. Some crematoria in the UK, especially where there are large communities of Hindus, have made special provision for mourners to witness the cremation of the body by building special furnaces. The River Soar in Leicestershire is officially approved as the British 'Ganges' where British Hindus and Sikhs can scatter the ashes of their dead. The Environment Agency has authorised a section of the river to be used for that purpose. Altogether, there are three places in England where ashes can be legally scattered on a river.

We have been brief here as members of other cultures are probably more aware of their death rituals than are nominal Christians. However, there are nominal Jews, Muslims and Hindus, etc., just as there are nominal Christians, and they will have to make the same sort of funeral decisions.

The timing of the burial or cremation

Once the decision has been taken to bury or cremate, and the place of burial chosen, you will then need to book a date and a time for the burial to take place in a cemetery, churchyard or woodland burial spot, or for a slot at the crematorium.

A burial usually involves gravediggers and someone to officiate at the burial. In the winter it is unusual to have a burial much after 1 p.m. for health and safety reasons, as the gravediggers have to fill in the grave while it is still light. Timing also has to be co-ordinated with the time of day when you feel most people who would want to come are able to attend the funeral. This is what you pay the funeral director for. They tend to know those in charge of crematoria and graveyards very well and are used to the juggling of diaries, so they can often come back to you with confirmation of a time and date very quickly, even sometimes at your first meeting. However, as mentioned previously, you may have to consult with other people before you can determine exactly when it will take place.

There are a surprising number of decisions that you now have to take in relation to the preparation for the interment or cremation.

Choosing the coffin

Your funeral director will almost certainly produce a booklet containing pictures of the coffins that are available to purchase on your behalf. Your decision as to burial or cremation may have an effect on the type of coffin you choose. Coffins vary greatly in their cost. The cheapest, and one that might appeal to you if you and your family are ecologically minded, is a cardboard one. However, you may be surprised at how much even this costs. Cardboard coffins can be white or brown. One benefit of such a coffin is that if you have children or other members of your family who might want to be involved, they would be able to decorate this coffin with pictures and messages. Your funeral director could deliver it to your house, and you could even have a coffin-decorating event where everyone comes together and you supply them with food and drink. If you are artistic yourself, or have artist friends, you may want them to paint or draw a picture of something or somewhere that meant a lot to you and your loved one – your honeymoon, a special holiday, a sporting event. This may sound odd to some ears, but being involved in such a way is helpful in enabling people of all ages to come to terms with their loss and feel that they are making a contribution to the valedictory process.

The next in price is a wooden coffin followed by bamboo and banana coffins, with an English willow being the most expensive. All these come in a variety of designs. One quirk is in the shape. If you choose a shaped coffin, for example one that is more diamond shaped, not only will it cost more but you will also be asked to pay more for the gravediggers, who have to prepare a larger grave to accommodate this shape. You can ornament the coffin with special handles and finishes according to your taste, which will add to the cost.

You can have a custom-made coffin to commemorate your loved one. Some examples are in the shape of mobile phones, cars and ballerina pumps. You need to use a search engine to find companies to do this, but they are relatively easy to find. Such coffins are also more expensive, and you will have to liaise with your funeral director. Having a custom-made coffin could delay the funeral too, as it might take longer to get it made.

Perhaps surprisingly there is no legal requirement for using a coffin for burials in the UK. Do not feel that you have to have one. A body can be buried in a cloth or shroud. A funeral director can supply this for you or it can be custom-made. A lady in Devon makes beautiful felt shrouds (Yuli Somme). Most crematoria expect a coffin to be used, although there are some that now allow shroud cremations. If you wanted to go down this route, you would have to check with your local crematorium or find a crematorium that allowed this; it might be some way off, and therefore costly in terms of travelling expenses for yourself and for mourners. A presiding minister of religion would need to be willing to have an un-coffined body in their church or the cemetery chapel. Those we spoke to were happy to do so and said that it was up to the family to arrange this with the funeral director. It might come as a bit of a shock to other mourners, so you would do well to warn them. A more likely scenario for this would be a woodland or garden burial. It is possible to organise an electric cold blanket, which keeps the body cool and rigid, if you want to retain the body in your own home until burial, which is perfectly legal. There are companies that produce equipment specifically for this purpose: see www.flexmort.com for a Mini Mortuary Cooling System.

What goes in the coffin

Your undertaker will inevitably ask you what you would like your loved one to be dressed in and if there is anything else that you would like to be put in the coffin to be either buried or burnt. There may be some special clothes that you would like worn or a particular item that is meaningful to you. Alternatively, you can ask for a simple cotton shroud. We have encountered items including a teddy, a watch and a Jawbone running monitor being put in the coffin. This is another opportunity to involve children and family in the process of arranging the funeral. Children or grandchildren, especially, might want to put something in the coffin that is a link between them and their parent or grandparent. Make sure that someone is designated with the task of collecting the clothes for your partner to be dressed in and any other items to be put in the coffin, and ensuring they get to the undertaker's in good time. However, bear in mind the example of the poet and artist Dante Gabriel Rossetti, who buried a bound collection of manuscript poems in the coffin of his late wife, Lizzie Siddal. Seven years later, Rossetti, then publishing a collection of his poems, reconsidered, and instructed a friend to exhume the body and recover the manuscript. He was thwarted in that the particular poem he had wanted to retrieve was beyond recovery.

Viewing the body

Most funeral directors have a chapel of rest and can make arrangements for mourners to come and see the body after it has been suitably prepared. This might involve a decision about embalming. You may want to see your partner to say goodbye to them for one last time. One lady I know went to see her husband to tell him what a fool he had been and how angry she was with him for getting electrocuted while trying to mend their refrigerator. This was a cathartic experience for her and a brave thing to do. People feel very differently about this and, of course, it may depend on the nature of the death.

You also have to decide whether you want other people to see your loved one's body. To some extent this will also depend on the nature of the death. You are the principal organiser of the funeral and can take the decision as to whether you want your loved one to be available for viewing. Some relatives and friends may feel very strongly that they do wish to pay their respects in this way, especially close members of the family who were not able to get to the bedside in time for the death or where the death was sudden and unexpected.

Young children should always be consulted if you wish them to see the body, and they should be questioned closely if they themselves have expressed such a wish. It can be an extremely traumatising event and may add immeasurably to their grief. Alternatively, if the body looks peaceful, it can be very consoling. If you want the body to be viewed, it is likely that you will need to have it embalmed, especially if potential mourners cannot arrive within a short time of the death. This will add to the cost.

Alternatively, in some families, there is a tradition that the body is laid out at home and stays there for viewing if required until the actual funeral. However, this is not recommended if the funeral is delayed more than a few days and especially where the temperature cannot be controlled (though see p. 153 for details of a special cooling blanket you can buy or maybe borrow from your funeral director).

34
Planning the Funeral Service

Unless you have already agreed with your partner before they died what they wanted their funeral to be like, the next decision you have to take involves the funeral service itself. You may feel that a service at the crematorium is sufficient, as neither you nor your loved one had strong religious beliefs. On the other hand, you may feel that a church service is what you want or what your loved one would have wanted, followed by a burial or cremation. This is something of a balancing act. If there is only yourself to please, you may decide to do things the way you want, especially if it was not something you previously discussed with your partner. On the other hand, if there are several people whose views have to be taken into account, focusing on what the dead person might have wanted can be a useful way of dealing with dissent and gaining consensus, for example where there are children, stepchildren, parents or siblings with strong views.

Planning a church service

If you and/or your partner were regular churchgoers, there is unlikely to be a problem with the service being held in the church you attended, wherever it is. Be aware, too, that you are legally entitled to a funeral service at the church in whose parish you live. In other circumstances – for example, where you want a religious service in a cemetery chapel or a crematorium – you may have to find a vicar or minister prepared to conduct the service, especially if you were not part of his or her flock. If you have a friend who is an ordained minister and you want them to conduct the service, the minister of the church you want to use will have to agree. Your friend will also have to be vetted by the minister, and the service will probably be shared.

The funeral service and the committal

There are two parts to the funeral process: the funeral service and the committal, which is the burial or cremation. If you decide on a church service and a burial, the church may or may not be next to the burial place. If you are using a church where burials are still taking place in the churchyard, and you have permission for your loved one to be buried there, the congregation can simply walk out of the church and cluster around the grave while the minister conducts a short committal service. This is also the case if you are using the chapel attached to a cemetery, which is always a possible alternative.

If the church is some distance from the burial place, you will need to give some thought as to how to transport everyone to the cemetery from the church and if indeed you want everyone to be present. This is also true of a church service followed by a cremation. Sometimes this is solved by restricting the cremation ceremony to 'invitation only' or 'family only'. You will be reasonably sure of who is coming and can arrange transport accordingly. However, that then leads to a problem of what to do with the residue of mourners. You can ask them to go straight on to the reception or wake without you, and join them later, but this is a difficult situation that requires a 'meeter and greeter' at the reception who stands in for you until your return. One solution to this problem is to have a short committal service beside the hearse after the service. The body is then taken to the crematorium by the undertakers, while you and your guests go to the reception. Most, though, will probably feel this is an unsatisfactory solution, so you will have to come to an arrangement that suits you best.

A civil or humanist service

You do not have to have a religious service. If neither you nor your partner had religious views, you might feel a civil or humanist service is more appropriate. Your undertaker will normally have a list of people who conduct services of this nature in your area or you can contact Humanists UK. People who take these services are known as celebrants. A humanist funeral is a non-religious service that is both a dignified farewell and a celebration of life. It recognises the profound sadness of saying goodbye while celebrating the life and legacy of a loved one. The celebrant works closely with you to create a unique and personal ceremony. They will usually pay you a visit and glean as much information as possible about the life of the person for whom they are conducting the service.

Splitting the funeral from a celebration of life

A humanist funeral aims to embrace both mourning and celebration. You may feel that this is more difficult to achieve in a religious service and therefore decide to have two services. The funeral service could be followed at a later date by a celebration of your loved one's life. It may be that we are more used to this happening to well-known or famous people, but there is nothing to stop you doing this. It is especially appropriate if the death of your loved one was a shocking and unexpected one, and the funeral is being held before anyone has really come to terms with the death and is consequently very definitely more in the nature of grief and mourning than celebration.

Floral tributes

Your next decision involves the flowers for the coffin and whether you want to have floral tributes from other people.

Choosing your tribute

The funeral director will produce a book of floral tributes and their cost, from which you can choose. They usually do this in collaboration with a local florist. However, you may wish to use a florist of your own or a friend may offer to prepare a floral tribute as a loving contribution of their own. This is another way that you can demonstrate your individuality and express your feelings. For example, your loved one might have had a preference for a certain flower or particular colours. You may want to replicate your wedding bouquet or some other occasion when flowers were a motif. Perhaps your loved one came from overseas. You may want to indicate this in your choice of plant, which might be native to that country. Depending on the time of year and the type of plant, this could provide a challenge for the florist. You may want to go to a flower market and pick the flowers yourself. At a recent funeral, the flowers requested were replicating a wedding bouquet of seventy years ago and came from Brazil. This was quite a challenge for the florist, but they rose to the occasion. Clearly, this will all be reflected in what you are prepared to pay. You can also have floral tributes in the shape of MUM or GRANDAD, which your children or grandchildren might appreciate. Some flowers are synonymous with certain countries and cultures, for example chrysanthemums at Chinese funerals; on occasion, flowers are to be avoided, such as in Jewish or Muslim funerals. You will know your own cultural traditions.

People sometimes feel, in the case of a burial, that it is appropriate to have flowers to cast onto the coffin when it is lowered into the ground but before it is covered with earth. Often a single rose is given to the principal mourners, or it could be a different flower of choice. Again, this is something to discuss with those people who you want to participate in the arrangements. After this brief ceremony, it is usual for the funeral director to hand round a box of earth for mourners to cast onto the coffin.

Floral arrangements from other people

Another decision you need to make is whether to accept floral tributes from other mourners. Many funeral notices say that only family flowers are acceptable and please could the sender donate to a good cause that you specify instead. Or you may feel that it is up to the person wishing to send a tribute what they want to do. You may feel that the sending of flowers is a waste of money much better spent on charitable giving; equally, your thinking may be that your loved one would have loved lots of flowers and it is good business for florists. It's a personal decision, and it is up to you, your family and close friends to decide. After the burial the flowers are usually placed on the grave mound to rot. If it's a cremation, often the family flowers are burnt with the coffin but the others are arranged in a special place for the other mourners to see and admire. As they die off, they are removed by crematorium staff and composted.

Transport arrangements

Most people are happy with a simple black hearse, but there are other forms of transport that you may think are more appropriate for your partner's funeral and better reflect their personality and wishes.

If your loved one was a motorcycle enthusiast, you may want to consider Motorcycle Funerals. Founded in 2002 by Revd Paul Sinclair, it enables the coffin to be transported in a hearse sidecar, protected behind clear glass. The company offers a variety of motorcycles to choose from. Based in Leicestershire, the fleet serves all of the United Kingdom. There are other organisations that offer this service. This is just one example and the oldest.

Alternatively, you may want to create a bit of a splash and select a horse-drawn funeral complete with plumes and drapes. There are several organisations that offer this service and your funeral director will be able to contact them for you or they can be found easily on the internet.

You will have to decide where you and the funeral party – the principal mourners – will be joining the hearse. Often the hearse and limousine will come to your house, where those to be transported will have assembled. On other occasions it is more appropriate if you all assemble at the funeral directors.

No matter whether it is a religious service or a service at the crematorium, the minister/celebrant and funeral director will both want to know if you intend to be already in the place where the funeral is taking place when the coffin arrives, or if you want to follow the coffin in. The former is the more common.

It was a sign of Queen Elizabeth's respect for Sir Winston Churchill that at his funeral, instead of coming in last as is her right as sovereign, she entered St Paul's Cathedral before the Churchill family and the coffin.

While we are on the subject of the funeral, it is a good opportunity to think about the clothes you will be wearing. What you want to wear, and what you might want others to wear at the funeral, is entirely your own choice. You may be of a conservative nature and feel that, taking everything into consideration, black is the colour you feel most comfortable in. Alternatively, you may feel that the service is above all the celebration of a good life and so you want everyone to wear 'bright colours'. Or perhaps your loved one had a favourite colour and you want the accent to be on that. You can then ask mourners to wear something of that colour.

The order of service

Depending on the type of funeral service you have decided upon, the exact nature of the service will vary. The order of service you choose will go hand in hand with deciding who is to be involved in the service. Many partners do not feel they are able to participate without breaking down in public, and are happy to leave it to other people to give a tribute or a reading. You are likely to select someone close to your partner to give a tribute. The focus should be on giving those in the congregation a rounded idea of your partner's life and why they will be so sorely missed. Children, grandchildren and godchildren could participate, together with friends, in giving this picture. Here again is an opportunity to involve people in your choices and make other bereaved members feel a part of the service.

A religious service

If you have chosen a church service, the officiating minister will come and see you or you will meet with them once you know the date of the funeral. They will explain the procedure to you and will usually ask to see the order of service once you have made up your mind and before it is printed. Depending on the denomination, there is a clear order that the service follows, beginning with the coffin being brought in, while the presiding minister says some words laid down in the funeral service. Thereafter, as long as you keep to this order, you can intersperse it with items of your own choice, such as hymns, music, poems, singing and tributes. The minister usually gives an address relating to the life of your partner, and will often ask you for copies of what other members of the family or friends intend to say, so that they can craft their own words in accordance with what has been said, usually picking up the themes and weaving them into an uplifting message.

In a High Anglican or Roman Catholic service, there may be a requiem or funeral mass in addition, and the service may take up to two hours.

A civil or humanist service

If you are having a civil or humanist service – for example, one at a crematorium or in a chapel at the cemetery – there is much more choice as to what you might include in it, particularly with regards to the music, even if the service is being taken by a minister. Thus you might include songs that were important to the pair of you or were special to your loved one, pop songs from your youth or from your courting days. You might have their favourite hymns or one that would have had particular associations for your partner. For example, 'Jerusalem' is a great favourite for people who were involved in the Women's Institute. You are likely to want tributes, poems and passages from secular books, but as part of a much more relaxed order of service. Your celebrant will be able to help you. Again, this is an opportunity to involve the family in making the service a collaborative effort that all can think is worthy of their loved one. The idea of the service is to reflect the life of your partner as far as possible, within a context.

The service sheet

The service sheet is there to help those attending participate in the service and also to act as a memento of the service.

The funeral director will show you a selection of styles to choose from, and in nearly all cases they will offer to print the service sheet for you for a fee, which is usually based upon numbers. Always have more printed than you think you will need, as more people may turn up at the funeral than you are expecting and you will also have some left over to send to people who could not attend the funeral in person. Someone of our acquaintance sent out over one hundred service booklets with a personal letter following the funeral of her husband. This is also a courteous way to thank someone for a condolence letter or card.

It is usual nowadays to have a photograph of the loved one on the front of the service sheet, and sometimes also on the back, but it is up you to decide if you want this. Further information about the committal can be written at the end of the service sheet, for example concerning the burial or cremation. You may want to make it clear who should go to the cemetery or crematorium. You can also thank people for coming and for the support you have received, invite them to the reception for refreshments, perhaps giving directions, and also state where any donations can be sent.

You will need to have the details finalised for printing three or four working days prior to the funeral. You also need to arrange for someone to take the service sheets to wherever the funeral is taking place. Often this is done by the funeral director, but for reasons of your own you may wish to take on this task. Bear in mind that, for various reasons, people might arrive there quite early.

If you are expecting many people at the funeral, you may not be able to greet everyone or even know that they had attended. In this case you may want to have slips of paper printed and placed in the order of service or pew, asking people to enter their name and address, so that you can write to them afterwards. Make sure that you get someone to collect these safely.

Choosing a charity

Many people now feel that the money spent on funeral flowers could be better donated to a charity. Your loved one may have had a favourite charity that they supported, or you may have one that you support. Often the charity chosen is related to the type of illness that your loved one died of, or to special help that you received – for example, the air ambulance in the case of an accident, or a hospice – or to support others going through what you have endured, possibly in the case of a suicide or murder (charities such as SOBS or SAMM).

Setting up your own charity or trust

There may have been little or no research into the illness that you lost your partner to, and therefore you might decide to set up a charity to give money to in memory of your partner, and then to support it by raising money for it. If you decide to set up your own charity, you will need to contact the Charities Commission. At the time of writing, charities with an income of more than £5,000 a year need to register with them. In the case of a trust, you will need the help of a solicitor. In either case, you will need a method of accounting for the funds that you receive. A useful source of information on charity registration is www.resourcecentre.org.uk.

Arrangements for mourners

Once you know the date, time and place of the funeral, you will want to let those people who you think might attend know when it is. For close family and friends this probably means compiling a list. You may have already done that to inform them of the death. In addition, you may want to decide who you want to transport to the funeral and how many people will come in their own vehicles. This will determine the number of limousines you need. Very close family usually travel together, with the elderly and infirm. You may also wish to inform people of how to get to the funeral by supplying information such as car parking, park-and-ride facilities, and nearby cafes and pubs, should they arrive some time prior to the service.

Trying to assess numbers attending the funeral

Unfortunately, unlike a wedding, you can never be sure how many people will attend a funeral, which can make the arrangements rather difficult to finalise. Obviously, some people who you might expect to attend may not be able to come because they already have appointments on that day that they cannot break without inconveniencing large numbers of people. Some might be abroad and not even contactable, although in this day and age this is more unlikely.

It can be hurtful if those you expect to attend the funeral do not do so, especially close relatives. It may feel to you that they are paying insufficient respect to your loved one. One long-lasting family feud we know of started because a family who were abroad could not afford to cut short their holiday and pay for the extra flights home to attend a funeral, as their insurance did not cover the extra cost. In these circumstances, you need to be generous and gracious. It may be very upsetting for those who cannot attend also.

Having a 'meeter and greeter' at the church, crematorium or reception

You may ask someone who is a friend of the family and familiar with many who will be attending if they will act as a 'meeter and greeter' in your absence at the venue. They might be the person you task with getting the order of service there also. They can welcome people, make sure they have an order of service, stop them from sitting in the pews reserved for the family and ensure they know how to get to the reception. This person might also be responsible for getting people into waiting taxis to get to the reception, if it is some way from the funeral and you think it is necessary. They may also be able to look to the comfort of those who have travelled a long way, by knowing where the nearest toilet is available. You could also provide hot and cold drinks if the venue is agreeable.

Planning the reception or wake

It is a little difficult to know what to call the part of the funeral proceedings where you entertain those who have attended the funeral, but for want of a better word we will call it the reception. Although it is not obligatory, it is usual to have some sort of refreshment offered after the funeral service, in order for people to offer you their condolences in person and for you to thank them for coming. Be prepared for a few surprises, as there may be some there who you were not expecting.

Sometimes the reception is the most difficult part of the funeral to co-ordinate, as it has to be on the day you have chosen and at a time to follow the service. The venue also should be reasonably near to where the service took place. The church hall adjacent to the church is an obvious candidate, as they often have decent kitchens and church people who are available to help. The same applies to village or community halls. Local hotels or pubs might be suitable. The latter will also provide catering, but for the church or village halls you might have to find a professional caterer. The secretaries of the halls might be able to supply possible names or you could ask among your friends if it is your local hall.

What you offer may well depend on what time of day the service takes place. If it is in the morning, you may wish to supply a reasonable lunch, whereas if it is in the early afternoon maybe only sandwiches, cake and tea will suffice. You will have to decide about the provision of alcohol. Some traditions demand copious amounts of this, but in general if people are driving, they tend to drink very little and this might not be necessary.

Once you have decided on the venue for the reception, you need to let people know and find out what help they require in getting there. It is the norm nowadays to ask people if they have any dietary requirements before they attend lunches or dinners. This is difficult to do when you are unsure who will be attending, but you should at the very least try to be prepared for the requirements of vegetarians, maybe vegans if you know there are some among your acquaintance, and people who are allergic to gluten and lactose. I was reminded of this recently when my sister went to a funeral where there was literally nothing she could eat as she is allergic to wheat and mustard. All these foods should be clearly labelled, either by you if you are catering or by the caterer you have paid to do it.

35
The Death Notice

Local and national papers

You may want to have notice of the death put into the local newspaper or, if you feel that it is worth the considerable extra cost, into a national newspaper like *The Times*. Most newspapers have rules about how these are written and will help you with the actual wording, although you can also ask your funeral director to do this for you. It is usual to start with the surname, followed by forenames and any names the deceased was known by, the date and place that they died, and their age. Sometimes a reference is made to how they died – for example, 'peacefully' or 'after a long fight, bravely borne' – before the date and place. Then comes a reference to any honours they held or any positions they were well known for, especially of a local nature if the notice is for the local paper, or nationally if for the national papers. For members of the armed services, ranks are nearly always mentioned, especially if the one who's died was still serving. This is then followed by a reference to you and your children, stepchildren and grandchildren, as appropriate, usually named. Sometimes this section contains references to parents and siblings, and possibly uncles and aunts, depending on age and relevance. Next comes the place, time and date of the funeral (if it is known) and whether only family flowers are requested. You can follow this up by saying that donations in lieu can be made to whatever charity you have chosen to commemorate your loved one. The notice usually ends by directing interested readers to the name, address and telephone number of the funeral director for further enquiries, especially if a date has not yet been set for the funeral.

You can also pay to have an obituary, as opposed to a death notice, in a local or national paper.

Responding to condolence letters and cards

You will have already received condolence cards and letters from your family and close friends, but the notice in a paper or similar will alert even more people to what has happened. I have sent condolence cards to bereaved friends and relatives, but I never realised how comforting they are until I received them myself. Knowing that your loved one was loved by others, and what they meant to other people, can be balm to the soul. Of course, it is also a double-edged sword – it rubs in what you are missing. Opening these cards and letters was the last thing I did at night in bed before trying to sleep. It felt as though my late husband and I were doing it together. Responding to them is probably the last thing on your mind at this time, but it is a courtesy to respond to these offers of sympathy in some way. Following the funeral of her husband, a friend sent handwritten letters to over a hundred people with the order of service, and this despite the fact that over 120 people had come to the funeral.

If your community is very local, you could think of putting something in the local paper to thank people generally for their support. One positive outcome is that it is likely you will hear from long-lost friends and can resume your friendship. I had a letter more than five years after the event from just such a person. Be prepared for letters coming as word gets round. Sometimes, after a lengthy interval, they can give you a bit of a jolt, which you have to overcome.

Online funeral notice

Some funeral directors offer something called an 'online funeral notice'. A website is set up in the name of the deceased, and participants can exchange photographs and anecdotes on it. You can put up information about the funeral, ask people to contact you, give information about travel arrangements and also show a map of the location of the church, crematorium, chapel or burial site and of the venue for the reception. You can provide a convenient way for family and friends to send flowers on the day of the funeral and they can also donate on the site through JustGiving, which lists 25,000 charities. Gift Aid can be added to eligible online donations, meaning that the charity receives more. Be aware that the names of donors, the amounts they donate and their messages can also be seen by everyone, unless your donors choose to remain anonymous by pressing the appropriate button. You may feel that this is private and something for just yourself to be able to see. You may also wish to put up a simple obituary before the funeral or record the tributes from the funeral on the site. In the current situation, with restricted numbers of mourners attending funerals, the sites are being used to tell people that the funeral is by 'invitation only'.

Clearly, this is a great boon for a computer-savvy selection of mourners and for young people, but not perhaps so useful for elderly people who might not have a computer or an email address, and even if they did, might find this an odd way to go about things. If you are not very computer literate yourself, you may decide to delegate this task to another person, a child or grandchild, who might be very glad of such an involvement and work in collaboration with you.

36
Dealing With the Press

If your partner was a well-known personality, either locally or internationally, or the death was newsworthy, through an accident or murder, you may find yourself receiving the attention of the press. This can feel very frightening, oppressive and intrusive, especially at such a sensitive time, but they have a job to do, and the surest course is to face the issue head-on. If you know someone with journalistic experience among your friends, they would probably be happy to support you by taking on this task. Between you, you can issue a statement giving appropriate information, including your version of the facts, if relevant, and supplying a photograph. If the attention is ongoing, you would be advised to ask your friends and relatives to say as little as possible and leave it all to the person to whom you have delegated the task. In very rare situations it might be necessary to hire a public relations firm, to protect yourself and your family and preserve your reputation. As very few people would know where to begin in this search, we have included details of the Chartered Institute of Public Relations.

If there is an inquest or court case, the press are also more likely to be in attendance, so here again it will help your cause if you are gracious and helpful, either in person or through someone else.

37
Further Dealings with the Funeral Director

There will be numerous reasons for you to want to be in contact with the funeral director, but from their point of view the most important thing will be for them to have the Certificate of Burial or Cremation, without which there can be no funeral or cremation. This is issued by the registrar. Should the case have been referred to the coroner, he or she can issue an interim certificate, if having reviewed the facts they do not think there is any reason for the funeral to be delayed. It might be different in the case of an accident or murder, where forensic tests could be ongoing and the funeral might have to be delayed. This can be very distressing, but the coroner and registrar, who work closely together, are very aware of what you are going through and will keep you aware of what is happening as much as they can. In the case of a friend who was wrongfully accused of murdering his mother, the coroner telephoned him personally to let him know that the results of all the tests were that death was of natural causes, which was a very kind and thoughtful thing to have done.

Where there has been a cremation, you will want to liaise with the funeral director concerning collection of the ashes, and possibly a memorial stone.

Having a memorial stone erected

If you have opted for burial in a churchyard or conventional cemetery, you will probably want to erect a memorial over the grave. Your funeral director may raise this at your initial meeting. They will be able to give you a brochure containing examples of materials that are traditionally used, memorial designs and costs. They will also put you in touch with a monumental mason. If you do not think any of the designs suits your personal requirements, you can always arrange to meet the mason and talk through a unique memorial. If you expect to be buried with your loved one and have left space for that, then leave a space on the stone for your own details. Someone we knew did not want a headstone for her husband. This made finding him in the cemetery extremely difficult every time.

If you do not think you can deal with the headstone immediately, this is one task that you can postpone for a while.

Paying for the funeral

The funeral director will want to know who their client is, as that person will be the one who signs the papers and will be responsible for payment. We are assuming that in this case it is you, the widow, widower, civil partner or partner.

Funeral directors vary on the way that they ask for payment. You have to bear in mind that not only are they providing you with services themselves, but they are also paying for items, such as a coffin, and for the services of other people. These latter are called disbursements and should be clearly shown as such on your invoice. The funeral director will pay for the burial plot, if any, or the cremation slot, the church fees, the florist, if you use one recommended by them, and so on. As a result, they often ask for half the likely cost before the funeral and the rest later. If you have not got the money, but will be able to pay from your loved one's estate, you should explain this to the funeral director. They can be very patient. As mentioned above, someone known to the authors was accused (wrongly) of murdering his mother and had to wait for the subsequent police inquiry to finish and exonerate him, before he could gain possession of the original will. A 'caveat' had been put on this and the solicitors had to hand it over to the police, so he was unable to obtain probate. As a result, he had no money to pay for the funeral until a few years later when he finally obtained probate. In these circumstances the funeral director was remarkably sympathetic.

Sometimes a bank can advance you the money required, on

presentation of the invoice, especially if there is money locked in your partner's account but unavailable to you. Funeral expenses are nearly always exempt from inheritance tax. If someone else pays the bill, they can be reimbursed by the executors.

38
Commemorating Your Loved One

You may feel that you want to commemorate your loved one in a more tangible way. Many people sponsor a seat in a park or one that overlooks a view that their loved one admired. Sometimes your local theatre conducts a refurbishment and asks for seats to be sponsored; if you were theatregoers, you might feel this is a fitting memorial. More ambitiously, you may want to set up awards in your partner's name, perhaps at their local school or where they were at university. Do not be conned into thinking that you can have a star named after them. The only body that can do this is the International Astronomical Union. Stars are now usually named after the discoverer.

The ashes
Once the curtains close at the cremation ceremony and the coffin is transported to the furnace, it may not be cremated immediately, depending on the numbers being processed by the crematorium. However, the ashes are usually available to be collected by you from the funeral director or the crematorium itself within seven to ten days. You can pay for a casket or urn to hold them in, otherwise they are typically in some other receptacle. The next decision is deciding what to do with them.

Burial
You may decide to bury the ashes at the crematorium. Most crematoria have what are called Memorial Gardens. Because of the high amount of phosphate in ashes, the gardens are often planted with rose bushes, which benefit most from this. You can arrange to have a plaque affixed in a suitable place. If you decide to bury the ashes in a cemetery or

churchyard, you will need to buy a plot, organise the services of someone appropriate to hold a small service, and arrange to have a plot dug. A consideration might be where you yourself want to be after your death and if you decide to be buried with your loved one.

If you decide on the cemetery or churchyard, you may need to have a stone put over the ashes, in which case you will need the services of a monumental mason. Your funeral director will usually have a brochure showing cremation-size memorials as opposed to headstones, types of stone and lettering, and the name of a local firm.

Scattering

The law on scattering ashes in the UK is fairly relaxed. There is nothing explicit in the legislation to stop you scattering ashes over land or water, but strictly speaking you need the landowner's permission. Perhaps your own garden is the safest thing here. If you choose to scatter on a river, you don't need permission, but you should consult the Environment Agencies Guide. An organisation called Scattering Ashes can be helpful here. They are a business dedicated to the distribution of the ashes by various means. They even have a photograph of a replica Viking longship on their site. The ashes of a former colonel-in-chief of The Sealed Knot, a battle re-enactment group, were shot from a cannon. According to a National Trust Coastal Values Survey, 16 per cent of us want to have our ashes scattered on a beach or at sea. Another idea is to mix the ashes with wildflower seed so that you can visibly see where they were scattered the following year.

Coral reefs

If you are ecologically minded, the following might appeal to you. Reef balls are an innovative semi-natural wonder, plants and fish colonising artificial coral reefs that are made of a combination of crematoria ashes and moulded concrete (see YouTube Reef balls/National Geographic: https://www.youtube.com/watch?v=yrUErAQWo9s). Organisations such as the US-based Eternal Reef combine a cremation urn, ash scattering and a green burial at sea into an environmental memorial.

Other organisations include One World Memorials. YouTube has several videos giving more explanation. This can be an expensive option.

Keeping the ashes at home

You may decide to keep the ashes at home. Many people are now doing this. In that case, you may decide to buy a suitable container such as a special urn from an organisation such as Cherished Urns. Or you may decide to have the ashes made into a stone for a ring or a paperweight, for example by the organisation above or EverWith Memorial Jewellery, Forever Together Jewellery or an organisation recommended by your funeral director. The high carbon content of ashes enables such items to be made.

Sometimes there are disputes over ashes and occasionally the dispute ends up in court. If it was your husband who died or you were in a civil partnership, a dispute seems a bit unlikely, but if you were in a less formal relationship, but have been organising the funeral, this might occur with parents or siblings. In such an eventuality, the simplest solution is to divide the ashes up, although this might be painful for you.

39
When Someone Dies Abroad

Having someone die abroad, if it is not in a holiday home you own, can be particularly distressing, as you are having to deal with a difficult situation in a foreign country with different laws, regulations and customs, and it is likely that you do not speak the language sufficiently well to manage the process, as you would be able to if you were in the UK.

If you are with your loved one when they die abroad, you should contact the nearest British Embassy, High Commission or Consulate. They will be able to offer advice and help you with arrangements. If you are on a package holiday, tour operators or reps may be able to put you in touch with the right authorities. The Foreign, Commonwealth and Development Office (FOCD) has bereavement packs for nearly every country in the world, which are very helpful; at the very least, you can consult their website.

If your loved one dies abroad but you are not with them, and the death has been reported to the British Consulate in the country where the person died, they will ask the police to come and tell you. If you hear of the death from someone else, such as a tour operator, you should contact the FCO in the UK. You will need to register the death according to local regulations and get a death certificate. The local police, British Consul or tour guide can advise you on how to do this.

If someone dies on a foreign-registered ship such as a cruise ship or an aeroplane, the death has to be registered in the country where that ship or plane is registered.

40
Conclusion

What we have tried to do in this Part of the book is to take you through what is required for the funeral, the burial or cremation, and explain all the decisions that you might have to take. Do not be rushed into making decisions that you are not comfortable with. If you need a funeral director, by all means use one, but do not be deterred if you think that you can plan and execute the service yourself, especially with a little help from your family and friends. You want to have something that you think is fitting for your loved one, and if you wish to have something a little different, a little unorthodox, then go ahead. Involve as many people as you think should have a say. Planning the funeral can be a very cathartic experience for those involved and help in the grieving process.

The next Part goes into more detail concerning the registration of the death, probate, and all the other issues that you now have to contend with.

Organisations

Adfam, a national charity working to improve life for families affected by drugs or alcohol, www.adfam.org.uk, 020 3817 9410 (not a helpline).

Bereaved through Alcohol or Drugs (BEAD), a partnership set up by Cruse Bereavement Care and Adfam, www.beadproject.org.uk.

Bereavement Advice Centre, a free service that gives practical information and advice on the issues you will face after the death of someone close, www.bereavementadvice.org.uk. Advice line open Monday to Friday 9 a.m. to 5 p.m., 0800 634 9494.

British Institute of Funeral Directors, www.bifd.org.uk, 0800 032 2733.

The Charity Commission for England and Wales, www.gov.uk. Phone line open Monday to Friday 9 a.m. to 12 p.m. and 1 p.m. to 4 p.m., 0300 066 9197.

The Chartered Institute of Public Relations, www.cipr.co.uk, 020 7631 6900.

Cherished Urns, www.cherished-urns.co.uk, 01872 487101.

Department for Environment, Food and Rural Affairs (DEFRA), www.gov.uk, 03459 335577.

The Environment Agency, non-departmental public body, www.gov.uk, enquiries@environment-agency.gov.uk. Phone line open Monday to Friday 8 a.m. to 6 p.m., 0114 282 5312.

Eternal Reefs, funeral director, www.efbox.co.uk, 01294 465402.

EverWith Memorial Jewellery, www.everwith.org.uk, 01452 379379.

Foreign, Commonwealth and Development Office (FOCD), www.gov.uk, 020 7008 1500.

Forever Together, cremation ashes and remembrance jewellery, www.forevertogetherjewellery.co.uk, 01942 417315.

Human Tissue Authority, www.hta.gov.uk, 0207 972 4551.

Humanists UK, www.humanism.org.uk, 020 7324 3060.

Judicial Conduct Investigations Office, www.judicialconduct.judiciary.gov.uk, 020 7073 4719.

The Law Society of England and Wales, www.lawsociety.org.uk, 020 7320 5650.

Missing People, www.missingpeople.org.uk, you can call the charity at any time of the day or night on Freefone 116 000.

Motorcycle Funerals, www.motorcyclefunerals.com, info@motorcyclefunerals.com or phone 01530 274888 or 0845 375 2106.

National Association of Funeral Directors, www.nafd.org.uk. Phone line open Monday to Friday 9 a.m. to 5 p.m., 0121 711 1343.

National Society of Allied and Independent Funeral Directors, www.saif.org.uk, 020 7520 3800.

The Natural Death Centre, independent funeral advice, www.naturaldeath.org.uk. Helpline: 01962 712 690.

Scattering Ashes, www.scattering-ashes.co.uk, 03192 581012.

Simplicity Cremations, www.simplicitycremations.co.uk, 0800 484 051.

Simplicity Funerals, www.simplicity.co.uk, 0330 021 1010.

The Suicide Bereavement Support Partnership (SBSP), umbrella organisation for suicide support groups, www.uksobs.org.

Support after Murder or Manslaughter (SAMM), www.samm.org.uk, 0121 472 2912 or 0845 872 3440.

Support after Suicide, does not give individual support but exists to ensure support is available through various means, including research, signposting, advocacy and campaigning, www.supportaftersuicide.org.uk.

Survivors of Bereavement by Suicide UK, www.sobs.org. Helpline open Monday to Friday 9 a.m. to 9 p.m., 0300 111 5065.

Yuli Somme, felt shroud maker, www.bellacouche.com, 01647 441405.

Books and publications

Mannix, Kathryn, *With the End in Mind: How to Live and Die Well*, William Collins, 2017.

Oliver, Jamie, *Get Dead*, Friday Books, 2006.

Wienrich, Stephanie, *The Natural Death Handbook*, Ebury Publishing, 2006.

Websites

www.flexmort.com: For a Mini Mortuary Cooling System (CuddleBlanket) for keeping bodies cool.

www.funeralzone.co.uk: An online resource for all things to do with funerals.

www.gov.scot: Government Services in Scotland.

www.gov.uk: Government Services and Information in the UK, but mainly England and Wales.

www.lawscot.org.uk: Law Society of Scotland. You can find a solicitor on this site or phone 0131 226 7411.

www.macmillan.org.uk/information: For information on support to improve the lives of people with cancer.

www.mariecurie.org.uk/help: For information on benefit rules and grants for the terminally ill and their carers. Or call 0800 090 2309.

www.mywishes.co.uk: An app for digitally having your partner's wishes known in terms of your will, advance planning, funeral and bucket list.

www.nidirect.gov.uk: Government Services in Northern Ireland.

www.resourcecentre.org.uk: For information on charities.

Part Four

After Death Has Occurred – Registration of the Death, Probate and Looking to the Future

41
Introduction

This Part covers all the other things you need to do after the death of your partner besides the funeral. Under the law, you or another acceptable person has to register the death within certain time limits. In some circumstances, your partner's death may not be thought to be 'natural' or it may be 'unexplained'. We will tell you what might happen if this is the case and when this can lead to an inquest, although in the vast majority of situations this does not happen.

We also go into the subject of obtaining probate, so that you inherit the estate of your partner smoothly. We explain the situation if you were not married and if there is no will. We look at your finances and suggest some ways that you might make ends meet, particularly concerning paying your mortgage, if you have one. We look at what your partner's place of work might be able to do for you and what help you might get from the state, especially if you have children. Lastly, we talk about that painful process of disposing of your loved one's effects and how you might go about this.

42
Registering the Death

In England, Wales and Northern Ireland a death should be registered within five days, but registration can be delayed for another nine days if the registrar is told a medical certificate of cause of death (MCCD) has been issued. If you do not feel able to register the death yourself, it can be done by someone else. If the death has been reported to the coroner (or procurator fiscal in Scotland), you cannot register it until the coroner's investigations are finished and then it is normal for them to do it for you. If, having reviewed the facts of the case, the coroner is satisfied that a funeral can take place, they can issue an interim death certificate, even when there is to be an inquest.

If your loved one died in hospital or a nursing or care home, but was under the supervision of medical staff, and there were no unusual circumstances, a doctor at the hospital or attending the care home will give you a medical certificate that shows the cause of death. If your loved one died at home, the doctor attending them during the last fourteen days of their life is generally the person who signs it. Once you have the certificate, you can register the death.

If you are planning to have a cremation, the current system normally requires that the doctor who signed the death certificate signs a Certificate of Medical Attendant (Cremation 4) and a different doctor will sign the Confirmatory Medical Certificate (Cremation 5). Obviously, cremation is very final, and as there is no opportunity for possible later exhumation, these precautions are taken to ensure that the cremation can go ahead with no possibility of a miscarriage of justice. This process is usually carried out by the funeral director when they know you want a cremation.

If you are not using a funeral director, you will have to arrange to do it yourself. Hospital doctors have colleagues in the same hospital who can sign the Confirmatory Medical Certificate. General Practitioners usually have an arrangement with another practice. A doctor from the same practice cannot do this. At the time of writing, the certificates cost £82 each, but they are not payable if the coroner has become involved. If you do not think you want cremation, but are thinking of a burial, you are in a bit of a dilemma. Cremations are much cheaper and if you change your mind later on whether to have one, there might be some difficulty in arranging for a second certificate, although it is not impossible. Equally, whether or not you want to pay for a second certificate and then not use it is a difficult decision. If the death goes to the coroner, there is no need to pay for the forms to be signed, because they will have determined the cause of death.

What follows assumes that the death took place in England or Wales, the person died at home, in hospital or in a nursing home, and the death was expected – in legal terms, that is, it was normal and explained.

Your appointment with the registrar

You have to book an appointment to register a death with the registrar at the registrar's office, which sometimes delays the registration. Most large towns have an office, but if you live in the country or are incapacitated, you may not be able to attend within the five days stipulated. However, you can explain this to the registrar's clerk, or someone can do so on your behalf. When you contact the office, you will need to tell them about the medical certificate(s).

If you use the register office in the area where the person died, you will be given the documents you need at the time. However, if you use a different register office – for example, if your partner died a long way from home, you may have chosen to use a register office more convenient to you – the documents will be sent to the office in the area where the person died, before they are issued to you. This means you will have to wait a few days for them.

The person who registers the death

It is likely that you will want to take on the task of registering your loved one's death yourself. However, if you cannot do it, for whatever reason, the law provides for several other people who can (in England and Wales):

- A relative.

- Someone there at the time of death, such as the matron of a nursing home.

- An administrator from the hospital if the person died there.

- The person in charge of making the funeral arrangements, such as a godchild or friend.

You cannot register a death if you are none of these things.

There is a slightly different list for other parts of the UK, which is detailed below.

The paperwork required

Whoever registers the death will need to tell the registrar:

- Your partner's full name at the time of death.

- Any names previously used. This is unlikely in the case of a man, but they may have changed their name by deed poll or the terms of an inheritance. In the case of a woman, it might be the maiden name or previous marriages.

- Your partner's date and place of birth.

- Their occupation.

- The full name, date of birth and occupation of the surviving spouse or civil partner.

- Whether your partner was getting a state pension or any other benefits.

You should also take supporting documents that show your name and address, such as a utility bill or phone bill, if you can.

If you have them available, you should also take in the following documents for your partner:

- NHS card (also called the medical card)

- Birth certificate

- Driving licence

- Council tax bill

- Marriage or civil partnership certificate

- National Insurance number as well as your own

- Passport

- Blue Badge (if they had one)

The documents you will get from the registrar

During the meeting with the registrar, you will receive a number of documents that you need in order to finalise the funeral and arrange probate:

- A certified copy of the death certificate.

- A certificate for burial or cremation.

- A certificate of notification or registration of death.

The death certificate

This is the entry in the death register. It is essential that you give the registrar the correct details for the register. If the details are subsequently found to be wrong, the registration has to be done again, with a consequent charge. This happened recently at a registration I was attending, where the dead spouse of the person being registered had an unusual spelling of one of their given names. The person registering gave the registrar the incorrect spelling. In this case it was decided to leave things as they were (hopefully not to the confusion of future generations of family history enthusiasts) as nothing depended on the spelling being correct, but in other circumstances there might have been a significant cost to put this right: £150 at the time of writing.

You can buy extra certified death certificates, which you will find useful in sorting out your loved one's estate, for sending off to banks and insurance companies. It is sensible to do this, as not all organisations return the original and photocopies are usually not accepted. At the time of registration, copies currently cost £11 in England and Wales, £8 in Northern Ireland and £10 in Scotland. If you ask for them at a later date, they cost £11 in England and Wales, £15 for the first copy and £8 thereafter in Northern Ireland, and £12 online or £15 by post, phone or in person in Scotland.

A Certificate for Burial or Cremation

Sometimes known as the 'green form', this gives permission for burial or an application for cremation. You need to give this to your funeral director if you have one, as soon as possible, for without it nothing can take place. If you do not have a funeral director, you give it to the crematorium or cemetery office. Once the cremation or burial has taken place, the relevant office staff returns part of the form to the registrar. If a coroner has carried out a post-mortem examination and your loved one is to be cremated, the green form is replaced by an authorisation from the coroner, which is usually collected by the funeral director on your behalf although you would have to collect it yourself if you were not using one.

A certificate of notification or registration of death (form BD8)

This white form is used to notify government departments about your partner's death. After your partner has died, you need to let government departments know so that any benefits or pensions they were receiving can be stopped.

'Tell Us Once' is a service that is offered by most local authorities on behalf of the Department for Work and Pensions. The service allows you to inform central and local government services of the death of your partner through a single contact, rather than you having to write, telephone or even go in person to each service individually. The service is free and can save you a great deal of time and effort. You will be told about the service either when you book an appointment with the registrar or when you or your representative attends to register the death. In most cases, the registrar will offer you the service immediately after you register the death. They will check with you what central and local government services need to be notified. The notification is sent through immediately and you will be given a letter of confirmation. If this is difficult for you, the registrar can offer a telephone and online 'Tell Us Once' service instead. Many of the items mentioned above in the list on p. 189 are covered by this. In addition, if you are registering your spouse, you should have with you your own National Insurance number and date of birth.

If you choose not to use the 'Tell Us Once' service you can use the form on the back of the certificate of notification or registration of death to notify the Department of Work and Pensions so that they can adjust any payments and prevent overpayments. They will forward the information to HM Revenue and Customs. It will come with a prepaid envelope. You will then have to notify all the other agencies yourself, such as the Passport Office.

Registering a death in Scotland

In Scotland, the list of those who can register a death is widened to include:

- The deceased's executor or other legal representative.

- The occupier of the property where the person died.

- If there is no such person, anyone else who knows the information to be registered.

You have eight days to register a death in Scotland, and it can be registered in any registration district there.

The Scottish government booklet, 'What to do after a death in Scotland', is available on the Scottish government website and is available in registration offices, or you can telephone 0131 244 2193.

In Scotland, the certificate of notification or registration of death is called Form 3344SI.

Registering a death in Northern Ireland

In Northern Ireland, the time allowed is five days, as in England and Wales, but the list of persons who can register the death is similar to that in Scotland, with the addition of:

- The governor, matron or chief officer of a public building where the death occurred.

- A person finding, or a person taking charge of, the body.

The latter would likely be the police, but hopefully this would not be the case for the circumstances we are writing about.

Information needed by the registrar, in addition to that for England and Wales, includes:

- The name and address of the deceased's GP.

- Details of any pension apart from a state pension that the deceased might have held.

In Northern Ireland, the certificate of notification or registration of death is known as Form 36/BD8. You can also contact the Bereavement Service on the Northern Ireland government website to report the death of someone who was receiving social security benefits.

Which? issued guidance on registering a death in April 2019, which you may find useful.

43

A Death That is Considered Unnatural, Unknown, Sudden, Violent or Unexplained

In all these cases, the death will have to be reported to the coroner. Where the death is thought to be unnatural, such as in a murder, accident or drugs overdose, or where there is not enough evidence of natural causes, say because the person had not been seen by a doctor in the prescribed time, there will be a post-mortem and an inquest. Next-of-kin permission is not required for a post-mortem.

The role of the coroner

The office of the coroner is one of the oldest institutions in England and Wales. The role was originally established in the eleventh century shortly after the Norman Conquest in England and in Wales in the thirteenth century. The coroner was a crown official whose primary duty was to protect the financial interest of the Crown in criminal proceedings. It was meant to counterbalance the role of the sheriff. Nowadays, coroners are independent judicial officers who investigate deaths reported to them. Perhaps surprisingly, 43 per cent of deaths were reported to coroners in 2017, so do not be concerned if this is what happens in your case. Only 37 per cent of them resulted in post-mortems and only 14 per cent required an inquest – a very small proportion of those reported. The coroner will make whatever inquiries are necessary to find out the cause of death, including ordering a post-mortem examination, obtaining witness statements and medical records, or holding an inquest. The job of the coroner is to order and conduct an inquest into the manner or cause of a death when it is deemed to be violent, unnatural, sudden or unexplained. In some cases, for example after an accident in the workplace, the coroner may do so in front of a jury, but in the majority of cases they will preside on their own.

The coroner is a public servant paid for by the local authority and is usually qualified as a doctor or a lawyer. In Scotland, the role of the coroner has been abolished. Deaths requiring judicial examination are reported to the procurator fiscal and are dealt with by Fatal Accident Inquiries.

In February 2014, the Ministry of Justice published a 'Guide to Coroner Services'.

Reporting a death to the coroner

The registrar, a doctor or the police can report deaths to the coroner in certain circumstances, such as where:

- No doctor attended the deceased during their last illness.

- Although a doctor attended during the last illness, the deceased was not seen either within fourteen days before death or after death.

- The cause of death appears to be unknown.

- The death occurred during an operation or before recovery from the effects of an anaesthetic.

- The death occurred at work or was due to industrial disease or poisoning.

- The death was sudden or unexpected.

- The death was unnatural.

- The death was due to violence or neglect.

- The death took place in other suspicious circumstances.

- The death occurred in prison, police custody or other state detention.

- There is a possibility of negligence or misadventure related to the treatment of the person who died in hospital or a nursing home (listed under Northern Ireland specifically).

The involvement of the coroner necessitates considerable distress and particular difficulties for you as the partner of the dead person, although at the same time it is important for you to know what caused the death of your partner, so you can have peace of mind. In many cases the coroner will decide that even though it is necessary to have an inquest to determine the cause of death, there is no reason to delay the registration and therefore the issuing of an interim death certificate. In these circumstances, the coroner will pass the appropriate documents to do this to the registrar. Sometimes these may be given to you by the coroner to pass on to the registrar, but generally the coroner's and registrar's office work together.

The inquest

A doctor or the police will typically contact you if there is likely to be an inquest, but probably the first contact you will have with the coroner is when the coroner's clerk contacts you to explain what is happening. They are usually very helpful and sympathetic, and will keep you updated on progress and particularly the date of the inquest. Although this is normally held a few days after the death, it is likely to be opened and adjourned, and there is usually a delay of several months before the inquest proper takes place.

An inquest takes place in a courtroom with the usual places for witnesses and officials giving evidence. The coroner, who presides rather like a judge, will decide who needs to be called as a witness. Sometimes they will simply decide to rely on witness statements rather than having someone there in person. You are advised to take along someone to support you, as the details of the death and any explanations concerning it can be distressing, especially if any blame is being attached to your partner's actions by the investigating officer.

I must declare an interest here, as my husband drowned and an inquest was held. My experience of coroners (limited to this one occasion and one other when I was on a jury for a work accident) is that they are very aware of how difficult it is for you, especially to hear criticism of your loved one's behaviour. They try as hard as they can to shield you from pain, including asking you if you would care for an adjournment or whether you need the inquest to be halted for a time in order for you to regain your composure. They also ask if you have any questions and ensure that queries you may have about the facts of the death are answered. This is your opportunity to ask the questions you might have about the whole affair. Do not be afraid to do this.

The inquest is also very likely to attract the attention of the press, who have a job to do in reporting the findings of the coroner. You are advised to treat them with courtesy and to follow the suggestions given on p. 169, under 'Dealing with the Press'.

Copies of all the appropriate papers, witness statements and post-mortem reports, plus any statements given by ambulance personnel and first responders, will be made available to you before the inquest.

In Northern Ireland, there are coroner liaison officers who contact the family and forward written information to them about the preliminary cause of death, and enclose documents to assist with financial matters.

The conclusion of the inquest

The coroner comes to a conclusion at the end of an inquest. This includes the legal 'determination', which states who died, and where, when and how they died. A coroner's jury may be convened if your partner died in custody of an unnatural cause, or if their death was linked to their own or someone else's actions while at work, or to certain health and safety issues. The coroner may also decide to use a jury in other cases should they feel it would be helpful or in the public interest. Either the coroner or jury also make 'findings' to allow the cause of death to be registered. One of the following terms may be used:

- Accident or misadventure

- Alcohol/drug-related

- Industrial disease

- Natural causes

- Lawful killing

- Unlawful killing

- Open

- Road traffic collision

- Stillbirth

- Suicide

The coroner may also make a brief 'narrative' conclusion, setting out the facts surrounding the death in more detail and explaining the reason for the decision.

They may also make a report concerning what they have found, especially if it has significance beyond the individual case.

If there is a jury, instead of the coroner deciding the outcome, he or she will give the jury a choice of possible conclusions and the jury will select the one it feels best fits the facts.

You may challenge the coroner's decision or the conclusion of the inquest. You should do this as soon as possible and should seek advice from a solicitor. If you are unhappy with the personal conduct of the coroner, you should complain to the Judicial Conduct Investigations

Office. If you wish to complain about the standard of service you have received, you should first do so to the coroner.

Where there is no body

You may be in the very sad and unfortunate position of having your partner go missing, and over time have to assume that they are dead. In England and Wales, you can apply to the High Court under the Presumption of Death Act 2013 for a missing person to be declared presumed dead. This declaration will enable any property, money and other possessions of the missing person to be administered and will dissolve the missing person's marriage or civil partnership. You are advised to use the services of an experienced lawyer who has the expertise to deal with your case. There is an organisation to which you can apply for information, called Missing People.

Once you have received the declaration, you can apply to the General Registry Office for a Certificate of Presumed Death and apply for probate. The declaration only becomes final once the appeal window that follows the declaration has closed and is subject to the outcome of any appeal made. An appeal may be brought within twenty-one days, unless the court specifies differently when making the declaration.

The declaration is granted if the court is satisfied either that the missing person has died or has not been known to be alive for at least seven years. If there is clear evidence of death, an application can be made immediately. What matters is the strength of the evidence, not the period of time. Suicide notes would be seen as strong evidence. If there is insufficient evidence that the person has died, you will have to show that the person has not been known to be alive for at least seven years.

If this happens to you, you may have financial commitments and no means of fulfilling them, as the missing person was the breadwinner. It is a good idea in these circumstances to inform all the interested parties, such as building societies and banks, about what is happening and ask for clarification of the situation from their perspective. This can help avoid any repossession proceedings.

44
Probate

When people talk about 'probate' what they mean is that the executors' or administrators' powers to administer the estate of a dead person have been officially confirmed. The person who applies for probate is also often called the personal representative. The aims of probate are to safeguard creditors of the deceased, to ensure reasonable provision is made for the deceased dependants, and to distribute the balance of the estate in accordance with the intentions of the person whose will it is, if there is one. Note that creditors come first! You do this by applying to an office of the High Court known as the probate registry. Most cities and big towns have a probate registry or a sub-registry. Citizens Advice and Age UK all have accessible web pages to describe how to obtain probate, but the most reliable is the government's, as it contains the official information from the registry.

Where there is a will, a document called a Grant of Representation is given, which enables those administering the estate to gain access to all relevant information, financial or otherwise, concerning the person's estate. You may be the sole executor or you may be acting in tandem with someone else, such as your solicitor or one of your children or a friend. If you are good with figures and are up for a challenge, by all means undertake the process of obtaining probate yourself without professional help, but in many cases you will not be in a condition to take on this task and you may want to leave it to someone else, perhaps your solicitor or another legal representative.

If there is no will then it will be necessary to obtain letters of administration, which involves a similar procedure. You can usually apply if you're the person's next of kin, usually their spouse or civil partner, but any of your joint children or a child of theirs can also do it.

You can still apply if you were separated at the time of death but you had been married or in a civil partnership. You cannot apply if you are the partner of the person who has died but you were not married or in a civil partnership, as you are not automatically entitled to any of your partner's estate.

You may not need probate if the person who died had jointly owned land, property, shares or money. These will automatically pass to the surviving owner(s), but that person isn't necessarily you. If you are unmarried but your name is on joint accounts and the deeds, provided it is a beneficial joint tenancy, you will inherit these.

You may not need probate or letters of administration if:

- The estate is just made up of cash (notes and coins) and personal possessions such as a car, furniture and jewellery.

- All the property in the estate is owned as beneficial joint owners.

- You had joint bank accounts.

- The amount of money is small.

- The estate is insolvent and there is insufficient money to pay all the debts, taxes and expenses.

- There are certain life insurance policies and pension benefits in the estate.

A small estate is difficult to define, but usually if an estate contains property or has a value of more than £5,000, it will not be deemed a small estate and probate will be needed.

You need to contact each asset holder – for example, banks or building societies – to find out if you'll need probate to get access to their respective assets as long as they follow the small estate provision. Every organisation has its own rules. Many have a specialist department that deals with deaths and inheritance. For example, Halifax has a Specialist Bereavement Team who you can call on 0800 028 1057, open 8 a.m. to 8 p.m., seven days a week, or you can make an appointment to see someone in your local branch. They also have a very helpful booklet entitled 'A guide to our bereavement support services' available in branches or by phoning the above number. In this they explain the threshold for closing a sole account, what payments can be made from it, and at what threshold the accounts will be frozen until probate has been received, together with lots of other useful information.

The process is different in Scotland and Northern Ireland, so you would need to check the procedure there on their respective government websites.

How a probate application works

What follows are the steps you should take to get probate granted:

1   Check if there is a will. There is a different process if there is no will. You then have to apply for letters of administration.

2   Value the estate and report it to HMRC.

3   Apply for probate.

4   Pay any inheritance tax that is due.

5   Collect the estate's assets.

6   Pay off any debts.

7   Keep a record of how any property money or possessions will be split.

8   Distribute the assets to the beneficiaries.

The person who does all this is the executor or a legal representative. If there is no will, you can apply as their spouse or civil partner. You cannot apply if you are their partner but not their spouse or civil partner.

When applying for probate, you always need the original will and not a photocopy. Only the most recent will is valid. If by any chance you know that a will was made but you do not know where it is, you can first contact your spouse's solicitor, if they had one, or try the London Probate Department – you'll need the death certificate and to prove you're the executor in order to be sent the will. Bear in mind that this cannot be done if you were neither married nor in a civil partnership. Or you can fill in a lost will questionnaire, which you can find online.

The process is different in Scotland and Northern Ireland, and you should check the appropriate government websites.

The ensuing paragraphs give some general guidance concerning things you need to know about probate, but they are by no means a comprehensive guide to obtaining this, which is complex.

Property held as 'beneficial joint tenants' and 'beneficial tenants in common'

In English law, where property is owned jointly as 'beneficial joint tenants', which is normal for couples, following the death of one of the owners that person's share does not become part of the estate but is inherited by the surviving joint owner regardless of what is contained within the will. It is only if property is held as 'tenants in common' (see p. 204) that on the death of one owner that person's share of the jointly owned property becomes part of his or her estate. An example of things held as joint tenants would be joint bank accounts or houses where two people are named as beneficial joint tenants on the deeds.

The largest part of most deceased persons' estate is their house, if they owned one. As the spouse or civil partner, you automatically inherit their half-share free of inheritance tax if you both owned the property as beneficial joint tenants. You also inherit anything else they left you, free of tax.

If you are not married but you own the property as beneficial joint tenants, you would automatically inherit their half-share of the house and anything else your partner left you in their will, but it would be subject to inheritance tax if the total was over £325,000. If there was no will, you would simply inherit the half-share of the property and pay inheritance tax over £325,000, but not inherit anything else.

If you are married and there is no will, but the house you own is held as beneficial joint tenants, the house would not form part of the estate and you would automatically be entitled to your husband or wife's half-share of the house. After this, there are restrictions as to the amount you may inherit, which is dealt with on p. 205. A husband, wife or civil partner can gift their spouse any amount of money before death, and inheritance tax would not be due on their death.

In English law, where property is owned jointly as 'beneficial tenants in common', meaning each person owns a defined share in the property either in equal or unequal shares, then, as stated above, following the death of one of the owners, that person's share will not automatically pass to the surviving owner but will form part of the estate of the person who has died.

If there is a will, it should say what is to happen to the share of the owner on death. This could be left to the surviving owner absolutely or the surviving owner may only be given an interest in the property for their life. This may be because the owner who has died may have children from a previous relationship to whom they wish to leave their share of the property on the death of the surviving owner. If you are married or in a civil partnership, the same rules of inheritance apply as to property held as 'beneficial joint tenants', meaning you would inherit anything else that your husband, wife or civil partner has left you in their will, free of inheritance tax.

If you are married and there is no will, there are restrictions as to the amount you may inherit, which is dealt with in 'The laws of inheritance and intestacy' (p. 205).

If you are not married and there is no will, the share of the deceased owner will pass to their next of kin.

Small estates

A lot depends on the size of the estate. If the value of the estate before deducting the cost of the funeral and any debts left by the deceased is less than £5,000, probate may not be required. It is worth contacting banks or building societies holding assets to request that they make payment to the personal representative. They may only require a copy of the death certificate, a copy of any existing will and/or proof that you are the remaining spouse or civil law partner. Many of these organisations have special departments dealing with just such a set of circumstances, and if the sums are relatively small, they should be willing to co-operate. If you have known for some time that your spouse, civil law partner or partner was dying, you may have already made arrangements to transfer all your assets into joint accounts or transferred them to yourself.

If there is no will – the laws of inheritance and intestacy

The laws of inheritance and intestacy are complex and if you are not already using a solicitor or other legal adviser you are advised to seek professional help if there is any doubt in your mind about who is entitled to what, especially if there are children from previous relationships, legally adopted children and stepchildren. We have summed the law up below as simply as we can on the basis of a person with only a surviving spouse or a spouse with children.

Under the Inheritance and Trustee Powers Act 2014:

If you are married (or in a civil partnership) and your estate is worth less than £270,000. Under the intestacy rules, your surviving spouse/civil partner inherits everything.

If you are married (or in a civil partnership), your estate is worth more than £270,000 and you have no children. Again, under the intestacy rules, your surviving spouse/civil partner inherits it all.

If you are married (or in a civil partnership), your estate is worth more than £270,000 and you have children. Under the intestacy rules, it now starts to get interesting and potentially problematic for the surviving spouse/civil partner. The first £270,000 and the personal possessions will go to the spouse/civil partner. The remainder of the estate will be divided in half, with half going to the surviving spouse and the other half being divided between surviving children. If any child should predecease you, then their own children (your grandchildren) would get their parent's share and so on if a grandchild has predeceased, etc.

If you are not married (or in a civil partnership) and have children. Under the intestacy rules, your children will inherit everything equally. Again, if a child has predeceased you, then their children with get their parent's share (or children's children, etc.).

If you are not married (or in a civil partnership) and have no children. Under the intestacy rules, your surviving relatives will inherit in the following order:

- Parents

- Brothers or sisters or their children (or children's children, etc.)

- Half-brothers or half-sisters or their children (or children's children, etc.)

- Grandparents

- Uncles and aunts (brothers and sisters of the whole blood of a parent) or their children (or children's children, etc.)

- Uncles and aunts (brothers and sisters of the half blood of a parent) or their children (or children's children etc.)

- If you have no surviving spouse/civil partner, children, parents, siblings, grandparents, uncles, aunts, cousins, first cousins, etc. then, under the intestacy rules, everything will go to the Crown.

If you are married or in a civil partnership in England and Wales, your partner can make a will leaving their estate to whosoever they choose; there is no 'forced heirship'. In Scotland the rules are different. A surviving spouse and children have a statutory claim to parts of the estate. You cannot disinherit your spouse and children, including adopted and illegitimate children. The link https://beyond.life/help-centre/admin-legal/dying-intestate-in-scotland-scottish-inheritance-law-explained/ has a helpful flow chart explaining this.

As the surviving spouse you will not pay inheritance tax. If you owned your home together with your partner in a beneficial joint tenancy, you will also inherit their half-share together with their share of any joint accounts. If any property was in your spouse's name, the same rules of intestacy apply as stated above: you inherit the personal property and belongings of your spouse plus the first £270,000, and then the estate is divided between you and your children. The threshold of £270,000 came into force on 6 February 2020. At least every five years the government raises the amount partners can inherit in line with the consumer price index.

If you are unmarried, you inherit nothing from your partner's estate, but if you owned your home together with your partner in a beneficial joint tenancy (not a beneficial tenancy in common) you will inherit their half-share together with their share of any joint accounts. You may have to pay inheritance tax on this if the part you inherit is worth more than the £325,000 inheritance tax threshold.

Inheritance tax

At the time of writing, the tax threshold for inheritance tax on an estate is £325,000. The allowance has remained the same since 2010/11 and is set to remain at £325,000 until the end of 2020/21. The standard inheritance tax rate is 40 per cent of anything over the £325,000. Spouses and civil partners do not pay inheritance tax. It is worth pointing out here that although many people worry about paying inheritance tax, according to HM Revenue and Customs only one in twenty actually do so.

There are complex rules about the value of your home and passing on your allowance, which need to be tackled professionally.

Employing a solicitor or someone else, or doing it yourself

When it comes to probate, you have a choice of routes, organisations and people you can use. You can employ a solicitor, perhaps the person who drew up your wills, if you have them, or bought and sold your houses for you. You can use your accountant, who deals with your business affairs and has dealt with HMRC on your behalf. You can employ a probate administrator, whom you may not have met before but who specialises in probate. Or you can do it yourself, probably with the help of the internet and a few books from the library.

The pros of employing a solicitor include the fact that they are properly qualified and should know the law, plus they are regulated so you would be covered if you had grounds for complaint and were proved to be correct. This is important because, according to a 2014 report by the Legal Ombudsman, wills and probate-related legal services were the third-most-complained-about area of law, making up around 13 per cent of the 8,000 complaints resolved. Solicitors are insured so that they can make reparation and, most importantly, they have a set of standards that they should adhere to. The cons are that their fees are relatively high. The number of people using a solicitor for probate has fallen quite dramatically in the last few years. However, if you think the will is complex and it might be challenged, employing a solicitor may save you money in the long run.

The pros of using an accountant are that they may be from the firm you habitually use for your tax returns or business returns, so they know you and you know them. Their fees are likely to be lower than a solicitor's. While not specialising in probate law, they do have a good knowledge of company law, tax law and dealing with the HMRC.

The pros of using a probate administrator are that they are specialised and therefore do a lot of applications. They will come to see you, size up the job to be done, and most of them will offer you a fixed price, which would add up to well below the total bill that you would have to pay using the hourly rate of a solicitor, which is open-ended. Your funeral director might have experience of a local person who does this. They can charge less and are practised at knowing what to do. They have often worked at some stage in a solicitor's office. Reports we have had are good. Unlike solicitors, they are often hot on communication and some will send you a weekly update indicating progress. The cons are that although they are normally licensed and insured, you might only have recourse to the courts if things go wrong. If the estate is very complicated, they may not have the experience to deal with it.

The big pro of doing it yourself is that you have control of the process the whole time. However, it is a steep learning curve. You can use a search engine to find literature you can buy to help you with a DIY probate. One DIY probate pack we researched was £9.99, one £29 and yet another £97, so the price varies considerably. The latter two came with free access to customer-only help and support. Your funeral director may also be able to supply you with a helpful booklet. Again, if the estate is large and/or complicated, this might not be the best route. Additionally, you may not be in a fit state to undertake this task yourself, although you could ask a friend or relative to do it for you.

Online probate application

HM Courts and Tribunals (HMCTS) has an online application service, allowing people to apply for probate from home on the www.gov.uk site. The service lets you apply for, pay for and swear a statement of truth online, whereas previously you were required to visit a probate registry or solicitor's office to obtain permission to deal with the estate and wind up the deceased's affairs. You can use this service if you're the executor or administrator and you:

- Have the original will if you're the executor (you do not need the will if you're an administrator).

- Have the original death certificate or an interim death certificate from the coroner.

- Have already reported the estate's value.

The person who died must have lived in England or Wales most of the time. It is not available where the deceased lived in Northern Ireland or Scotland.

A very helpful aspect of this method is that the system will guide you through the process telling you what information is required. You may have the information to hand and can retrieve it from your records, or you know you need to find it out. Either way, ensure you do not arrive at the probate registry with inadequate documentation.

Probate fees

There is no fee if the estate is under £5,000. The application fee is currently £215 if made by an individual. You can call the probate registry to pay by debit or credit card. You will be given a reference to send with your documents. At the time of writing, probate fees were due to rise considerably, but this has been delayed by Brexit.

Insolvent estates

You may find that you are unable to access any money after the death of your spouse or civil partner, either because you did not deal with the finances of your household or you or your deceased partner have debts. You will probably need the help of a solicitor, as you may have creditors; at the very least, seek some help from a debt counselling organisation. You can go to Citizens Advice or Age UK, both of whom have specialist debt advisors. The StepChange Debt Charity is the trading name of the Foundation for Credit Counselling and is a debt charity operating across the United Kingdom. You will be able to find other similar organisations by using a search engine. If you think your partner had debts, you are expected to make a search for creditors. Your solicitor will explain the procedure and place the necessary advertisements.

45
Sorting Out Your Finances

Sorting out your financial situation might be the last thing you feel like doing in the circumstances, but it has to be done sooner or later and you should at least give it some thought as soon as you are up to it. Alternatively, it might be the thing that gives you nightmares, so as soon as you tackle it you will start to feel a good deal better. There is a lot of help out there for you to tap into. If it seems particularly daunting, ask a friend whose discretion you trust and who has a practical head on their shoulders to give you a hand. They can steer you in the right direction.

It is important that you are aware of your sources of income and your outgoings, so that you can live within your budget, especially if this has been severely curtailed by the loss of your partner. There is a large section in Part Two on stabilising your financial affairs (see p. 76), which you might like to read in conjunction with this section. Below are some of the most important ways that you can plan to make ends meet.

Getting to grips with your finances

The problems you will have in sorting out your money situation after your partner's death will depend very much on what arrangements were in place before they died and whether or not you are used to handling money. If you have your own sources of income, such as a salary or a state pension of your own, it is likely that these will continue, provided you carry on working. If you were entirely dependent on your spouse for money, you will probably soon run out, especially if you have no savings of your own. Any money in a joint account, whether a current or savings account, immediately becomes yours, as does your house if the mortgage is in your joint names and it is a joint tenancy. It is also useful if the bank or building society will let you have small amounts from accounts in your spouse's name on production of a death certificate and without getting probate. This relieves the immediate pressure on you. The only problem here might be if an account was overdrawn. A bank or building society might pay itself from another account if there is one, before letting you have the residue.

If there are utility accounts on which the two of you are named, then you become fully liable for continued payments if you are continuing to benefit from them, even if the money came out of an account of your partner's. If they were in the name of your partner, you need to let the appropriate authorities know, and unless you want to be left with no heating and lighting or telephone and internet services, you will need to terminate them and commence new contracts in your own name. Many organisations have departments for handling such cases and are very helpful. The fact remains, however, that, at the time of death, the contract ends and will have to be paid for up to that point. It may be that you can ask your executor or solicitor, if you have one, to handle this for you, although some organisations do ask to speak to the surviving account holder.

You are advised to make a list of all the bills that you have to pay and systematically sort them into date order, so that you can work out what needs to be done in the short, medium, and long term. If you are using a solicitor, they can be very helpful in this process. If you are used to this sort of management process, you shouldn't find it too difficult. If not, it can be onerous. Probably the best way is to start with the paperwork, if it has not all been done online, and sort it out into piles. Usually, there is a customer service telephone number. If you ring this and explain what has happened, you will receive the help you need. An additional bonus to doing this is that it can be quite distressing to receive letters and bills in your partner's name, so the sooner these are changed into your name the better.

You may be able to receive some money from the state, your husband's place of work or your own. These are detailed below.

Bereavement Support Payment

Bereavement Support Payment is a benefit paid to widows, widowers or surviving civil partners who have been bereaved on or after 6 April 2017. It replaces Bereavement Allowance, Widowed Parents Allowance and Bereavement Payment for those whose husband died on or after 6 April 2017. You may be able to get Bereavement Support Payment if, when your spouse or civil partner died, you were under the state pension age yourself, or over the state pension age but your spouse or civil partner wasn't entitled to a state pension based on their own National Insurance contributions. Your spouse or civil partner must have either paid enough National Insurance contributions (at least twenty-five weeks currently) or died because of an industrial accident or disease caused by work. You must be living in the UK or a country that pays bereavement benefits. You aren't eligible to receive such a payment if you were divorced, you are living with another person or you are in prison. You must claim within three months for the full benefit and up to eighteen months for any benefit, as it tapers off.

If you want to claim, you should either download a Bereavement Benefits pack (form BB1), telephone for one, or go in person to your JobCentre Plus, where they will be able to advise you. The pack contains notes to help you fill in the claim form. You can return the completed form to your JobCentre Plus or send it to:

Dover Benefit Centre
Post Handling Site B, Wolverhampton, WV99 1LA

If you need an alternative format such as Braille, large print or audio CD, you should call the Bereavement Service Helpline.

If you are living abroad, you should contact the International Pension Centre to see what you are entitled to:

Mail Handling Site A, Wolverhampton, WV98 1LW

You could also access the Bereavement Service Helpline, where there is an online enquiry form, or call 0191 218 7608.

Making your own will

If you have not already made your own will, it is now more necessary than ever, especially if you have children or other dependants, as there is now only one parent. If you were to die, your children would need a guardian. If there is no will stating your wishes, they could be put with people you would not have chosen. The website www.farewill.com has a good section on guardianship.

Mortgages

If you and your partner were buying a property together and your name is on the deeds as beneficial joint tenants, you automatically inherit your partner's half of the house, but unless you had some sort of mortgage protection insurance, you are still responsible for paying off what remains of the mortgage. You are advised to go and see your mortgage provider as soon as you can face it and tell them what has happened. Take a friend with you so that you know you have understood everything correctly by checking with them afterwards. The bank or building society will help you as much as they can. The question is: can you afford to keep up the mortgage payments? There may be several solutions to this dilemma, which we detail below.

If you have paid off quite a lot of your mortgage already, you may be able to remortgage and pay lower premiums that you can manage. Do not automatically use the same provider. Shop around or use a broker if you think they can do a better job, or one of the price-comparison sites. If your house has increased in value, another solution might be to raise money on it. This is known as 'equity release'. Ask your financial advisor about this if you have one. There are usually advertisements selling equity release on daytime television or you can approach the industry body, which is the Equity Release Council. Do not do this without a lot of thought and advice, and if you do decide to go ahead, use someone reputable and preferably someone that your friends have used and found satisfactory. There is sometimes an age restriction on equity release.

You may decide to 'downsize' and thereby release equity from your house or reduce the size of the mortgage payments. This is an enormous thing to contemplate so soon after your bereavement and you should think twice about it. Only do it if it really is the only solution. For one thing, it will force you into making decisions about disposing of your partner's belongings perhaps a lot sooner than you would have done if you'd stayed put, which may have a negative effect on your grieving process.

If you were married but for some reason the property you lived in was in your spouse or civil partner's name, and they have left it to you in their will, the house will form part of their estate, but you will inherit it by virtue of the gift of this in the will and you will not have to pay inheritance tax on it as no inheritance tax is payable between spouses. However, if you wish to keep living there and there is an outstanding amount still to pay, then it is likely that you will have to take out a new mortgage in your sole name unless there was some sort of insurance scheme such as a mortgage protection that your partner paid for, out of which the outstanding amount will be paid. If you are the only person left in your home, whether you own it or not, don't forget to apply for the single person's allowance on your council tax. This is usually a saving of 25 per cent.

If you are not married and there is no will or a joint beneficial tenancy, then you are in dire straits and at the mercy of those who inherit the house. Hopefully, this is not the case.

Benefits from your partner's place of work

You should contact your partner's workplace concerning the death of your partner and should arrange to see a representative of the organisation – usually a human resources team member, depending on the size of the organisation – to discuss what, if anything, you will receive from them. Depending on the size of the organisation, you may receive a pension of your own, a lump sum or other benefits. If they have any humanity, they will make the effort to come and see you, but you may have to go to the workplace itself. Benefits often apply only to those who were married, but in some schemes, employees are asked to nominate a person they want to be their beneficiary.

If your partner was a union member, you should also contact their shop steward and through them the local paid official. Unions exist partly for just such an emergency as this and you may find that the union will not only fight your corner with respect to the benefits owed to you from the employer, but also might have funds of their own that they can make available to you.

If your partner was a doctor, dentist, lawyer, accountant or in a similar profession, they may have been in a practice and the other principals will probably be familiar to you. They are most likely to rally round at a time like this and give you what help they can. Here, you have the added complication of a possible partnership that may need a solicitor to sort out.

If your partner ran their own business or was a director of a family firm or business, there might be quite complicated financial arrangements to deal with, and again you will need a solicitor.

Your work situation

You may have given up your own paid work when you realised that you needed to care for your partner in a terminal situation, or you may have reduced your hours or changed your role to one less demanding for the same reason. In which case your employer will know about your circumstances and you may have had a discussion with them about how much compassionate leave you can take, for such reasons as hospital appointments. The sad fact that the inevitable has happened and that your partner has died will not come as a surprise to the place where you work, and you will simply continue the conversation you began following the original diagnosis.

If your partner's death was sudden and unexpected, you will now have to begin that conversation. There is no statutory right for you to have paid compassionate leave after bereavement, but employees are entitled to a reasonable period of unpaid leave and, when the deceased was a partner, this will almost certainly be longer than for other dependants, except children. Most companies will have a policy on this, and you can find out what yours is by talking to your human resources department or from a staff handbook if you have one.

Apart from showing considerable sympathy, there is not much more that your own organisation will do for you in terms of benefits, but it may agree to change your hours and give you more flexible working, at least in the short term. If the company is big enough, it might have its own counselling service, which you might like to use, or it may give you time off to use one.

Leaving work or changing your job

You are going to have to get some money from somewhere to look after yourself and any children still at home, and continuing working would seem the obvious thing to do. Perhaps the consideration here is what kind of work? If you have a high-powered job in which you are away a lot, work long hours with tight deadlines and it is stressful, and you have a family, you are going to have to ask yourself whether you can cope with all this. It could be that your partner was the person who worked from home, had a less stressful job and you were the main breadwinner. If you change your job to something less demanding, it may not bring in the same amount of money.

Can you afford to pay for childcare? Do you think it would be of benefit to you and your children if you worked less? That might sound an odd question, but if you are not a very maternal or paternal person you may find that having a less high-powered job is not good for your self-esteem and could cause feelings of resentment. This is helpful neither for you nor for your children. Alternatively, do you want your children to be brought up by somebody else? Can your parents help, if you have any? How much stress will that put on them? What happens if one of your children is ill or has an accident and you are abroad and now their only parent? All these questions require you to take a long, hard look at what you are doing.

If your work is less stressful but nevertheless full time and demanding, can you juggle all the things you need to do with the help of your parents, neighbours, other family and friends? Do you need to reduce your hours, at least in the short term?

You are not really in the best of states to look at this dispassionately, and certainly for the first few weeks it is unlikely that anyone will expect you to be paying attention to anything other than the most pressing needs of your children's grief, the funeral, obtaining probate and getting through day by day. However, at some stage you will have to be making some decisions. Your place of work will require this from you. They have needs too; nothing like yours, but a business to run.

When you are feeling a bit stronger, perhaps you could sit down with a good friend and talk through all the alternatives, discuss what is available with your employer, and come to some conclusions.

Rent a Room

One solution would be to take on a lodger. You may feel that this is not something you could face at the moment, but we have put it in for completeness for when you feel ready for it. The Rent a Room scheme provides up to £7,500 of tax relief to people letting out accommodation in their own homes. From April 2019, a new condition will mean that you must be living in the property at the same time as the tenant for at least some of the letting period – a condition that possibly suits your situation.

There is a privacy issue here and a question of how far you can cope with having a stranger in your house. If you have a spare bedroom with en suite facilities, this would solve the problem of having to share a bathroom with a stranger. If you are just going to rent out your box room, it is only fair to allow your lodger the run of the house as well, which might not be what you want.

Organisations like Spare Room bring those needing a room together with those wanting to rent one out. They offer a Monday-to-Friday rental scheme for those prospective tenants who want this arrangement, which could be convenient for your situation, although of course this will bring in less money. Their services are free and they provide a free guide to 'dos' and 'don'ts'. You might find that having someone Monday to Friday only, so that you have your weekends free with your children, is easier to cope with. Consult your children on the idea. For less rent, you may be able to negotiate some childcare from this person and they will also provide someone else for your children to relate to. Obviously, there are security issues. You will want to take up references, for example, and study them carefully. Do not take this on together with all the other things you are coping with too early. You are far too vulnerable!

Insurance

It is likely that you will have some type of insurance, be it for your house, car or travel. These will have to be changed to your name. Be aware that your policy premiums may go up as a result. There are various reasons for this, some of which are based on actuarial tables. Not all insurers use the same risk tables. Usually, bereaved customers are dealt with sympathetically by the insurance companies, but if your premiums do increase, the reasons for it should be clearly stated. This might be an opportunity to shop around, but that's not something you may want to do just at this moment. Perhaps you have someone who might be prepared to take the task on for you?

You may want to take out some life insurance of your own to provide some security for your dependants.

46
Parenting

One in twenty-nine children in the UK under the age of sixteen will suffer the death of a parent. Children often have an overwhelming sense of confusion, fear and anxiety alongside their grief, which must be dealt with in order for them to continue into adulthood with a sense of confidence and long-lasting happiness.

If your children are still dependent on you, they will require a lot of support. There is a section on parenting and your relationship with your children's schools towards the end of Part Two (p. 115), which is as pertinent to before your partner's death as after it. If there has been some time to adjust to having a terminally ill parent, then your children might have settled into a new routine, difficult though that may have been. Death when it comes will be a shock, as the chances are that they were still hoping for recovery. If the death is sudden, you will have the needs of your children to cope with on top of everything else. Their well-being must be a priority for you, and the fact that discussing it comes towards the end of this Part of the book, after all the other practical things you need to do, in no way represents the importance that we think it deserves.

This will be an area where you will have to turn to friends and family for help. Charities that specialise in child bereavement include Cruse Bereavement Care, Jigsaw and Grief Encounter Child Bereavement Charity, who support children and their families to help alleviate the pain caused by the death of someone close.

You may find that older children, who you might expect to be able to support you, are so overwhelmed themselves that they cannot do this. This will be very difficult for you and you may need some assistance in enabling you to understand their position. That is where counselling might be helpful – see Part Six (p. 293).

47
Disposing of Your Partner's Effects

There is no hard-and-fast rule as to when you should dispose of your loved one's things. Everyone feels differently about this. Some people feel that they want to dispose of everything immediately. For others this is such a painful thing to have to do that they spend a very long time over it and sometimes never get round to it at all. I found that I wanted to give each of a small number of my husband's closest friends a significant item to remember him by. These items included his cherished number plate, a painting, some ceramics, his bicycles, his cashmere jumpers and his shirts. I wanted to give as much as I could, such as his cycling clothes and equipment, to good homes. Other items reminded me of him so much and were so very 'him' that it took me a while to be able to part with them. You do not have to do it all at once. You can do it in bits. A friend of mine recently disposed of her late husband's opera CDs. Opera was his great love. However, she is having to move and is asking herself what is the point of carrying these items off to yet another temporary place. Quite often it is moving house, whether self-instigated or enforced, that makes you realise that unwittingly you are carrying around a lot of baggage and you have the opportunity for a rethink.

Sometimes the answer is that you want to keep things for your children's sake. They may not want them now, but they may in the future. Books are another item that need consideration. Some building work and redecoration gave me less bookshelf space and I had to divest myself of substantial numbers of books. My rule concerned reference books. I got rid of all the paperback fiction I had and just kept things that I could refer to or that interested me. If your partner had a lot of books on a specific subject, you may find that someone might be interested in them. For example, someone I know who is the widow of a bishop wants his copious library to go to a theological college or department. I have known second-hand booksellers pay well for substantial libraries. If you want to give your books to a charity, then Oxfam is probably the best one as they have specialist bookshops and employees who know what things are worth. Use a search engine to locate a shop in your area or use the information at the end of this Part of the book.

You should only be concerned if keeping your loved one's effects is stopping you from coming to terms with your loss and assimilating your dead partner into the life you live now (see Part Five, 'Grieving and Mourning', for a more detailed description of what that means).

48
Conclusion

In this Part we have looked at the things you need to do in the immediate aftermath of your partner's death, such as registering it, obtaining probate, sorting out your financial situation and disposing of your loved one's personal possessions.

We have described what might happen if the circumstances of your partner's death warrant a referral to the coroner, a post-mortem and then an inquest.

We have asked you to think about your own work situation, if you have children, and how much you can reasonably be expected to do to juggle everything that previously may have been done by two of you. The answer is that there will never be enough hours in the day, but you can and will manage!

In the next Part we describe how you might be feeling under the weight of grief. We want you to be reassured that, no matter how bad you feel, it is very unlikely that you are going mad. It is important that you get a sense of the emotions you might be feeling, their contradictory nature, and the huge sense of confusion that will be with you every waking minute. We also offer some theories, ideas and practical advice to help you cope with them.

Organisations
Age UK, a charity that supports older people, www.ageuk.org.uk. Advice line: 0800 678 1602, open every day from 8 a.m. to 7 p.m.

Citizens Advice, a network of independent charities that give free, confidential information and advice to assist people with a variety of problems, www.citizensadvice.org.uk. Advice line open Monday to Friday 9 a.m. to 5 p.m., 03444 111 444. Specialist debt chat line open Monday to Friday 8 a.m. to 7 p.m. Be aware that the advice will vary depending on which part of the United Kingdom you live in. Either phone or use a search engine to contact your nearest branch.

Cruse Bereavement Care, a national charity that supports all bereaved people, www.cruse.org.uk. National helpline open Monday to Friday, 9.30 a.m. to 5 p.m., 0808 808 1677, or use a search engine to find your local Cruse centre.

Equity Release Council, industry body for the UK equity release sector, representing qualified financial advisors, solicitors and others, www.equityreleasecouncil.com, 0300 012 0239.

Grief Encounter Child Bereavement Charity, a charity that supports bereaved children and young people across the UK, www.griefencounter.org.uk, 0808 802 0111.

Halifax, Specialist Bereavement Team, helpline open 8 a.m. to 8 p.m., seven days a week, 0800 028 1057 or +44 (0) 113 366 0145 from abroad.

HM Inspector of Anatomy, information on organ donation, www.organdonation.nhs.uk, 020 7972 4551.

International Pension Centre, a government office providing advice on all matters to do with the state pension for people living abroad, www.gov.uk, 0191 218 7777.

Jigsaw, offers grief support to children and young people who have experienced the death of a significant family member and for those who have a family member with a life-limiting condition, www.jigsaw4u.org.uk, 020 8687 1384.

Judicial Conduct Investigations Office, an independent office that supports the Lord Chancellor and Lord Chief Justice in considering complaints about the personal conduct of judicial office holders, www.ojc.judiciary.gov.uk/OJC/complaintlink.do, 020 7073 4719.

The Law Society of England and Wales, www.lawsociety.org.uk, 020 7320 5650.

London Probate Department, email enquiries: londonprobate@justice.gov.uk, phone enquiries: 020 7421 8509, probate helpline: 0300 123 1072, court counter open Monday to Friday 10 a.m. to 4.30 p.m.

Ministry of Justice, www.justice.gov.uk, 0203 334 3555.

Missing People, a charity that offers a lifeline for the 180,000 people who run away and go missing each year, together with providing support for their family and friends, www.missingpeople.org.uk. You can call the charity at any time of the day or night on Freefone 116 000.

Oxfam, charity focused on the alleviation of poverty, www.oxfam.org.uk, 0300 200 133.

Spare Room, an organisation that puts those who need to rent a room with those who have one to rent, www.spareroom.co.uk. Phone line open Monday to Friday 9 a.m. to 8.30 p.m., weekends 10 a.m. to 7.30 p.m., 0161 768 1162.

StepChange Debt Charity, provides the UK's most comprehensive debt advice service. It helps people with debt problems take back control of their finances and their lives, www.stepchange.org. Helpline open Monday to Friday 8 a.m. to 8 p.m., Saturday 8 a.m. to 4 p.m., 0800 138 1111.

Books and publications

Oliver, Jamie, *Get Dead*, Friday Books, 2006.

The Scottish Government, 'What to do after a death in Scotland', The Scottish Government Law Reform Division, 2017, https://www.gov.scot/collections/what-to-do-after-a-death-in-scotland/.

Websites

www.bereavementadvice.org: Bereavement Advice Centre, 0800 634 9494, Monday to Friday 9 a.m. to 5 p.m. This is a free helpline and web-based information service provided by Co-op Legal Services.

www.farewill.com: '... blending smart technology with outstanding customer service making everything to do with death easier, faster and fairer for people all over the UK'.

www.gov.uk: the website for the UK and more specifically England and Wales.

www.gov.uk/bereavement-payment: Bereavement Service helpline, 0800 731 0469, Monday to Friday 8 a.m. to 6 p.m. This is a government-funded helpline.

www.nidirect.gov.uk is the website for Northern Ireland and where their Bereavement Services can be accessed, 0800 085 2463, Monday to Friday 9.00 a.m. to 5.00 p.m.

www.gov.scot: the website for Scotland.

Part Five

Grief and Mourning

49
Introduction

The aim of this Part is to help you understand more about your grief and what is happening to you, while you adjust to the new set of circumstances in which you find yourself. The most important thing to say at this point is that grief is an entirely normal and natural reaction to loss. It is the price we pay for caring so much about someone. It is neither a pathological condition nor a personality disorder, no matter how extremely you may be suffering. Sometimes grief becomes 'complicated'. When this happens, you are no longer able to function – that is, get up in the morning, do the things you have to do to keep body and soul together and carry out the responsibilities that you have. It often has its roots in feelings and behaviours that existed, but were perhaps hidden or denied, long before the death occurred. We will talk about this later in more detail. Sometimes, too, owing to the breakdown of your relationship, the grief may not be so much about losing the person, but about the loss of a life that you could have had in different circumstances or a partnership that can never be set right.

For most people, however, the overwhelming feelings of sadness, disjuncture and loss have to be worked through and come to terms with in the ways that we describe below, until the new person that you will be emerges – the person who can 'manage' without the love and support of their partner, perhaps not as well, but sufficiently to give you hope that a relatively happy life is possible. Having said all that, this transition period can be a frightening time for you. You may behave in ways that are quite alien to you; you may not feel in control of yourself and your emotions; you may find it difficult to take decisions and you can feel very alone and isolated. Be assured that in most cases this period will pass and you will arrive in time at a place of tranquillity, even if that is the last thing that you will think will happen.

If you have children, you may feel that you have to be strong for them and that you cannot indulge in your own grief as much as you would want. There are dangers to this that we will discuss later, as delayed grief can cause its own problems and be a cause of complicated grief or the need for grief work later in life.

Grief is the intense sorrow caused by someone's death, although, of course, it can be caused by other tragic losses such as divorce. Mourning is the outward expression of that grief and in some cultures is accompanied by certain rituals intended to help the bereaved person through the period immediately after the death and for some time afterwards, with the help of their friends and family. If you come from cultures where there are mourning rituals, you may find them very supportive.

We start with loss in its broadest terms to familiarise you with the concept and remind you that you have already suffered from this many times, although perhaps not as acutely. We then go on to talk about the loss and grief you are likely to feel even before your loved one has died – pre-bereavement grieving. We next describe your state of mind before, during and after your loss, and identify the emotions you might feel, what the tasks of grief are, and what theories are available that will help you to understand the process. We look at grief arising from specific circumstances and where you can turn to for support.

Lastly, we suggest how to cope with dealing with your loved one's personal possessions, and anniversaries. Most important is the understanding that your loss is not something to 'get over' but a process of keeping memories alive, integrating the person who has died into your being, together with recognising and appreciating the legacy of their personality that they have left you with. At the end of the Part are the sources of the theories, should you wish to read more about them. Some of the books are memoirs by people who have been in the same situation as you are now (see Further Reading). Often these books have been read and found helpful by people we know, in which case we have added a few words from them about why they found the book helpful.

50
Loss

We do not have to lose a person to feel grief at a loss. For example, we have all lost keys and know what it is like to search for them in ever more unlikely places until either they are found or we reconcile ourselves to the fact that they are gone for ever and we set about the tedious task of replacing them. While it's unlikely you will mourn the loss of your keys, we can feel a very strong emotional attachment to things, to the point that when we lose them it is as if a part of our personality goes with them. This feeling is exacerbated if the item was costly or, perhaps more importantly, was tied to our memories of an event or a person. It may have been given to us as a memento and that link is now broken as there is nothing tangible to remind us of the person, or it may have been a physical reminder of an achievement or an anniversary. When these items are stolen, they are often described as being of 'sentimental value'. This is a poor description of their value to us and what they meant to us. This type of loss can be felt very keenly, and the older you get the worse is the loss and grief, as more things are likely to become irreplaceable.

To some extent we are prepared for loss from a very early age. As young infants we feel the loss of our mother or primary caregiver very keenly, even if they are away from us physically for only short periods. It is how we come to terms with this that affects our psychological health in later life (see p. 286 for a longer discussion on attachment). As we grow older, we may lose pets and beloved grandparents. This helps us to adjust to the idea that nothing is permanent but that we can still retain memories of the animal or person we have lost and talk of them fondly. This being able to assimilate the lost loved one into our persona is a very important part of grieving and we will return to it later at some length.

However, although we may have felt the grief that comes with a loss before, the grief that we feel when our loved one dies is of a different order of magnitude and is overwhelming in its nature.

51
Pre-bereavement Grieving

If your partner has had a terminal diagnosis or an accident, attempted suicide or taken an overdose that renders them incapable but not dead, your immediate reaction will be numbed shock. In the latter situation, as the condition might have come out of the blue, your shock will be the greater. In cases where your partner has been suffering for a while and has been undergoing tests, you may now realise that your worst nightmare is coming to pass. Where it has been clear for some time that they are entering the tunnel of dementia or their health is deteriorating visibly, the shock might not be as great, but you will nevertheless feel enormous sadness and distress, as you have been hoping against hope that things weren't as bad as they now obviously are.

When someone is dying your mind leaps ahead to imagine a life without them and as a result of this anguish you may exhibit many of the signs of grieving that are discussed below, the emotions commonly felt after bereavement. This is known as pre-bereavement grieving. You may worry about these feelings as you were not expecting them. Please be aware that this is a normal reaction to what you are going through and do not let concerns about it being odd or strange add to the heavy burden that you are already carrying.

As a person's illness progresses, they often stop being the person you know and take on a quite different persona. It is obviously true in dementia situations, where the individual starts to lose their personality and memories and eventually gets to the stage where they do not know you, so that you are faced with a virtual stranger rather than your partner. It is also true in other debilitating diseases such as Parkinson's or motor neurone disease, where the privations of the illness have their effect on the dignity and confidence of the person concerned. In all these cases, your utmost attention must be focused on looking after yourself sufficiently to enable you to care for them to the best of your ability so that you have nothing to reproach yourself for or feel guilty about afterwards. They may become petty or bad-tempered or complain, but who can blame them? Make sure that you stay as tranquil and open-hearted as you possibly can. You will be so glad that you made that demanding extra effort when they are gone. The aim of this Part of the book is to help you to do this, as well as to understand your feelings and emotions after the death takes place. If you are in a pre-bereavement situation, you may find the following descriptions helpful, as they describe not only what you may be feeling now but also what to expect after the death, so that you are more prepared when it comes.

52
How Bereavement Can Affect You

Being bereaved affects absolutely every part of your life, so much so that sometimes you may think that you are quite literally going mad with grief. Please be assured that this is very unlikely. However, what your mind and body are doing is adjusting almost every thought, feeling and action you have to the new situation. No wonder your mind feels that it is suffering from overload! Instead of coasting along, as most of us do for most of the time, you are constantly having to question and correct yourself from thinking, feeling and doing exactly what you did before. Here are some of the ways that you will be affected:

- Intellectually – you are suffering from a threat to the structure of your world so profound that nothing seems 'safe' any more and the world suddenly feels a very hostile and lonely place.

- Behaviourally – the old ways of doing things can no longer serve you, and you have to create new ones to serve you better in your present circumstances, which is very demanding in terms of energy.

- Spiritually – having this happen to you may challenge your faith, so that a crisis in your beliefs is added to everything else you are suffering, which might cause you great pain.

- Physically – you may find that the enormity of what is happening to you taxes you to the limit physically and you exhibit stress-related illnesses and symptoms as well as frustration.

- Emotionally – you may find that you cannot control your emotions as much as you would want to and that you are prey to being overwhelmed when you least expect it.

- Practically – the old arrangements won't work any more and you have to make new ones in your daily life for yourself and your dependants or those who rely on you.

- Socially – people will see you differently now that you are no longer part of a couple and you may find that some see you as a threat.

At the beginning of Part One we talked about some of the emotions that you might be going through – denial, anger, bargaining, depression and acceptance – and quoted Elisabeth Kübler-Ross as the authority on the theory of the stages of grief that every bereaved person supposedly moves through chronologically. We also said that her work was actually with the dying and that her stages have been adapted to cover the grieving process. Some people find this idea of stages very helpful to their understanding, though rarely do sufferers move through them as a linear model and some people do not suffer all the stages. The concept does not always mirror reality, as this was originally a theory about the emotions of the terminally ill rather than about grieving. We will show in some detail the way in which Kübler-Ross's views have been superseded by rather more sophisticated models of what brings relief to the bereaved.

Somewhat more practical and helpful is a description of the 'tasks of grief', a theory that was suggested by William Worden. They are:

- To accept the reality of the loss.

- To work through the pain of grief.

- To adjust to an environment in which the deceased is missing.

- To emotionally relocate the deceased and move on in life.

Let's examine these tasks in a bit more detail.

Accepting the reality of the loss

At first you might be quite numb with shock, and you may not want to accept the reality of what is happening. You may be in denial. This is a common reaction as your mind seeks to come to terms with the enormity of what is happening to you and the ramifications of all it means start to sink in. A behaviour associated with this denial is 'searching'. Searching is when you are continually looking for the person who has died, see them in other people's faces and gestures, and expect them to walk through the door or be at home when you get there. It is very distressing when they do not and are not. This is somewhat different from feeling that they are there with you and that you can talk to them. There is more acceptance involved here in that you are aware they are not really there, but it is comforting to talk to them as if they were, just as you used to. It is perfectly OK to talk to your partner, only do not try to do so in public places or you may get some strange looks! Gradually, you will get used to the idea that your loved one is not there, especially at times when you feel you need them most, but it does take time.

Working through the pain of grief

Grief is painful. There is no getting away from this or sugar-coating it in any way. You simply have to gradually face up to all that is involved and work through the feelings as they arise. Here are the feelings and experiences you might have, although you are unlikely to feel all of them:

You don't feel anything. This is a common reaction at the beginning and can be a necessary defence against so much pain that it is unbearable. Gradually, however, you will begin to feel and the numbness wears off.

You feel ill. It is hardly surprising that your body cannot cope with everything it is being asked to do. Be aware that your immune system is being put under considerable strain. Depending on the time of year, you might find you are much more susceptible to colds and viruses, and any particular weakness that you already suffer from, especially when stressed – headaches, stomach problems, a bad back – will get worse. Try to protect yourself as much as possible by eating properly, particularly fruit and vegetables. Soups are a particularly useful way of getting a good source of nourishment and are easy to throw together. If you cannot face cooking, it can be one of the things that you ask your friends to do for you (see p. 260). Take supplements if you think they can help. You may find that you have no appetite at all and are losing weight. If this is the case, you should seriously think about consulting your GP, as there might be another cause for this.

You feel guilty and/or remorseful. It is extremely sad if you feel this, but it is quite common. You may feel that you have not said what you wanted to say before your partner died and now no longer can. You may feel that you said too much or too little about how you felt about your partner or that on occasion you said things that should have been left unsaid. You may feel that you did not go the extra mile for them or that – and it is really difficult to admit to this – you actually began to dislike them before they died, even though you still loved them and would have done anything for them. None of this is surprising, as you were under enormous strain, caring for them and keeping your home and family going. A human being can only do so much. If this is how you feel, one way of assuaging your feelings might be to write your loved one a letter explaining your conflicting emotions, which you can either keep safely or destroy. You will find this very cathartic and helpful. Alternatively, you may need to talk to someone about it; doing so will help you come to terms with the feelings. In that case you may need bereavement counselling or psychotherapy (see Part Six for a fuller explanation of these topics).

You feel angry. You may feel angry with a lot of people – your partner for leaving you, the ambulance service that you thought were too late arriving, the medical staff who were so incompetent. The list is endless. You may feel particular anger towards your partner because they did something stupid that killed them. The husband of a lady I know fell off the roof trying to fix a slate. She was furious with him in a very honest and open way. I am sure that helped her come to terms with his death. She didn't try to pretend she didn't feel angry, which would have caused the resentment to grow and embitter her. This casual dicing with death on the part of people with responsibilities can be devastating for those left behind. As explained in Part Six, you can unwittingly aim to punish your missing loved one by neglecting yourself or behaving in odd ways: 'See what you've made me do, how you've made me behave.' Only when this behaviour is seen for what it is and responsibility taken for it can the healing start to take place.

The other side of the coin to feeling angry is **idolising the dead**. Your dead partner did no wrong in their life and was angelic in every way. This is plainly ridiculous to other people, but for you what they did and said and wanted becomes sacred and non-negotiable. This will be a problem for your children, family and friends especially, as they will not want to upset you by presenting a contrary view, but they may also feel that upholding such an idea may not be working in your best current interests and they may want to point this out. You might feel that you should do things in a certain way because that's what your loved one liked or the way they wanted it done. Perhaps you feel that by doing so you are paying homage to them, keeping the memory of them alive and maintaining things as much as they were as far as you can. This is comforting, if rather Canute-like, and we do not want to take it away from you, but it can only be temporary. Life changes, you change, the things of the past do not necessarily serve you well now, and you have to think to the future and what is best for you going forward.

You feel afraid. If you have always had the supporting arm of your partner to rely on, whether man or woman, being on your own can make you feel very fearful. One woman who I am aware of has not slept on her own for two years since her husband died. She simply can't bear to be on her own. Imagine the strain this puts on the rest of the family, who have had to devise a rota of sleeping at their mother's/sister's regardless of what plans they have.

The loss may make you feel that you want to check all the locks several times over each night and indeed have new locks fitted that are more secure than the ones you felt were adequate before your partner died. Or perhaps a dog would make you feel safer? This is a big decision and should not be taken without a lot of thought, although we do know of people who have acquired dogs both before and after a death as a way of helping to assuage grief. What you must face up to is that your security has gone and you can either go through the rest of life thinking that you are a victim and that every bad hat in the area knows how vulnerable you are, or that this is part of what you have to go through to be an independent person. If you are a woman, console yourself with the thought that, according to Statista, more than 4 million of us lived alone in the UK in 2017, with far more women than men living alone over the age of sixty-five. As women live longer than men and average life expectancy increases, this number is likely to grow.

You feel like crying all the time or you can't cry. Crying is nature's way of dealing with emotion and gradually it will lessen, but it can be very debilitating as you can never be certain what will set you off. Going to a friend's mother's funeral several months after my husband died had this effect on me. It was very embarrassing. There was a man there whose mother had also died recently, and the funeral had the same effect on him. We were able to commiserate with each other and it didn't seem quite so bad. That was a rather obvious example of a cause, but sometimes it can be the oddest things that set you off. There is no answer to this but a good supply of tissues and perhaps spare make-up, especially if you are a woman, to repair the ravages of tears as much as you can. Most people will understand and sympathise. Conversely, not being able to cry might make you feel abnormal, as you feel that you look uncaring and you worry that indeed you are uncaring. *Why can't I cry?* Here again, nature is trying to protect you from pain that is almost unbearable. The tears will come when they are good and ready, and probably at the most inconvenient time!

You feel exhausted. This is hardly surprising, is it? You are coping with so much that is new and strange, and each day presents itself with fresh pain and new challenges to be overcome. If you are not sleeping, you may feel you want to resort to your doctor for some help in this area. Or you can develop a routine that is helpful. I found myself having a bath every night, much to the annoyance, I imagine, of my neighbours, who had to cope with my bathroom fan sounding off about midnight each night, although they were nice enough not to say anything at the time, and I only realised afterwards how much I owed to their forbearance. A hot milky drink or hot chocolate; having a television where you can watch it from bed; listening to music or a story on the radio; above all keeping snug and warm, can all help to lull you into sleep. As mentioned earlier, I opened the condolence cards I received in bed each night. It made me feel as though we were doing this 'together' and gave me some comfort.

You feel thoroughly bad-tempered. You are stressed; there is only so much patience and forbearance that you can muster from your depleted energy, and the people around you, especially probably your children or siblings, insist on trying to thwart you and generally making life difficult for you. Is this how you feel? Be aware that what you are going through limits your resources to cope and you are not as resilient as you were. You are bound to feel crotchety, out of sorts and worse. Try to nurture what energy you have by reserving time for yourself in which you indulge in whatever gives you some pleasure, although beware of binge eating, overdoing the sweet stuff, or turning to alcohol, drugs or sex for relief. These may make you feel better in the short term, but it will only be temporary and you will in turn be disgusted with yourself for your lack of willpower. Thus begins a downward spiral that you want to avoid at all costs.

You feel you are going mad. If madness means you are temporarily out of control, then you probably are, but it doesn't. Psychologically you are at a low ebb. But this does not mean that you are going mad. It is a normal reaction to what you are coping with and in most cases it will pass. The confusion and uncertainty can be overwhelming. Even the most down-to-earth people will feel the ground sway beneath them. If you are seriously concerned about psychological impairment, you should consult your GP. Doctors can provide reassurance and methods of coping. It may mean you need some sort of medication for a short while. Being bereaved can be like being in a pit in the centre of a forest. Before you get out of the forest you have to get out of the pit. Drugs can help you get out of the pit and enable you to find your way through the forest. Even sleeping pills, which give you a good night's sleep, can be helpful. Endless nights of not sleeping, when you can't relax physically and your mind is going round like a whirlpool, sinking lower and lower, are detrimental to your health. And need to be stopped. Make sure you consult your GP before taking any medication. MIND is also a useful organisation to be aware of. They have a helpline providing advice and support for anyone experiencing a mental health problem.

You feel jealous of other people. This feeling may take you by surprise. You are not generally a jealous or envious person, but suddenly you are overwhelmed when you see couples together with their children enjoying the simple pleasures of the park, the cinema or even McDonald's. You want to go up to them to tell them how lucky they are to have one another and to urge them to make the most of every day they have together. Of course, the practical side of your mind tells you that nothing is what it seems and that being in a partnership is not really a bowl of cherries, but you will still be concentrating on the best of what you have lost and want it back. Even as you get a more pragmatic perspective on your partner, warts and all, you will miss being together and envy those who still have their partner.

This might also make its presence felt with your friends. Depending on your age and circumstances, some of the people you thought were your friends are now no longer interested in you and you never hear from them. There could be several reasons for this. Many people genuinely do not know what to say to you and are so embarrassed by their inadequacy that they literally shun you. For others it was your partner who was their friend and they are not really interested in you, hard as this may seem. Some will see you as a threat perhaps to their already shaky relationships. You will find that some of your friends cannot bear to be with you. One friend admitted to me years later with an apology that he could not cope with my pain as well as his own, which knowing him as I did, I understood completely, although at the time I found his disappearance difficult to comprehend.

You may feel worse after a few weeks or months than you did at the beginning. The pain of grief accumulates. First of all, you feel numb so that you are protected from the pain and you have all the arrangements for the funeral to see to, which is distracting. However, once that is over, friends and relatives who have been helping you have to return to their own lives and they expect you to be starting to cope, little realising that the full sense of what loss means is only just beginning to dawn on you and you are at your most exhausted. People are often prepared to help in the short term, but if you begin to look as if you are needy, they tend to shy away. On p. 260 there is a section on asking people for help and being clear about what you want. The counterpart to that is beginning to be self-sufficient and learning as you go along, so that you do not have to keep asking people for the same thing over and over again.

You feel alone. Sadly, you are alone. Everyone feels lonely sometimes, even in a successful partnership, but actually being on your own is of a different order of magnitude. There is now no one you have the right and expectation to turn to when you need some support, even your children; not that it was always necessarily forthcoming when your partner was alive. Grieving is a lonely business, even if you have supportive relatives and friends. You have to learn to rely on yourself more than you ever have done before.

In summary, confusion is probably the strongest feeling that you may have. You have so many conflicting emotions – anger, guilt, longing, jealousy. You will want to feel better but worry that by doing so you appear uncaring. You fear that you will forget the voice and features of your loved one. You see them everywhere, but it turns out not to be them at all but some stranger who from a distance looked similar. Everything is a reminder of their presence, so that your home, which was such a safe place for you, is now a place of horrors with a memory waiting to ambush you in every part of it. Your favourite places are now taboo, as the thought of being there without your loved one is unbearable.

Everything you did together, which you now might try to do on your own, makes you feel their loss all the more. If your partner has committed suicide, been murdered, taken an overdose or been killed in another violent or traumatic way, anguish over their death is multiplied as you wonder how much they suffered before they died, and are overwhelmed with the pain of knowing that you were not there when they needed you. If you were at their side when they died and were able to hold their hand, how much comfort this must give you, knowing that they were not alone. How great the feeling of distress if you have not been able to do that.

Are there any theories that can help me understand?

This brings us to the third of the tasks of grief. There are some theories discussed here. Please do not let that put you off; don't assume that you are a practical person and that theories are not for you. A good theory should be practical and be of help in determining action, whether thinking or behaving. This is what these theories do. They give an explanation of what is happening to you and why, and try to explain what that means to you and how it can support you.

Adjusting to an environment in which your partner is missing

According to Stroebe and Schut in their dual process model, most bereaved people cope by oscillating between a) confronting grief, which is a loss-oriented behaviour, and includes such things as thinking about your partner, pining, holding on to memories and expressing feelings; and b) seeking distraction in order to manage everyday life, which is known as restoration-oriented behaviour, such as suppressing memories and taking 'time off' from grief by keeping busy, behaving as normally as possible and regulating emotions. You can think you are coping quite well and then suddenly you are overwhelmed in a way you were not expecting and that takes you by surprise. This is perfectly normal and is evidence that you are oscillating between the two states.

Loss-oriented behaviour involves grief work such as counselling and psychotherapy, where you get the opportunity to talk about your feelings and about your partner to someone who is dedicated to listening to you, no matter how many times you repeat yourself. It involves allowing yourself to feel sad, to cry and not feel the need to apologise for it. Sometimes it means that you are in denial about the fact that you are feeling better. The first time you laugh or feel happy even for an instant may feel like a gross betrayal of your love for your partner and sends you plummeting down into the depths again. This behaviour is sometimes referred to as 'feminine' and it is probable that most women feel like this.

Restoration-oriented behaviour involves getting on with the things you have to do to support yourself and your children. It means doing new things, perhaps filling each evening with plans like going to a quiz night, having your brother over for dinner or going away on your own for the first time – generally being distracted from the grieving process. You may find your house has never been cleaner because you have thrown yourself into cleaning it with a fervour that you never showed before, or you have sorted out your paperwork from what was akin to an archaeological dig, all this helping to take your mind off the distress you are feeling. You may find that you have new roles to fulfil, a new identity (see p. 284) and even, after some time, new relationships. This type of behaviour is sometimes referred to as 'masculine', and it is likely that more men behave like this.

References to the feminine and masculine are important. Stroebe and Schut suggest that other grief-work theories undervalue the male experience of grief and are based on the female experience, which is more expressive and willing to confront difficult emotion.

Some people are able to enter into new relationships very soon after their partner dies, while others will feel that they can never replace the person they lost. It is a matter of individual choice. One man I know of was distressed that his recently deceased wife's relatives had shunned him because he had taken a new partner. However, his wife had been ill when he first met her, so all their married life he had taken care of her and nursed her at home until her death. If anyone needed to be cut a bit of slack in the matter of relationships, it was him.

There is more about how you can adjust to an environment in which your partner isn't there in Part Six.

Emotionally relocating my partner and moving on in life

What practical help can we give you to enable you to gradually do this? Luckily, there are several theories and ideas that are helpful in this respect.

Elisabeth Kübler-Ross's model of grief seems to indicate that people pass through the stages, work through their emotion, move on and live without the person who dies. However, it is not really like that. It can benefit bereaved people more to integrate the memory of the dead person into their lives. This continuing relationship with the dead person involves bereaved people in a process of adaptation and change during which, over time, they may reconstruct their own identity and view of the world. It is important and valuable to bereaved people to talk and think about the person who has died, rather than expecting them to 'get over it'. When you are first bereaved, your grief consumes you totally, filling every part of your life, waking and sleeping. As the days, weeks and months go by, you might expect the grief to shrink and become more manageable, although you would not expect it to go away altogether. This does happen for some people. However, for others, the grief remains the same size as in the beginning. It is your life that grows round it. There will be times such as anniversaries and Christmas when your grief feels just as intense as it ever did, but increasingly you are able to experience life without the grief. What is helpful about this idea is that it relieves you of the expectation that your grief will largely go away. It explains the dark days (rather like the Stroebe and Schut dual process model mentioned above) and also describes the richness and depth that the experience of grief has given you. You will grow a new life, but there is no need to feel a sense of disloyalty to your partner, as you will be integrating the loss into your life and moving forwards. This model was developed by a lady called Lois Tonkin in New Zealand and you can read more about it, if you find it helpful, in her article, 'Growing Around Grief'.

Many recent ideas about grief have concentrated on the concept that the work of grief is not about closure and the severing of ties with your loved one, but the integrating of their memory into your continuing life. Tony Walter's view is that the purpose of grief is the construction of a durable biography that enables you to integrate the memory of the dead person into your ongoing life. How you do this is by talking to others, particularly those who knew your partner. You can do this with your children, other members of your family and with friends. You can keep photographs by your bedside, visit the grave or place where you scattered the ashes on certain special days, or have parties to celebrate their birthday. You may want to keep up certain traditions that you had with your partner and children, especially at Christmas. A friend has kept a complete set of the Marx brothers films that her husband loved, and she watches them with her children. This is a good way of bringing 'Dad' and his particular personality back to life.

Similarly, Klass, Silverman and Nickman believe that your relationship with your dead partner will continue and evolve over time. You may remember us talking earlier about idolising your partner in the first few days and weeks of your loss. That idolisation gradually fades away and you are able to see your partner in the round. These integrated relationships are called 'continuing bonds'. You renegotiate what the loss means to you over time. You will be changed by the process and, unbelievably, you may be able to see that some good did come out of it. 'Accommodation' is probably a more appropriate term to describe what is happening. It is a continual activity. The past is incorporated into the whole. We are the person we are now because they were the person they were. This is to a large extent their legacy to us, but now we will grow and develop in other ways.

Robert Niemeyer regards grief not as a symptom to be overcome but as a process of reconstructing meaning. The loss of your relationship has fractured your sense of identity, your understanding of the world as well as your place in it. Hence the distressing symptoms that we suffer mentioned earlier. This has to be reflected upon. In grieving we try to relearn the world and our place in it. We also try to communicate to others the effect this loss has had not only on our thinking and emotions but also on our perceptions of ourselves, our place and our belief systems. The woman mentioned earlier who cannot sleep on her own has been unable to adapt to the new situation. The aim is to reconstruct our identity, discover new purpose or meaning in our lives, and reorder our sense of the world, perhaps with greater strength and realism than before. Such reflections usually take the form of an internal narrative, a retelling of events, perceptions, responsibilities or roles. It is important that you tell this story in a safe environment, where you can rehearse to yourself what you are manifesting. Do not be afraid to repeat things. You are trying to understand your new place in the world and to reconstruct your own meaning of your life after your loss.

Your partner will have left a legacy that has nothing to do with the money in their estate. It is a legacy of their being. You are not the same, because you were part of their life and they were part of yours. Some parts of this legacy are clearer than others. I know widows who see their lost partner as a teacher who enabled them to grow. For whatever reason, that form of development with that person physically present is now over, but they continue to influence the thinking and behaviour of the one left behind. Similarly, there are others who feel that the deceased partner taught them all they could and that they have now handed the baton on, so to speak – perhaps to the person left behind, perhaps to others.

Some people find the loss of love in their life – loving and being loved – so overwhelming that they cannot cope without it, and turn quite quickly to someone else to fill that gap in their lives. Often it is someone they already know in their social circle, who is helping them through the process, or someone in a group that they belong to, who they now see in a different light. Sometimes this happens very quickly and the person concerned finds themselves being criticised for their behaviour, even though they might have lost the support of their partner long before they died. It is important to work through the tasks of grief, but everyone does this in their own way and at the speed that is right for them.

Overall, it is important to realise that every bereavement and every person's grieving is unique; your loss and your grief are unique. Only *you* are experiencing it in this particular way. Similarly, you are the only person who can resolve your issues and work through the tasks of grief. No one else can do it for you. You are not grieving for your partner alone. Other people are involved and you can mutually help each other. There is no known standard emotional sequence in grieving. It is unlikely that you will work through a series of stages, be able to detach yourself from the bereaved, or that you will achieve closure and an end to grieving. It is more likely that you will assimilate the loss of your loved one into your life as a whole, recognise their legacy for what it is, and commence a new life around which you reconstruct meaning, maybe even with a different persona and a new partner. You can certainly be happy again, even though there will still be times of sadness and feelings of loss.

53
Supporting Others Through Their Grief

The people who are likely to be grieving most besides yourself, following the loss of your partner, will be your children, stepchildren and adopted children, if you have any. If the death does not follow a terminal illness, the shock will be just as sudden for them as it was for you. How you talk to your children depends to some extent on their ages. If they are very small, you may not be able to explain it to them, even though they may be clearly registering that someone is missing. The KidsHealth website, which we quoted from earlier, suggests doing the following when speaking to children about the death of a loved one:

- When talking about death, use simple clear words.

- Listen and comfort.

- Put emotions into words.

- Tell your child what to expect.

- Talk about funerals and rituals.

- Give your child a role.

- Help your child to remember the person.

- Respond to emotions with comfort and reassurance.

When planning the funeral, you can involve them by asking them what part they want to play and how you might achieve this. Talk often about their father or mother, what they would have said had they been there, how they would have reacted to things, how proud they would have been of what they have achieved.

You might find a memory box helpful. This is where the child or children put together items that remind them of their parent. At times of distress this can be brought out and looked at, thereby supplying comfort. Keep their routine the same as far as this is possible, asking friends and family to help you. Children have a horror of being different from their peers, and anything that singles them out in most cases is deeply distressing. Simply being the son or daughter of someone who has died is sufficiently different to give them anguish, without the added burden of keeping them from things or insisting they do things differently. If you think your children might need professional help, try Jigsaw, Winston's Wish or, in Norfolk, Nelson's Journey.

The next group who will be grieving most will be your partner's family. They may have lost a child, a sibling or a niece, nephew or even a grandchild. If you are in a big family, having to cope with the grief of all these other people can be overwhelming. This is especially true if there are previous husbands, wives or partners and their children. Be as big and open-hearted about this as you can possibly be, given your depleted resources. Involve them in your plans as much as you can; give them roles and specific jobs to do. You may have to swallow hard on occasion and bite your lip, but they have lost a treasured person too.

Hopefully, the group you can really rely on are your own family and your friends. They will give you the support you need, when you need it, although they too will have lost someone they cared for.

54

What is Complicated Grief?

People always worry about what is 'normal' when they are grieving, but almost everything is normal because we are all unique and we grieve in our own particular way. As we have tried to show you, denial, confusion, preoccupation, absent-mindedness and even sensing the presence of your partner are all what we might consider quite normal. However, on some occasions, some people do suffer from a condition rather more serious called 'complicated grief'. We would like to reassure you, however, that most of the time such cases stem from a situation that existed before the death and may have been hidden or denied. In other words, it has been exacerbated by death but does not originate from it.

What might be the symptoms of complicated grief? If your grief lasts for a very long time, you may need professional help (please see Part Six for what that professional help might involve). If you have delayed grief reactions, such as following a death other than, and prior to, your partner's, it may mean that you did not process your original grief and that this might be adding to the grief you feel for the loss of your partner, or if you are bereaved again soon after losing your partner. If you are suffering from any of the following: severe loss of interest in anything and anyone, loss of appetite or sleep, pangs of severe emotional distress, excessive feelings of emptiness and aloneness, and excessive avoidance or preoccupation, you may indeed be suffering from complicated grief. Of course, it is difficult to make an objective judgement when you are the sufferer, but generally speaking, if you are unable to function in any way, are totally depressed and can hardly rise from your bed, you should seek help.

55

Bereavement by Murder, Manslaughter, Suicide, Drug Overdose or Accident

You have a very particular bereavement challenge if the death of your loved one has been caused by murder, manslaughter, suicide, drug overdose or accident. Together with the loss suffered by all bereaved people, you have the added anguish of not knowing how much your partner suffered and coming to terms with the fact that – except perhaps in the case of an accident – you were unable to be with them in their final moments. It is the not knowing and the uncertainty that can eat into your soul. In the case of suicide and drug overdose, there is also the consuming guilt and fear that you could have prevented it, that you were not aware of how they felt and that you have let them down.

In these situations there will almost certainly be a post-mortem, and the thought of this may be very upsetting for you, especially if you are the person who identifies the body. You will find that the police and hospital staff are sympathetic and helpful, and the post-mortem will normally be carried out after the viewing.

In most cases there will also be a police presence, particularly so if it is a case of murder or manslaughter. Sadly, you yourself might find yourself under suspicion. One per cent of male victims over sixteen were killed by their partner or ex-partner in 2018, according to the Office for National Statistics, whereas 33 per cent of women were killed by their partner or ex-partner. This was the fewest number of women aged sixteen or over killed by a partner or ex-partner in the last forty years. Most males are killed by a stranger. Most women are killed by someone they know. Where there has been a murder or manslaughter, you are likely to be allocated a police Family Liaison Officer, who will support you through the process.

Then there will have to be an inquest, and in the case of murder or manslaughter, where a perpetrator has been apprehended, a trial. We have dealt in some detail with what to expect if there is an inquest in Part Four. Although an inquest is usually opened and adjourned within a short time of the death, the inquest proper to find the cause of death is usually delayed for several months while all the information is collected. The court case will take even longer, and sometimes the inquest is delayed until after this.

All the officials involved in these have a job to do and, like all of us, some are good at being aware of the sufferings of others and some are not. You are always advised to take a friend to any meeting you have, to give you moral support and enable you to talk over the situation afterwards.

You also have other issues to contend with. It is likely that what happened to your partner will attract the attention of the local and national press and you will have reporters and journalists to contend with, together with a lot of possibly unpleasant publicity. We have spelt this out in more detail in Part Three, 'Dealing with the Press' on p. 169.

There are specialist agencies that can help you through this difficult period. Support after Murder and Manslaughter (SAMM) is a national UK charity supporting families bereaved by murder and manslaughter. You can ask a friend or family member to make the call – you do not have to refer yourself, unlike, for example, at Cruse Bereavement Care. All the trained volunteers at SAMM have been bereaved in this way themselves, and so can understand your pain and what you are going through.

For those bereaved by suicide, there is Survivors of Bereavement by Suicide (SOBS). If the parents and/or grandparents of your murdered spouse are alive, they might be interested in The Compassionate Friends, which is a charitable organisation of bereaved parents, siblings and grandparents. It is dedicated to the support and care of bereaved family members who have suffered the death of a child of any age and of any cause.

Scotland has Victim Support Scotland, and PETAL, which supports people experiencing trauma and loss. BEAD is a project jointly set up by Cruse Bereavement Care and Adfam (the national charity that works to improve life for families affected by drugs or alcohol). And last, but not least, there are The Samaritans, who exist to give confidential emotional support for people experiencing distress, despair and suicidal thoughts. If you have any thoughts of suicide yourself, you should immediately contact your GP for an urgent appointment. Do not be fobbed off by the receptionist but explain your need. They will have been trained to respond. You may be thinking that suicide would be an easy way to end the pain; you might even have reached the point of thinking how you might do it and be making plans. Either way, you need help quickly, and your GP can give you that.

56
Transgender Issues

If you are reading this book, it is possible that you may have changed gender from a man to a woman or a woman to a man, and it may be that it is your wife or husband who has died. You may have managed to keep together as a family and stayed on friendly terms. In this case you will have the same grieving reactions as anyone losing their partner. Alternatively, you may have divorced or parted in a very acrimonious way. Your previous partner may have been angry with you, confused by your behaviour and feel that you have damaged both them and your children. However, you may on some level have retained enough affection for your husband or wife to perhaps have wanted to see them in their final illness and to have effected some sort of reconciliation. Or perhaps you agonised over whether to visit them, or were prevented from doing so by your children. You are not involved in the funeral arrangements and now you are wondering if you ought to go to the funeral. We know of at least one situation where this was the case.

There is no easy answer to this. You have to ask yourself what attending a funeral is really for and then what the person who has died, as well as your children, would want you to do. Only you will know the answer to these questions.

This does not mean that you may not be suffering from grief. The death of your partner or ex-partner may remind you of a lot of distressing situations that you both had to face and bring up many memories from the past.

You may find the charity GIRES (Gender Identity Research and Education Society) helpful if you do not know of it already, or Sparkle, the national transgender charity.

57
Seeking Solace

You should make the most of whatever gives you comfort, even some things that might be bad for you over the long term but that, if they help get you over the immediate aftermath in one piece, may be useful crutches. But that is all they are – crutches. You cannot rely on unhealthy food, alcohol, sex and drugs for ever.

You may find that your religious faith is a great support to you. You may feel that you will reunite with your loved one after your death or have a belief in reincarnation and the development of souls, which may lead you to some karmic understanding of what has happened. However, if your loss was particularly cruel, you may wonder about a benign deity and it might make you lose your faith altogether. If this is the case, talk to your religious leader and, if you can, put your doubts to them. They will have heard it all before and may be able to help you through this dark patch.

You may feel you want to turn to a quite different form of spirituality. Perhaps you might want to learn to meditate. This has a very calming effect and will be good for you anyway. Perhaps you would like to explore other forms of belief such as shamanism, or non-duality. You might want to go to a spiritualist church to see if you can make contact with your loved one, or to attend a public meeting to hear a psychic medium. You might find that there is a lot of hostility to this idea from your family and friends, who do not want to see your hopes raised and then dashed. They have a point. Do be aware that only a few people can be contacted at any one session and that you must steel yourself to be disappointed. However, if you feel that this is what you want to do, don't be put off by other people's opinions. This is the beginning of the new you – the person who wants to do things for themselves and is prepared to confront people who do not agree.

Rituals

It may be that you have a faith in which the rituals of grieving and mourning are very clear, such as Judaism, where you are not allowed to make meals for yourself and your family, but your relatives, friends and neighbours sort out between themselves who will bring in food not only for you but for those people who come to pay their respects either to the deceased or to you. Christian mourning has very little in the way of ritual apart from the Irish concept of a wake.

Such rituals can be very helpful in that it is clear to everyone what your condition is and they will treat you accordingly. On the other hand, they can be quite constricting.

58
What Can Your Family and Friends Do?

The problem for your friends and family after you lose your partner is that they do not really know what to say or do. They do not want to add to your grief by, as they see it, bringing up painful subjects, so they often do not say anything at all. It may seem to you that they are blotting out the person who has died as if they hadn't existed. But they are doing it from the best of intentions. It is a matter of crossed communication or miscommunication.

It is up to you to give them a steer. If you talk about your partner, so will your friends and family. If you talk about how you are managing, they will follow suit. 'Managing' is a very good word to use in this context, as it allows for all sorts of interpretations, covering your physical health, emotional health and so on. If you can laugh occasionally, they will feel cheered; if you make plans, they will know that your life is carrying on.

There will be times when you don't want to talk about anything and your only recourse is to weep. Crying often upsets people as it makes them feel inadequate, but you are not in a position to worry about upsetting other people unless it is those equally affected, such as your children. You could warn people that you are likely to burst into tears without any explanation, so that they do not find it such a shock, but other than that they should allow you to grieve in your own way.

Of course, you will get lots of well-meaning advice, but unless people have gone through something similar, they will have no idea what it is like and, even then, everyone's grief is different. Follow your own intuition and what you think is right.

There will probably be times when you are needy and you will have to reconcile yourself to this. Being needy means that you ask too much of people, take their help for granted and keep asking them to do things for you that you should really be learning to do for yourself. Learning to be self-sufficient is difficult and made more so by your depleted resources and state of mind, but you should start to make the effort. You do not want to alienate your friends. You may feel that the easiest thing to do is to fall into another relationship; to just fill the gap with someone else. If you had been with your partner for a very long time and have never lived on your own, this might appear to be the best solution to you. It can work, but it is not really a very good basis on which to form another relationship, and it can also mean that you postpone the grieving process under the guise of the enjoyment of someone else.

Practically speaking, all your friends will want to help you, but may not know how. Be specific about what you want doing. At the beginning you may need someone to accompany you to meetings with your funeral director or to register the death. Providing meals is an easy way they can help, as well as shopping, housework such as washing and ironing, walking the dog. There is nothing worse than seeing your home descend into a slum, when there is someone who can do a bit of housework for you. You may have regular hospital appointments or visits to the doctor for which you need transport. Given some advance warning, this is an easy thing for a friend to commit to. I invited myself to friends' houses for dinner, but usually excused myself not long after eating as I found I could not cope with too many people around in the early stages. Most people will forgive you what they might in ordinary circumstances think is rudeness, just because they realise what you are going through. It is a question of knowing what you want and asking for it without taking advantage of people's kind-heartedness and generosity.

59
Anniversaries

We celebrate anniversaries all the time – birthdays, weddings, when we first met a loved one, our first date, our first kiss, and so on. They are part of our history together. It is hardly surprising then that anniversaries take on a completely new meaning when the date is not being celebrated but avoided and feared. Their birthday, the day they died, the day you got the news that their illness was terminal – all these dates remind us inexorably of what we have gone through and that we are still suffering. To others it is a day like any other, but to you it is a day when you would rather just huddle under the duvet and cry, because it is such a potent reminder. The first anniversary of everything is particularly hard.

Probably the best thing is to realise from the beginning that it is going to be difficult, and to decide how you are going to tackle it. This might include ignoring it. Or it might involve quiet reflection at the graveside or where the ashes have been buried or scattered, or somewhere you consider to be holy. It is completely up to you. You might think about how you have progressed since your partner died – what you can do now that you never thought you would be able to do. Or you might decide to go completely the other way and hold a party in which people talk about their year since the death and how they feel about it. You could in fact be enabling other members of your family to reconstruct their own meaning from the death and to talk openly about it. What was the legacy that your loved one left behind? Who did he or she inspire? On the strength of my husband's death, a friend decided to divorce her husband. It had made her realise that life was passing by and she was wasting it. I am not advocating this! I am simply making the point that your loved one's death will have affected many people, sometimes in ways that you have no idea about. This might be a way of celebrating those influences.

60
Conclusion

In this Part we have tried to do as much as we can to explain how grief can affect you, and particularly that, although you may sometimes feel that you are going mad, this is a normal reaction to the seismic events you are having to cope with. Loss is something that we have had to assimilate from an early age, even though we might not be aware that it is happening to us.

We start grieving as soon as changes take place in our partner and you might find yourself suffering from pre-bereavement grieving long before they die. There are a surprising number of emotions that we find ourselves prey to and very possibly some of them might take you by surprise, especially if you are not normally a person who feels angry or guilty or jealous. It used to be thought that we passed through certain stages of grief, and some people do find this concept helpful, but more in keeping with most people's experience is the idea of the tasks of grief, through which we learn to live in a world without our loved one and they become part of the person that we are.

In some circumstances, where there were issues prior to death, you might be suffering from complicated grief. This is where you simply cannot function on a day-to-day level rather than you oscillating between feeling grief-stricken and being able to disassociate yourself from your grief sufficiently for you to be able to carry out your daily tasks. Only you will know what help you need and there are several specialist organisations that can help you, including for drug-related deaths, suicide, murder and manslaughter. It is likely that besides your own grief you have to support others, particularly your children, through their grief, which can add an extra strain on your ability to function. Your family and friends long to support you, but often don't know how, so it is up to you to be clear about what help you want and to ask for it.

The pain does not go away, but you build your new life round it – a life that no longer contains your partner. You begin to see new opportunities for yourself – new ways of being. The next Part is all about this – rebuilding your life and creating the new you.

Organisations

Adfam, a national charity working to improve life for families affected by drugs or alcohol, www.adfam.org.uk, 020 3817 9410 (not a helpline).

Bereaved through Alcohol or Drugs (BEAD), a partnership set up by Cruse Bereavement Care and Adfam, www.beadproject.org.uk. Can also be accessed through Cruse Bereavement Care below.

The Compassionate Friends, offering support after the death of a child, helpline@tcf.org.uk, 0345 123 2304, Northern Ireland helpline: 0288 7788 016.

Cruse Bereavement Care, www.cruse.org.uk. National Helpline: 0808 808 1677, Monday and Friday 9.30 a.m. to 5 p.m., Tuesday, Wednesday, Thursday 9.30 a.m. to 8 p.m., weekends 10 a.m. to 2 p.m., Cruse chat, Monday to Friday 9 a.m. to 9 p.m., or use a search engine to find your local Cruse centre.

Cruse Bereavement Care Scotland, www.crusescotland.org.uk. National helpline (check website for opening hours): 0845 600 2227. Webchat also available.

DrugFAM, for those affected by someone else's drug or alcohol abuse, including those bereaved by addiction, www.drugfam.co.uk. Helpline: 0300 888 3853.

Gender Identity and Education Society (GIRES), a charity that aims to improve substantially the environment in which gender nonconforming people live, www.gires.org.uk, 0132 801 554. Contact by email on their site.

Jigsaw, information, advice and guidance to help support bereaved children and young people, and those who have a family member with a life-limiting condition, www.jigsaw4u.org.uk, 020 8687 1384.

Mind, www.mind.org.uk, infoline for mental health problems: 0300 123 3393.

Nelson's Journey, a charity for children in Norfolk up to the age of eighteen who have experienced the death of a parent, www.nelsonsjourney.org.uk. Helpline: 01603 431788.

Oxfam, charity focused on the alleviation of poverty, www.oxfam.org.uk, 0300 200 133.

PETAL, a charity for people experiencing trauma and loss through murder and culpable homicide in the Hamilton and Glasgow areas of Scotland, www.petalsupport.com. Helpline open Monday to Thursday 9 a.m. to 5 p.m., Friday 9 a.m. to 4 p.m., 01698 324 502.

The Samaritans, a charity offering confidential emotional support for people experiencing distress, despair and suicidal thoughts, www.samaritans.org. Helpline open twenty-four hours a day: 08457 909090.

Sparkle, the national transgender charity, www.sparkle.org.uk.

Support after Murder and Manslaughter (SAMM), for families bereaved by murder and manslaughter, www.samm.org.uk, 0121 472 2912 or 0845 872 3440.

Survivors of Bereavement by Suicide UK (SOBS), a charity to meet the needs of, and overcome the isolation experienced by, people over eighteen who have been bereaved by suicide, www.uksobs.org. Helpline open Monday to Friday 9 a.m. to 9 p.m., 0300 111 5065.

Victim Support Scotland, a charity providing emotional and practical bereavement support to children, young people and those who care for them. Helpline open weekdays 8 a.m. to 8 p.m., 0800 166 1985.

Winston's Wish, a charity supporting children and young people after the death of a parent or sibling, www.winstonswish.org. Helpline open Monday to Friday 9 a.m. to 5 p.m., 08088 020021.

Books and publications

Kessler, David, *The Sixth Stage of Grief*, Simon & Schuster, 2019.

Klass, D., Silverman, P., and Nickman, S.L., *Continuing Bonds: A New Understanding of Grief*, Routledge, 1996.

Kübler-Ross, Elisabeth, *On Death and Dying*, Macmillan, 1969.

Neimeyer, Robert A., et al., 'Grief Therapy and the Reconstruction of Meaning: From Principles to Practice', *Journal of Contemporary Psychotherapy*, 10, 2009.

Smith, Gordon, *Why Do Bad Things Happen?* Hay House, 2009.

Stroebe, Margaret, and Schut, Henk, 'The Dual Process Model of Coping with Bereavement: A Decade On', OMEGA – *Journal of Death and Dying*, 61 (4), 2010.

Tonkin, L., 'Growing Around Grief – Another Way of Looking at Grief and Recovery', *Bereavement Care Journal*, 15 (1), 1996.

Walter, Tony, 'A New Model of Grief', *Mortality Journal*, 1 (1), 1996.

Worden, J. William, *Grief Counselling and Grief Therapy: A Handbook for the Mental Health Practitioner*, Springer Publishing Company, 1991.

Websites

www.ons.gov.uk: Office for National Statistics.

www.statista.com: Statista.

Part Six

Rebuilding Your Life – Creating the New Self

61
Introduction

We have considered grief and how you might be experiencing it. Now we begin to look forward. Forward to the new you who will emerge as a result of this loss. The style in this Part is much more upbeat and when you first read it, it might jar or grate against how you are feeling. Persevere. Or if it really is too much to cope with, come back to it another time, but do keep trying!

A bereavement, whether it is a sudden crisis or an expected event, creates changes that can ripple out into every area of life. It's no longer possible to coast through life day to day on the familiar treadmill, staying within familiar territory. The profound changes brought about by the loss of a partner will force you to react, as there will be very specific tasks that need your attention. But beyond these reactive changes, this time of bereavement will give you an opportunity to consider some more proactive changes, so that you can rebuild your life in ways to bring you more satisfaction to come. Change is coming anyway, so you might as well have a hand in shaping it.

As well as thinking about the changes you would like to make in terms of your career or social life, for example, it is worth thinking about any potential barriers to change that may hinder you. These could be inner blocks such as a lack of confidence, or restrictive ideas about your role or identity. There are so many opportunities to learn and to connect with new people, and learning how to set goals, motivate yourself and manage the process of change will be time and effort well spent.

You could spend some time thinking about possibilities for the future. These thoughts begin to feel a little more definite when you write them down, or discuss them with a friend. But they become more definite still when you raise the stakes and make a commitment to a friend to take some action. Dr Gail Matthews, a psychology professor at the Dominican University of California, found that 76 per cent of those who wrote down their goals, rated them, shared them with a friend and sent weekly progress reports to the friend achieved them, or were at least halfway to achieving them after four weeks. Only 43 per cent of the group who merely thought about their goals made as much progress in four weeks. So, writing down your goals and having someone to answer to makes it much more likely that you will achieve something.

In bereavement, initially it may take all of your energy to do the bare minimum, but at some point you will know when it is time to start looking forward. When that time comes, we hope that some of the following information will help you.

62
A Golden Opportunity

How can I use this opportunity to develop the future I want?

The crisis of the loss provides the opportunity to think about the kind of future you would like. In the short term, there are many demands on your time and energy. To add yet another task to the list might seem unmanageable, but time moves on and the future will unfold. This could be the perfect time to shape it the way you'd like it to be.

In a relationship, there are many advantages to having a 'we' identity, rather than a 'me', but there are also disadvantages. Putting the 'we' first can mean sacrificing dreams or ambitions. Sometimes one partner's career will take precedence, and the other partner takes the supporting role, doing the largely unseen and unacknowledged emotional work and the mundane background work that facilitates family life and the advancement of the starring-role partner. Over time, there can be a loss of confidence, or even the death of dreams previously cherished for the future self. The antidote to this is planning, education, the support of friends and perhaps therapy.

SWOT analysis

If you work in business, you'll be familiar with a SWOT analysis. It's a useful way to 'climb up into the watchtower' and survey the landscape so that you can have a look at your territory from an elevated position, and gather the information you need to take the next steps.

All you have to do is get a big piece of paper and draw a cross, dividing the sheet into four boxes. Label the boxes, one each for Strengths, Weaknesses, Opportunities and Threats. Then just begin to jot down whatever comes to mind for each category. Or you can use the template at the back of the book in Appendix 2 to get you started.

One of the benefits of this exercise is that it will help you begin to recognise any catastrophising (viewing the situation as worse than it actually is, as if it were a catastrophe) that might be going on, and get a more realistic view of your current situation. This is something you can pick up and put down, adding ideas when they come, or jotting down points to research later.

Strengths can include aspects of your character, skills you have developed, and people who would be prepared to help you, for example. Weaknesses can include skills that you now need but that might have become rusty or that have not yet been acquired. They could also include your emotional state, and perhaps the needs of your children. They are absolutely normal and appropriate, and only labelled 'Weaknesses' as they are something for you to take into account as an area of life that may need some additional resources.

The Opportunities section is where you can let your imagination run wild and put down all sorts of ideas. They can always be trimmed back later. You could learn new skills, join new groups, stretch yourself in ways you hadn't considered before. Threats could include your own negative characteristics, such as self-sabotage or self-doubt, financial difficulties, or the unavailability of childcare, for example.

Getting this overview down on paper or on your computer can give you an easy way to take stock. You might do one comprehensive SWOT analysis, or several – one for each area of life you want to analyse, such as career, finances, social life or dating. Reviewing the SWOT analysis some weeks or months later can give you a sense of the progress you've made, as well as the ground yet to cover.

Healthy mind, healthy body

The Greeks and Romans knew that we have to think holistically about our well-being. This is as true now as it ever was, but we know today more about why that is. In navigating the aftermath of a loss and beginning to create yourself anew, it's helpful to bear 'both/and' in mind, as opposed to 'either/or'. *Both* – there will be times when you need to let the grief have its way with you, even if this means hours of crying curled up on the sofa; *and* – there will be times when you cannot afford to give in to the grief and will have to push yourself to get things done, robot-like, even though it feels as though you have no mental or physical energy left. There's a time for giving in to the sorrow, and a time for pushing beyond it. This is more natural and more realistic than '*Either* I keep going, *or* I'll cry, and if I start crying I'll never stop.' Please also see the paragraphs on the dual-purpose model on p. 245, which explain how you oscillate between the two.

The loss of a loved one, or of the familiar structure of a relationship, is a crisis, mentally and emotionally sending us out of the window of tolerance into fight, flight or freeze mode. Being plunged out of our emotional comfort zone alters our body chemistry, which results in our feeling off-kilter, whether restless and agitated, or with a sense of 'walking through treacle'. You may cycle through any and all of these unpleasant emotional states through the day, adding a new dimension of distress as you can't predict or account for your own reactions. Having a friend, or a grounded part of your own self, that can stand aside from these fluctuations and guide you through them, will aid your recovery. This is all common sense, not rocket science, but you won't necessarily feel like taking care of yourself. You'll benefit in the longer term from doing what used to be automatic a little bit more on purpose for a while.

As mentioned, do beware of 'either/or' -type thinking. 'Either I'll be completely healthy, or I won't bother at all.' 'Both/and' is better. 'It's understandable that my appetite and energy levels have gone haywire, yet I can make sure I take care of the basics.' If you're used to exercise, aim to follow your usual routine, maybe after a short break, even if less frequently or intensively than before. If you're new to exercise, keep your goals manageable. A brisk ten-minute walk once or twice per day is fine.

Brisk walking, jogging or running can produce chemicals in the body that give a feeling of well-being, or even bliss. Endocannabinoids are produced naturally by the body through aerobic exercise, and their molecular structure is similar to that of cannabis. Needless to say, exercise-induced endocannabinoids do not produce the negative effects of recreational drug use, according to Dietrich and McDaniel.

If you find you are using drugs or alcohol, or compulsively eating – or exhibiting any other compulsive behaviour for that matter – to manage your mood, then you are in the danger zone and need to make some changes, maybe with additional support. It is absolutely understandable to want to numb the pain of loss. But this is not the way; as Cantopher says, it just gives you more trouble down the line. Looking after your body will help you look after your mind, and vice versa.

For a calming, grounding practice, consider yoga. There is a form of yoga for all levels. You can join a class, or simply follow a YouTube tutorial. It is a very good way of reconnecting with your body, and has been shown to be helpful in allowing you to feel your emotions in a safe and self-accepting way. As van der Kolk demonstrates, this in turn allows the emotions to flow and be processed by the mind–body system, rather than becoming blocked.

Appetite is very often affected by the stress of loss or change. Again, you may need to look after yourself a little bit more purposefully than you're used to, and perhaps ask friends to cook for you in the short term, so that you have something in the freezer and can at least take care of one balanced meal per day. Friends often want to help, but don't know how and are afraid of saying the wrong thing and so withdraw. Help them by asking for the kind of help they can cope with, which can mean cooking something. The BBC Radio 4 *Food Programme* looked at Bereavement and Food, and is available on the iPlayer at the time of writing.

63

No Better Time Than Now

The expectations of society have evolved such that we do not feel as restricted as was once the case. Access to information has never been more open, although the accuracy of some of it is questionable. More and more people are creating businesses, either as their main focus or alongside an existing career. As a society we have shifted our collective attitudes towards gender roles, LGBTQ+ rights and children's rights, for example. We are so much freer to love whoever we choose to love.

Alongside this shift, we have enjoyed huge progress in terms of mental health awareness. We now know so much more about the causes of distress, and effective treatments for it. The stigma has largely gone today, thanks in no small part to the brave awareness-raising efforts of celebrities. In the bad old days, you could be carted off to the asylum and locked away indefinitely, put on brain-numbing sedatives, given electric shock therapy or even a lobotomy, if you went 'off the rails'. People were understandably terrified of admitting to any distress. Now we more or less know what to expect from the grieving process, and how to help if it gets stuck.

There is a huge amount of help available for your well-being via the NHS, mental health charities, private therapists, books, TV and radio programmes. There is also a great deal of help available for your financial education and work training via your local council, websites, books, magazines, TV and radio. Please see the resources available at the end of this Part of the book.

The way forward may be dictated by your immediate financial needs, or you may have enough room for manoeuvre to look for what would be satisfying. Either way, you may sometimes feel alone, but there is always someone or something to reach out to for help.

Assessing and working on priorities

In the example below, a woman with two children at primary school has lost her husband in a road traffic accident. She has been working part-time for some years as she has focused on childcare and her husband was the main breadwinner. He had a life insurance policy that has given her a financial cushion for the immediate future, but she will have to make some changes in order to support herself and her children in the longer term. They were a sociable couple and all of their friends were couples who were friends of both of them. Therefore, her bereavement profoundly impacts on all of her social relationships. Her husband's sudden death was a huge shock and has thrown her into a position where the day-to-day demands on her are amplified, at the very time when she is in need of care herself.

Filling in the following template gives her a quick snapshot of the changes she wants to make over the coming months. She can then use this as a basis for more detailed planning. Of course, she can't control everything in this equation, but she can identify the most important areas to focus on and begin to look at the What, When and How questions that will give her some clarity and a sense of control.

Example	What do I have?	What do I need?	Where to find help/ information	How satisfied am I currently? (0–10)
Professional				
Financial				
Health				
Social life				
Family life				

She needs to earn more, and so must decide on training, which will put her in a position to do that, while being able to support her children in their normal development as well as their grieving. In order to decide on her future career direction, she talks to friends, looks at student forums and speaks to recruitment agencies. At this point in her life she isn't prioritising personal fulfilment; she is looking for the convergence between her existing skills and personal strengths, availability of local well-paid work, and employment that will give her enough time to be an attentive parent.

Filling in the template

Example	What do I have?	What do I need?	Where to find help/ information	How satisfied am I currently? (0–10)
Professional	Transferrable skills. Updatable skills. Good personal qualities.	To increase earnings. Refresher course. Interview skills. An updated CV.	www.gov.uk www.reed.co.uk	6
Financial	Current assets and income. Ability to let a spare room?	Work out running costs of home, car, etc. Track spending.	Moneysaving expert.com	5
Health	A strong body. A good level of awareness and common sense.	Improved sleep. More self-belief. Help with the grieving process.	Dr Tim Cantopher's books. www.mind.org.uk Cruse.	7
Social life	Fewer options than when I was part of a couple. Less time, but more freedom to suit myself.	Fun. Companionship. Someone to motivate me. Running buddy. Friend for cinema or theatre.	www.meetup.com Park run.	6
Family life	A good relationship with children and in-laws.	Structure/rota. Childcare. More contact with wider family.	Friends and parents. www.griefencount er.org.uk	7

From here, she borrows a simple tool from business:

The Urgent/Important Matrix

Urgent and important Support the children in their grieving. Decide on career direction and training.	Important, not urgent Look after friendships, develop new ones. Look after mental and physical health. Financial planning.
Urgent, not important PTA commitments. Social diary.	Not urgent, not important (right now) Plan holiday.

From here she uses a year planner to begin a rough schedule that will help her sharpen her focus further regarding the What, When and How questions. All of this planning is subject to reviews and readjustments, with the help of friends, as time goes by and she gains confidence in her ability to step up and take charge. You can use the templates in Appendices 3 and 4 at the back of the book.

In the example below, a man with a stepson about to take his GCSEs and two daughters at primary school has lost his wife fairly suddenly to a brain tumour. He was the main breadwinner and she worked part-time and was the primary parent. He is a high earner, but is regularly expected to work late, including weekends, and travel at short notice. He has had very little input into managing the family diary, dealing with school admin or housework, and enjoyed the role of the fun parent rather than the disciplining parent. He is devastated by his wife's death and his grief is complicated by anger towards medical professionals for 'failing' to diagnose the illness until it was too late.

He has no financial pressures in the short term, but cannot easily stick to his usual work pattern and so may need to re-evaluate his career in the medium term. Filling in the template previously shown gives him a quick snapshot of the changes he wants to make over the coming months. He can then use this as a basis for more detailed planning. He is very aware that his elder daughter is on the cusp of adolescence and is keen to help her develop a closer relationship with a caring female relative.

Template example

Example	What do I have?	What do I need?	Where to find help/ information	How satisfied am I currently? (0–10)
Professional	A good track record, a high level of seniority and recognised competence.	To reduce work hours and achieve a more predictable work schedule.	Negotiate with employers.	6
Financial	Enough to live on for a year without working. An income protection policy.	To hire a childminder for school runs and holidays. To hire a cleaner and/or housekeeper.	www.childcare. co.uk www.mumswork. co.uk	8
Health	Good health, but some new health anxiety.	A detailed health check. Possibly genetic testing to check for heritable risks.	Check health insurance policy. Book a check-up.	8
Social life	A good network of friends. Diary previously managed by wife.	To transfer contacts list from wife's phone. More time, and to create the habit of proactively making arrangements. To think about dating at some point.	n/a	6
Family life	A good relationship with children and in-laws. The possibility of greater co-operation with stepson's father.	Structure/rota. Childcare. More contact with wider family. Someone to help the girls through adolescence, as well as their grieving process. Clarity on stepson's living arrangements going forward.	Friends and parents. www.griefencoun ter.org.uk	7

From here, he uses the Urgent/Important Matrix:

The Urgent/Important Matrix

Urgent and important	**Important, not urgent**
Support the children in their grieving. Discuss with stepson and his father any changes to living arrangements. Negotiate a new work schedule. Employ a childminder and housekeeper.	Look after friendships, ask sister to take the girls under her wing. Look after mental and physical health – do something about anger towards medics. Long-term career planning. Admin, for example buying uniform, grocery shopping.
Urgent, not important	**Not urgent, not important** (right now)
Next week's team meeting and appraisals.	Plan holiday.

From here, he uses a one-page year planner to begin a rough schedule that will help him sharpen his focus further regarding the What, When and How questions.

64
Creating a New Self

From twenty years of working closely with people as a psychotherapist, I believe that we each have a core self: the True Self, which is the essence of our personality and which can grow and develop, but remains recognisably stable (barring severe trauma). If conditions are not safe enough in early life, we will develop a False Self, a defensive structure, to get us through while protecting the True Self.

Around the core of the True Self, we have quite a lot of scope to shape ourselves. Our innate self-awareness means we can stand aside from our own self, observe and then choose to make improvements. Our ability to imagine into the future means we can delay gratification, and use our will and self-discipline to make changes now that will pay off in time to come. The self-improvement industry is a big industry, of course, and there is plenty of useful (and not so useful) information available.

The first step in this process is the idea. The second step, or maybe the parallel step, is self-knowledge. Getting an accurate assessment of yourself can be surprisingly difficult. So many people, it seems to me, wildly under or overestimate themselves rather than settle on an accurate assessment. Be prepared to ask yourself questions that might seem too obvious to bother with, in order to do some reality-testing. You can do this process alone, with a trusted friend, or with the help of a life coach, or working through a book that speaks to you. Expanding on the template above may give you all you need to make a start.

The third step is setting goals and taking action.

Your identity

The 'we' identity of a couple, as opposed to the 'me', occupies a smaller or larger part of the total identity, depending on the person and on the couple. If each partner in a couple were to draw a diagram of their individual and shared identity, they might be surprised to find that their diagram would not necessarily resemble their partner's, even in a happy, well-functioning relationship.

According to the wonderful Australian psychologist, Dorothy Rowe, every couple is made up of one introvert and one extrovert. While she was not keen on generalisations and labelling people as one type or another, Rowe did recognise some important differences here, a basic knowledge of which will aid your understanding of how you functioned as part of a couple and how you can begin to compensate for any deficits in functioning as you go it alone. She based her ideas and research on the earlier research of Carl Jung (on whose research the Myers–Briggs personality types were based). Jung's view was that identifying your type highlighted the work to be done on the personality to achieve greater balance. In short, it highlighted where introverts could benefit from learning social skills and increasing their tolerance of stimulating environments, and where extroverts could benefit from becoming more reflective and self-sufficient.

Main characteristics of introverts and extroverts

Introverts	Extroverts
The inner world is experienced as more real than the external world.	The external world is experienced as more real than the inner world.
Order and achievement are priorities.	A sense of belonging and the approval of others are priorities.
Chaos and disorder are feared.	The rejection or disapproval of others is feared.
Personal energy is recharged through calm time alone.	Personal energy is recharged through interaction with others and through stimulation.
Ideas are thought through internally before being expressed.	Ideas can be thought through by using others as a sounding board.
Enjoy deep one-to-one connections with people.	Enjoy the stimulation of a group of people.

Having potentially spent a long time as part of a couple, your 'me' identity may be very intertwined with your 'we' identity, and it may well feel alien and uncomfortable to have to turn inwards to your own self and your own thoughts, having had the familiarity of someone to bounce ideas off, or someone to validate you. 'Who am I?' is a very important question to address from time to time. It's a question that can take you down crazy-making rabbit holes if you spend too long on it, but the right amount of reflection and examination can help you keep pace with yourself as you evolve and adapt to the new demands of life.

Attachment theory

Beyond the introvert/extrovert difference, we each have our attachment style to contend with. This refers to the interplay between our innate temperament and our early experience with caregivers, and the template we then develop that informs our assumptions and expectation for subsequent close relationships. The main attachment styles are: secure attachment and insecure attachment. Insecure attachment styles are divided into six categories: preoccupied, fearful, dismissing, preoccupied-fearful, fearful-dismissing, and disorganised. The following is a brief description informed by the *DSM*, the American Psychiatric Association handbook of personality disorders. It is helpful to have an idea of these different attachment styles before you think of embarking on a new relationship, particularly if you are still grieving and are therefore emotionally vulnerable.

Preoccupied attachment style

This style is characterised by a sense of personal unworthiness and a high opinion of others. People with this attachment style need a lot of reassurance and validation from others and find it hard to bolster their own self-esteem.

Fearful attachment style

People with this style tend to have low self-esteem, along with an expectation that other people will reject or dislike them. They may look for the worst case in terms of others' intentions, and tend to catastrophise. If someone with this attachment style becomes anxious within a relationship, their behaviour could become quite dramatic.

Dismissing attachment style
This refers to a person with a high sense of self-worth, but with a low opinion of others, typically manifesting as a mistrust of others. People with this attachment style do not have a strong need to seek close relationships.

Preoccupied-fearful attachment style
This refers to a person with a negative self-view, and a view of the other that is sometimes positive and sometimes negative. A person with this attachment style desires to be liked and accepted by others, but fears rejection and abandonment. This gives rise to anxiety and avoidance behaviours, and possibly to manipulation and game-playing in relationships.

Fearful-dismissing attachment style
This refers to a person whose self-view is sometimes positive and sometimes negative. Their view of the other is negative. They may view themselves as special and entitled, but recognise that they may need the help of a person who could potentially hurt them. Accordingly, they use others to meet their needs, while being wary and dismissive of them. Personality disorders fitting this profile would include antisocial and narcissistic personality disorders.

Disorganised attachment style
This attachment style describes someone with an unstable personality structure, where both self and other are sometimes experienced positively and sometimes negatively. Their personality can shift between the above attachment styles, creating a disorganised profile. This would typically fit with a diagnosis of emotionally unstable personality disorder, also referred to as borderline personality disorder.

These different styles will affect how safe we feel to connect with another, how much intimacy we need or can tolerate, and how we interpret the intentions of our partner. When each partner is securely attached, the relationship is on the firmest foundations it can be, with each partner grounded in reality, able to take care of their own emotional needs, communicate clearly, and show affection and consideration to their partner. Secure attachment implies a good level of emotional intelligence and confidence. From this perspective, problems can be addressed, rather than defended against and distorted, and there will be room for fun as well as the ability to tackle the serious tasks of being in a relationship.

If you are securely attached, this bodes well for creating a positive relationship, but it can also leave you vulnerable to being caught off guard by a dismissive-avoidant or anxious-preoccupied potential partner who initially goes to great lengths to disguise the more unattractive elements of their personality. If things are initially going well, but then the partner blows hot and cold, or the relationship fails to progress to a deeper intimacy for no apparent reason, you can be left searching for reasons and may start doubting yourself. It could simply be that your partner has an internal struggle that they can't share with you, because they don't fully understand their own process. We all tend to replay unconscious scripts from early life when we get into intimate relationships.

Attachment styles are not fixed, but can be worked upon and strengthened in order to become more secure. The development of a healthier attachment style is one of the benefits of effective psychotherapy, and, obviously, if you are not already securely attached it may be worth considering some therapy before you embark on another relationship. There may be a sense of urgency to fill the emotional void by beginning another relationship, but there are benefits to first taking the time to work through the stages of grief (see p. 236). You will then be a stronger, calmer version of yourself and may connect with someone from that perspective who will be a better fit for you over the longer term.

Splitting

Linked to the relationship patterns formed by the different attachment styles is the idea of splitting. This can be quite a tricky psychological concept to grasp, as it entails the idea of projection, where you can see something in another person that actually belongs to you. Like the image on a cinema screen, it looks as if the screen is producing the image, but the image is actually produced by the projector some way away. If the projector were alive, it would look at the cinema screen and accuse the screen of creating the upsetting images, not believing that it, the projector, was actually responsible for creating those images.

Bear with me, because when you've understood splitting you'll find it easier to work out what may be going on in difficult interactions. This theory (the paranoid-schizoid position) was put forward by Melanie Klein, a student of Sigmund Freud. She studied infants from their earliest days, inferring mental and emotional states that greatly advanced the understanding of human development. Her theory suggests that the infant's mind cannot contain the extremes of Good and Bad together, and so one of these will be projected out, usually onto a parent. If, for whatever reason, the infant feels 'Bad', their 'Good' may be projected out for safekeeping; otherwise their innate Badness will annihilate the Goodness. If this pattern is not fully worked through during childhood, the adult will still have the tendency to fear their own Badness and will need to keep a partner close to them, to be the holder of their very precious Goodness. This could result in co-dependency or psychological game-playing.

Conversely, the infant may project out the 'Bad'. Again, if this is not fully worked through during childhood, the adult may have a tendency to misread others as hostile, and become hostile in 'revenge' or seek to control the other to limit the perceived threat that they pose. They may appear unreasonable or even paranoid to others.

If you recognise this in yourself, it will obviously be beneficial to work it through with the aid of a psychoanalyst or psychodynamic psychotherapist, who can interpret the unconscious forces at play and help you towards greater self-knowledge and self-acceptance. The ideal, in my opinion, would be a therapist trained in psychodynamic psychotherapy and Attachment Focused EMDR (Eye Movement Desensitisation and Reprocessing) (AF-EMDR). Therapists can be found on www.emdrfocus.com (UK-based source of therapists) and www.parnellemdr.com (an international list).

If your late partner was the repository of your Badness, the loss of the relationship will mean that you now have to contain your Badness rather than thinking it belongs to your partner. This can be destabilising at an already highly stressful time. It can give rise to anxiety, bewildering mood swings or self-loathing. If it is severe, you will need some psychological help. One of the dangers, if you have children, is that they, or one of them, become the new repository of your Badness and you start criticising them or putting them in situations where they can't win.

If your late partner was the repository of your Goodness, the loss of the relationship will mean that you now have to step up and be a grown-up when you may be used to your partner making all the difficult decisions and carrying out the responsible tasks. You will need to find a way to boost your self-esteem and confidence, and learn to trust yourself to get things done satisfactorily. Again, you may need help with this. One of the dangers, if you have children, is that they, or one of them, gets pushed to being the grown-up and bearing more responsibility than is appropriate.

Self-care

A bereavement can be a very traumatic transition in your life. During this transition you will need to look after yourself even when you don't feel like doing it. Stress causes changes in sleep patterns, mood, appetite, thinking processes and memory. You may need to set reminders on your phone or make lists for things you would usually find easy to hold in mind. You may even need to talk to yourself as you would to a child, 'Now it's bedtime so you're going to lock the doors, clean your teeth and set the alarm for tomorrow.' It's just one way of managing the transition, until you have created the next chapter of your life and you feel like yourself again.

Self-care means covering the bases in the main areas of life: eating, sleeping, finances, work, parenting, household chores and general mood.

Going deeper into the more unconscious motivations, for some, neglecting self-care can be a way of punishing the lost partner, as if to say, 'Look what you've done to me.' There can be some reluctance to attend to self-care, as if it would let the partner off the hook for the 'abandonment'. It's worth reflecting on your motivations, and bearing in mind the idea of sub-personalities, as it is often a young part of the personality that feels the pain of injustice most sharply that is fuelling the problematic behaviour. If this is at play, this 'young part' may be viewing the ex-partner as an internalised version of a withholding parent. In this scenario, the lost partner, as withholding parent, has the power to make everything OK, but in dying refuses to do anything, leaving you helpless in your distress. So, the danger in grieving is that you can slide into a deep, dark pit, from which it is increasingly difficult to find a way out.

Years ago, when a mourning period was a much more publicly acknowledged transition, there would be more support given by family and friends, and for a longer period of time, than tends to be the case now. We are expected to snap back to full functioning after a very brief period of compassionate leave from work; that is if any leave is given at all. There is also a tendency to pathologise and medicalise distress, even though this is a normal and natural reaction to loss. Having said that, there is nothing wrong with using medication to help you through this painful transition, as long as you have a wise and compassionate GP who will keep an eye on the appropriateness of the medication and the length of time you're on it.

Given the pressures of life and the need to function well for those relying on you, you might have to dip in and out of grief and self-care. You may even have to schedule in time to let yourself feel the pain and anxiety, and then time to switch out of that mode and get things done.

Certain times of day or daily activities can be particularly difficult. Going to bed alone can be such a painful reminder of your loss that the whole evening and night-time routine becomes associated with sadness and distress. Laurel Parnell's book *Tapping In* is an excellent source of suggestions for self-care. In it she teaches you how to install and activate a team of Resource Figures using active imagination and bilateral stimulation (tapping), so that you have a much greater ability to soothe sadness or anxiety, or motivate yourself to keep going. You first think of a calm place, or a safe place, and when you can imagine that strongly and feel a shift in your mood, say to a feeling of relief or satisfaction, you install it by crossing your arms across your chest so that you can tap your shoulders, left hand to right shoulder and vice versa, gently for a few seconds in a left-right-left-right pattern. Be aware, though, of her disclaimer, in particular that should you be suffering from PTSD or clinical depression you should consult a doctor before practising the exercises in the book.

In addition to the calm place, you can add any number of Nurturing figures, Protector figures or Wise figures, as well as tapping in to positive memories, such as having been resilient or determined, in order to help you keep your spirits up. Another idea is to install your Future Self, a version of yourself which has successfully made it through the difficult transition into a satisfying new chapter. This imagined Future Self can call you forward and motivate you to keep going. Give it a try and keep using it if it's helpful. If this works for you, you can call on the Resource Figures at night to help you feel safe and secure before you go to sleep. You can use them to help you feel motivated, protected or soothed, in virtually any situation in which you could do with a boost. It's one thing reading about these ideas, but to get the benefit you'll have to make time, repeatedly, to put them into practice.

As you will know if you're a parent, or if you've been responsible for others at work, a lot of care comes down to holding current and future needs in mind, and giving praise, validation and encouragement. This works so much better than cajoling and criticising, and is so much more pleasant for everyone involved. So do make sure your own self-talk isn't too critical or pessimistic.

65
Counselling, Psychotherapy and Other Therapies

There is not a clear distinction as to the difference between the definition of counselling and of psychotherapy. The title of my training was MA in Counselling and Psychotherapy, and one of the main professional bodies in this field is the British Association for Counselling and Psychotherapy.

For our purposes I will define counselling as short-term therapy – between six and twenty weekly sessions – centred around emotional support and aiming to bring about agreed-upon emotional and/or behavioural change. The relationship between therapist and client is the medium of change.

I will define psychotherapy as in-depth analytical therapy, of longer duration – perhaps a year or more, usually once or twice weekly – aiming to bring about change by increasing self-awareness of personal drives, needs, inner conflicts, strengths and vulnerabilities. Again, the medium of change is the relationship between therapist and client.

Counselling and psychotherapy are divided into three broad categories: cognitive and behavioural; humanistic; and psychoanalytic and psychodynamic therapies.

In simple terms, cognitive and behavioural therapies aim to help you identify and change the patterns of thoughts and behaviour that result in distress. Thinking more constructive thoughts, challenging patterns of catastrophising thinking, and reality-testing serve to reduce anxiety and increase resilience.

Humanistic therapy takes the inherent trustworthiness and appropriateness of the person as its foundation, and aims to create a supportive therapeutic relationship in order to help the client face their anxiety, distress and confusion. In this supportive relationship, the client can experience the freedom to live more fully, more authentically and therefore with greater satisfaction.

Psychoanalytic and psychodynamic psychotherapies aim to discover the roots of current distress and, in Freud's words, 'to make the unconscious conscious', in order to ease suffering. Freud aimed to help his patients successfully work, love and play, this being a measure of a well-functioning life. Hindrances to a well-functioning life are often early defence mechanisms, which are employed early in life to help tolerate difficult situations, but they then linger beyond their usefulness, creating their own problems. These defence mechanisms have to be identified, understood and overcome. An analogy would be the medieval knight putting on a suit of armour to protect him in battle, but then not being able to remove the armour when the battle was over and he went about his daily life. Identifying and overcoming the defence mechanisms happens within the relationship with a skilled analyst. There are many subsections within these three broad categories. For more detailed information, see the Counselling Directory or Mind websites. If you are considering private therapy, it's advisable to check the therapist's credentials such as training, accreditation and liability insurance by contacting the professional body and searching their therapist directory. The main professional bodies are UKCP, BACP, BPS and BPC.

There is a range of other therapies that can be helpful in times of grief, such as EMDR, arts-based therapies, equine therapy and body-focused therapies. The method, rather than the relationship, is the primary medium of change. Many therapists are trained in more than one method, in which case they usually refer to their therapy as integrative, meaning they draw upon various techniques or theoretical foundations.

Do you need counselling?

Counselling, here meaning short-term supportive therapy, tends to focus primarily on the here and now and how you can ease or better tolerate current distress. There are different schools of thought in counselling and psychotherapy, but what they have in common is an aim to offer a safe place where you will be met as an equal by a compassionate, sincere individual. At a simple level, counselling can offer a period of support, a regular time for you to talk and be heard, without your having to protect the other person from your pain, or worry that they won't keep your information private,[1] and without having to entertain the other. It's not a social relationship, and the emphasis is on you and your needs. At a more complex level, counselling can aim to help you understand yourself more thoroughly, allowing you to examine and own the aspects of yourself you'd rather disown, so that you can, paradoxically, more easily change the things about yourself that might have caused problems in your life.

Sadly, there is very little face-to-face counselling available on the NHS unless you're in a shockingly dysfunctional state, and then it might well be group therapy, which is anxiety-provoking in itself for some people. That leaves you with local charities, local private therapists, your insurance company if you have private insurance, or online cognitive behavioural therapy via the NHS.

Mind is a long-established national charity, providing counselling services across the country. Their website is an excellent resource for finding a counsellor privately or through Mind as well as other counselling charities. If you already know you would like to see a private counsellor, try the Counselling Directory, the BACP or the EMDR (Eye Movement Desensitisation and Reprocessing) Association. Cruse is a bereavement charity, with branches nationwide, which provides counselling services for the bereaved, although you might find there is a waiting list.

---

[1] There are caveats to the confidentiality of your private information. If you disclose that you intend to commit suicide or serious harm to another, or disclose knowledge of child abuse or terrorism, then the counsellor has a legal obligation to break confidentiality and contact the authorities, in practice your GP or the police.

It's hard to know if you really need counselling. A more pertinent question may be whether you think you would benefit from some professional support. This is a stressful time for most, but some people will find that the support of friends and family is enough. Some people in this transition aren't aware of the extent of their stress or distress, and it may take a kind and brave friend to suggest to you that you may need counselling. Typical reasons for seeking counselling can be, for example, a feeling of 'stuckness' or crisis, an alarming sense that 'this isn't me', or a low mood that makes it hard to get anything done or to see ahead with any optimism. If you are misusing drugs or alcohol, engaging in risky behaviours, having suicidal thoughts or self-harming, then it's much more urgent to seek help.

Do you need psychotherapy?

Psychotherapy, for our purposes, means longer-term, insight-driven therapy, aimed at helping you to understand yourself at a much deeper level. As you go through the often uncomfortable process of getting to know and to own the hidden or exiled parts of your own self, you gradually feel more whole, more responsible for yourself, more accepting of flaws and more grounded in your strengths. The medium of change is the relationship, with part of the therapist's role being to hold up a mirror to you, metaphorically, to help you see more fully who you are.

Psychotherapy is not a social relationship. The emphasis is on you and your needs. As you talk openly and candidly about your deeper feelings, the therapist will offer interpretations to help you gain clarity, through which you can gain self-knowledge and a greater ability to rationalise and tolerate distress, while understanding your strengths.

It would be worth considering psychotherapy if you feel you need more than short-term support to help you through the emotional crisis of grief. If you find you have encountered similar types of problems over and over, suggesting you might have a part in the dramas that erupt in your life, then psychotherapy can help you gain the mastery you need in order to step off the difficult treadmill of repeating dramas.

So which type would suit you? Psychoanalysis refers to intensive, two-or-three-times weekly analysis, so I will focus here on psychodynamic psychotherapy, which is more likely to be once weekly, and more likely to be one of a number of approaches used by integrative therapists, and is therefore more widely available. Sigmund Freud, Melanie Klein and Carl Jung were the originators of this approach, with their emphasis on early childhood development and its impact on the adult personality.

Freud placed an emphasis on unconscious drives, especially those arising from sexual and aggressive motivations. He was interested in Greek mythology and weaved this into his theories, for example the Oedipus complex, to aid his understanding of the human condition. Klein and Jung were students of his, and further developed and refined his ideas in their own directions. Klein developed a deep understanding of inner conflicts and defence mechanisms, and developed effective analysis to heal and integrate the split-off parts of the self. Jung was fascinated by Far Eastern mysticism, which influenced his form of therapy to embrace the spiritual and the universal archetypal dimensions of human experience, for example how our primal dramas, such as the Hero's Journey, are exemplified in fairy tales throughout the world.

There are more modern derivatives of these therapies, such as Cognitive Analytical Therapy (CAT) and blends of depth psychotherapy with short-term delivery, such as Dynamic Interpersonal Therapy, delivered over sixteen weekly sessions.

Despite the differences and similarities of these therapies, when outcomes have been investigated, one of the most crucial factors in the success of a therapy has been found to be the quality of the relationship between therapist and client. Put simply, chemistry matters, and so it is worth speaking to a few prospective therapists to see how you feel in their company before committing to working together.

I will include EMDR under this section, rather than 'Other Therapies', as in my experience many EMDR therapists have a psychodynamic or counselling psychology background. The psychodynamic theories provide a very good framework to understand the structure of the personality, and EMDR provides very good tools to effectively and efficiently solve problems and thereby bring a great deal of relief. This solution-focused method is particularly helpful if you are psychologically minded and able to tolerate brief spikes of what can sometimes be quite distressing emotion as traumatic memories are reprocessed and reworked. See the EMDR Association website for further information.

Other therapies

There are many complementary and alternative therapies available. Again, Mind is an excellent source of information here. Complementary therapies can be used in conjunction with conventional medicine, and comprise treatments such as massage or practices such as yoga or meditation. Alternative therapies comprise treatments such as herbal medicine, acupuncture or Ayurvedic medicine. These therapies tend to emphasise a holistic approach to well-being, rather than symptom reduction.

Complementary or alternative therapists are not currently regulated in England and Wales; however, therapists can voluntarily register with a professional association for their particular therapy, or with the Complementary and Natural Healthcare Council. In practice, therapists tend to have to be members of a professional body in order to get their professional liability insurance, and this is something you can check out with a prospective therapist.

We have a mind–body system, rather than purely a body, or purely a mind. Affecting something in one area of the system will therefore have an effect on the rest of the system. Soothing the body will help soothe the mind, and vice versa. Having a massage is a very nice way of allowing your body to let go of any accumulated stress and simply to feel good in the present moment. It is so nice to be able to come into the present moment with a sense of 'right here, right now, I'm OK'. The more you can do this, one way or another, the more you can trust that when the low feelings come, they will be temporary.

66
Taking Risks

If you've been in a long relationship, your role and identity may have become somewhat fixed. It may be a while since you've tried something new, or pushed yourself out of your comfort zone. The assumption may be that we have a greater appetite for risk when we're younger than when we're older, but some things are much easier to do when we're older and we are less sensitive to what other people think. Beyond that, with age we've hopefully gained wisdom and can better identify the boundary between appropriate and inappropriate risk. Even so, comfort zones in any area of life have a habit of shrinking in on you unless you take action now and then to push them out.

In simple terms, most people find they are more motivated by either moving towards a good thing, or moving away from a bad thing. One way isn't better than another. It's useful to know your style; then you can motivate yourself more effectively. In investing, for example, many people find it easier to make the decision to buy an investment than to make the decision to sell at a loss, even if selling at that point may well prevent them from suffering further losses. For many, the pain of a loss has a greater impact than the pleasure of a gain. We are social animals, and the loss might signify money, status, power, approval, or something else we consider vital to life. Our brains have evolved to take shortcuts to help us survive, and a lot of this means avoiding dangers. But, of course, our world now is very different from the world in which these survival mechanisms evolved and some of the things we instinctively fear aren't actually threatening.

As life has a habit of changing around us, decisions can't be avoided. Inaction is often effectively a decision, as the world doesn't stand still even if we do. Our tolerance for healthy risk can gradually be increased by doing more, bit by bit. It is interesting to notice how we all have problems in different areas. I might find it easy to take something back to a shop for a refund, but impossible to pick up a spider. Someone else might have the reverse. It's often not the thing itself that's the problem, but our confidence or attitude.

If you can easily identify an area of life in which it would help you to become more comfortable with risk, what can you do? If it's more than discomfort, and certainly if it's in phobia territory, then a solution-focused therapy such as EMDR is the best option in my opinion. If it's less severe than that, then some active imagination techniques followed up by action may be all you need. Say you have decided to apply for a job and will be having an interview for the first time in a long while, the thought of the interview will naturally be daunting. If you know someone who could handle the interview confidently, then a good start is to take a few minutes to get relaxed, turn your phone off and make sure you won't be interrupted, then imagine watching your friend in the interview. Notice their posture, their expression, eye contact and tone of voice. Notice, in your imagination, how they handle a question they're not sure of, how they ask questions about the job, rather than simply respond to questions put to them. If you find this imagination exercise quite easy to do, then maybe replay the movie in your mind's eye, but expand it to see how they prepare ahead of time, or how they support themselves with constructive self-talk, or how they debrief themselves afterwards by focusing on the parts that went well as well as the parts that went less well. If someone can do it, then it can be done. If it can be done, then maybe you can do it.

67
Conclusion

We have reason for optimism. It is said an Eastern monarch once charged his wise men to invent him a sentence that should be true and appropriate in all times and situations. They presented him with the words, 'And this, too, shall pass away.' How much it expresses. How chastening in the hour of pride. How consoling in the depths of affliction.

From the perspective of grief, or fear or depression, we cannot see clearly. We lose sight, for a while, of the joys and comforts in life. But it changes. Grief is a natural response to loss. We grieve, and then we emerge into a new chapter. In our interconnected world we share our knowledge with one another, and so we have the benefit of many lives' worth of experience to draw upon. We may feel alone in our grief, but we do not have to be alone in our transformation.

You know you are on the right path when you feel that tomorrow might just be worth looking forward to!

Organisations
British Psychoanalytical Council, www.bpc.org.uk, 020 7561 9240.

British Psychological Society, www.bps.org.uk, 0116 254 9568.

Cruse Bereavement Care, www.cruse.org.uk. National helpline open Monday and Friday, 9.30 a.m. to 5 p.m., 0808 808 1677, or use a search engine to find your local Cruse centre.

Cruse Bereavement Care Scotland, www.crusescotland.org.uk. National helpline (check website for opening hours): 0845 600 2227. Webchat also available.

Mind, www.mind.org.uk, infoline for mental health problems,
0300 123 3393.

Books and publications

Blaisdell, B., *The Wit and Wisdom of Abraham Lincoln*, Dover Thrift
Editions, 2005.

Cantopher, Tim, *Dying for a Drink*, Sheldon Press, 1996.

Dietrich, A., and McDaniel, W. F., 'Endocannabinoids and Exercise',
bmj.com, 2004.

Keogh, Abel, *Dating a Widower*, Ben Lomond Press, 2011.

Klein, Melanie, *The Psycho-Analysis of Children*, Vintage, 1932.

Rowe, Dorothy, *The Successful Self*, HarperCollins, 2010.

Parnell, Laurel, *Tapping In*, Sounds True Inc., 2008.

Van der Kolk, Bessel, *The Body Keeps the Score*, Penguin Books, 2014.

Websites

www.bacp.co.uk: Directory of private counsellors/psychotherapists,
01455 883300.

www.citizensadvice.org.uk: Information on financial help.

www.counselling-directory.org.uk: Directory of private
counsellors/psychotherapists, 0333 325 2500.

www.dominican.edu: 'Goal setting', findings presented in May 2015
at the Ninth Annual International Conference of the Psychology
Research Unit of Athens Institute of Education and Research (ATINER).

www.emdrassociation.org.uk: Directory of practitioners of EMDR (Eye Movement Desensitisation and Reprocessing).

www.familyandchildcaretrust.org: Help finding childcare, and general help and advice, 020 7239 7535.

www.familylives.org.uk: Advice and support for families. Helpline: 0808 800 2222.

www.gingerbread.org.uk: Advice and support for single parent families, 0207 428 5400.

www.gov.uk: For information on financial help, and free childcare for three- to four-year-olds.

www.kidshealth.org: Information on all aspects of children's health.

www.nationaldebtconsultant.co.uk: Help with debt.

www.nhs.uk: GP referral or self-referral for group or online therapy.

www.parnellemdr.com: Source of attachment-focused EMDR specialists.

www.pschotherapy.org.uk: UK Council for Psychotherapy, 020 7014 9955.

www.stepchange.org: Advice on debt.

www.turn2us.org: Information on financial help.

Conclusion

What we have tried to do in this book is give you the information and advice we think will be useful to you while you struggle with the shattering prospect that your loved one, be they spouse, civil partner, live-in lover or partner, has just received a terminal diagnosis or news of a life-threatening disease, or suffered a catastrophic trauma that ends in death. Any one of these is likely to turn you from a well-organised person into a jibbering wreck, as you try to assimilate the information and work out what to do and in what order.

There are no easy answers. You will need plenty of information. It is all out there waiting to be found, but what we have tried to do is to collate it into one place and to answer the sort of questions you might be asking if you could put words together and articulate them.

In Part One we began with news of the terminal illness and what you might be able to plan for in these circumstances. Depending on how well your partner is and how much energy you have, there are any number of things you can do. We discussed how you and your partner might be feeling. We explained what you might have to think about in having your partner at home or in a care or nursing home, if they are discharged from hospital. Where do you go to for help? Most importantly, we talked about you and your partner being in control of their treatment and palliative care and what might happen to them, through powers of attorney and advance decisions concerning treatment. We explained that unless these are completed, your partner might not be able to say what treatment they do or don't want, because they are unable to and you do not have the power to be able to speak for them.

In Part Two we looked at how you might manage your finances during this difficult time and what benefits you might be entitled to. We covered the writing of a will, if you have not already done so; who might be your executors; and all the issues associated with making one. We pointed out the benefits of marriage or a civil partnership in terms of inheritance. We also talked about your children and supporting them through this difficult time.

Part Three concentrated on the funeral. There are an astonishing number of decisions to be taken about a funeral, beginning with whether you want your partner to be buried or cremated. This is a very personal issue, but we offered you some ideas concerning the pros and cons of each. We looked at your dealings with the funeral director and what decisions he or she will want you to make. The message here is about consulting widely with those who are affected and not rushing into making decisions too soon.

Part Four covered all the other things you have to attend to after the death of your partner. This includes registering the death and obtaining probate, whether there is a will or not. We explained the role of the coroner and why you might have to have a post-mortem or an inquest. We then turned to your finances and how you might manage them. We discussed your work situation, assuming you have one, and practical ways to make ends meet. We ended with the difficulties relating to anniversaries and decisions concerning disposing of your partner's effects.

Part Five was about grieving and mourning. Grieving is a normal process after we lose someone we care for or who has had a large role in our lives. The emotions are strong and conflicting. The overall feeling is one of confusion. Sometimes people think they are going mad. We tried to support you through this period by explaining about the tasks of grief. The aim is to adjust to an environment in which your loved one is missing, to emotionally relocate them and to move on in life.

Part Six began the process of rebuilding your life. When our partner dies, we often do not know who we really are. The process of finding out is a painful one, but it also promises great rewards. As you develop skills and gain knowledge and understanding, you will become the person you can be. There are practical exercises and ideas to support you through this difficult period, including some guidance about your physical and psychological health. This is also an opportunity to tackle issues that you have not been able to face previously, and accordingly we discuss the pros and cons of counselling and psychotherapy.

If we have helped you on this journey from blackest night to a new dawn, we will have done what we set out to do. We have used our own experiences and those of many more people to try to achieve that. More than anything, we hope that you will find some happiness and that finally you will find something to look forward to: tomorrow.

Acknowledgements

We would like to thank all those people who have talked to us so openly about their bereavements and shared their experiences. Many of them have provided the anecdotes for the book.

We are indebted to our agent Robert Dudley for realising the potential of the book and taking us on, to our commissioning editor at Robinson, Tom Asker, for his enthusiasm and professionalism, and to Nick Fawcett, our copy-editor for tightening up the text and asking helpful questions.

We would particularly like to thank Alix Davenport, Pat Downs and Phil Robinson, who read the texts and were generous in their critical comments and suggestions; Doreen Spiers for checking the law so thoroughly not just once but twice, and also scrupulously checking for typos; and Revd John Spiers and his web-based group for ecclesiastical observations and advice. Thanks, too, to Amanda at St Luke's.

Appendix 1
Marriage, Civil Partnership and Cohabitation Agreements

Marriage is a culturally recognised union between two people, called spouses, which establishes rights and obligations between them and is recognised in law for such purposes as pension rights, house ownership, inheritance issues and making 'next of kin' decisions in medical matters. There are legal and financial protections for both parties in the event of the relationship ending.

Marriages are usually solemnised by saying a prescribed form of words or undertaking a ritual. After the form of words has been said or rituals performed, the official conducting the ceremony declares the couple to be married. Marriages can be conducted through either a civil ceremony or a religious ceremony by an officially designated person, such as a religious official, a humanist celebrant or a registrar. They can take place in various places such as a register office; premises approved by the local authority; any registered religious building; the home of one of the partners if one of them is housebound, or detained, such as in prison; and a place where one partner is seriously ill and not expected to recover, for example in a hospital or hospice. Private homes are unlikely to be approved by the local authority since they are not generally open to the public. Open-air spaces such as beaches, aeroplanes or hot-air balloons are not allowed, although permanently moored boats may be.

If the parties are intending to have a religious ceremony, unless this is in an Anglican, Church in Wales or a Roman Catholic building, they must give notice of their intention to marry in person at a register office to the superintendent registrar of the district where both parties live. Many religious establishments such as mosques, Hindu temples and chapels are registered for the solemnisation of marriage and the officiating person can issue a marriage certificate, but this does not apply to all and it should be checked with the registrar at the time that the couple give notification. If the religious venue is not registered, and in other establishments approved by the local authority for weddings, a registrar will normally be required to be involved.

Same-sex marriage was legalised in England, Wales and Scotland in 2014, and in Northern Ireland in 2020. However, many religious groups do not recognise same-sex marriages and will not allow their premises to be used for this purpose. The Church of England and the Church in Wales are legally banned from performing same-sex marriages, neither can they give such marriages their blessing. The Catholic Church, the Methodist Church, Islam and Orthodox Judaism are all opposed. The Scottish Episcopal Church allows same-sex marriages in its churches, as do the Quakers and the Unitarians. As above, if the officiating person is officially registered to perform marriages, a registrar will not be required; otherwise one will. However, individual ministers in these consenting churches are allowed by law to refuse to perform same-sex marriages, so consent is not automatic.

Civil partnership is an entirely civil event. It gives heterosexual and same-sex couples the same rights and responsibilities as marriage does, such as pension rights, house ownership, inheritance issues and making 'next of kin' decisions in medical matters. Any couple can convert a civil partnership into a marriage. There are legal and financial protections for both parties in the event of the relationship ending, just as in marriage.

It is not compulsory to have a ceremony to form a civil partnership; you just have to sign the civil partnership document. As soon as the second person signs the document, the couple are in a civil partnership. However, many people want to celebrate their union with an event in front of family and friends. The place you might hold this event does not need to be registered as there is no ceremony as such, just the signing of forms.

Many people choose a civil partnership over marriage because it is free of the religious connotations of marriage, and also because they believe that marriage is an institution and has associations with property and patriarchy.

Cohabitation agreements offer a third type of protection. They set out how you will support your children beyond legal duties to provide care and support, as well as defining how you will split any bank accounts, pension schemes, debts and joint purchases such as vehicles. You can also use it to outline who owns which assets while you live together and to explain your joint finances, such as how much you both pay towards the mortgage, rent or bills.

You can also enter into a beneficial joint tenancy with regards to your house ownership. This is mentioned in other places in the text.

As in many contracts, the most useful part of this agreement is the discussion that preceded it. One party should not present the other with a fait accompli and ask them to sign it.

As a cohabitation agreement is a legal document, it should be drawn up by a solicitor.

A note on protecting yourself

It is worth bearing in mind that only 50 per cent of those aged sixteen and over were married or in a civil partnership in England and Wales last year according to the Office of National Statistics. There is no doubt that if you want to ensure that you are protected as a partner, you need to get married or enter a civil partnership. If you do not do so, you may find that you have no rights and no expectations, even if you have been promised a share in your partner's estate when they were alive. If you are not the executor, and the executor does not think you are entitled to your share, no matter how long you were together with your partner, they can deprive you of it and you will not be in a fit state to contest this situation.

A detailed chart of the similarities and differences between heterosexual and same-sex marriages and civil partnerships can be found on the government website, www.gov.uk.

Citizens Advice has detailed advice on its website under the heading 'Getting Married' at www.citizensadvice.org.uk.

Other useful websites include The Registry Office and The Passport Office, both a part of gov.uk.

Appendix 2
SWOT Analysis for You to Complete

Strengths	Weaknesses

Opportunities	Threats

Appendix 3
Template to Assess Different Aspects of Your Life

Example	What do I have?	What do I need?	Where to find help/ information	How satisfied am I currently? (0–10)
Professional				
Financial				
Health				
Social life				
Family life				

Appendix 4
Urgent/Important Matrix

The Urgent/Important Matrix for you to complete

Urgent and important	Important, not urgent
Urgent, not important	**Not urgent, not important** (right now)

Appendix 5
Useful Organisations

Adfam, a national charity working to improve life for families affected by drugs or alcohol: www.adfam.org.uk. 020 3817 9410 (not a helpline).

Age UK, a charity that supports older people: www.ageuk.org.uk. Advice line: 0800 678 1602, open every day from 8 a.m. to 7 p.m.

The Benefit Agency: www.gov.uk, benefit enquiry line: 0800 882200.

Bereaved through Alcohol or Drugs (BEAD), a partnership set up by Cruse Bereavement: www.beadproject.org.uk. Can also be accessed through Cruse Bereavement Care below.

Bereavement Advice Centre, a free service that gives practical information and advice on the issues you will face after the death of someone close: www.bereavementadvice.org.uk. Advice line open Monday to Friday 9 a.m. to 5 p.m., 0800 634 9494.

Brains for Dementia Research, initiative to support brain donation for research: www.bdr.alzheimersresearchuk.org.

British Association for Counselling and Psychotherapy (BACP), offers a directory of private counsellors and psychotherapists: www.bacp.co.uk. 01455 883300.

British Institute of Funeral Directors: www.bifd.org.uk. 0800 032 2733.

British Psychoanalytical Council: www.bpc.org.uk. 020 7561 9240.

British Psychological Society: www.bps.org.uk. 0116 254 9568.

British Red Cross Society, offering support for any kind of human crisis: www.redcross.org.uk. 0344 871 11 11.

The Charity Commission for England and Wales: www.gov.uk. Phone line open Monday to Friday 9 a.m. to 12 p.m. and 1 p.m. to 4 p.m., 0300 066 9197.

The Chartered Institute of Public Relations: www.cipr.co.uk.
020 7631 6900.

Cherished Urns: www.cherished-urns.co.uk. 01872 487101.

Citizens Advice, a network of independent charities that give free,
confidential information and advice to assist people with a
variety of problems: www.citizensadvice.org.uk. Advice line
open Monday to Friday 9 a.m. to 5 p.m., 03444 111 444.
Specialist debt chat line open Monday to Friday 8 a.m. to 7 p.m.
Be aware that the advice will vary depending on which part of
the United Kingdom you live in. Either phone or use a search
engine to contact your nearest branch.

Compassion in Dying: www.compassionindying.org.uk. 0800 999 2434.

The Compassionate Friends, offering support after the death of a
child, email: helpline@tcf.org.uk, 0345 123 2304, Northern
Ireland helpline: 0288 7788 016.

Complete Care Shop, for mobility issues: ww.completecareshop.co.uk.

Coram Family and Childcare, help finding childcare, and general help
and advice: www.familyandchildcaretrust.org. 0207 239 7535.

Counselling Directory, a directory of private counsellors and
psychotherapists: www.counselling-directory.org.uk.
0333 325 2500.

Cruse Bereavement Care: www.cruse.org.uk. National helpline open
Monday and Friday, 9.30 a.m. to 5 p.m., 0808 808 1677, or use a
search engine to find your local Cruse centre.

Cruse Bereavement Care Scotland: www.crusescotland.org.uk.
National helpline (check website for opening hours):
0845 600 2227. Webchat also available.

Department for Environment, Food and Rural Affairs (DEFRA):
www.gov.uk. 03459 335577.

Dignity in Dying: www.dignityindying.org.uk. 020 7479 7730.

DrugFAM, for those affected by someone else's drug or alcohol abuse,
including those bereaved by addiction: www.drugfam.co.uk.
Helpline: 0300 888 3853.

EMDR Association, directory of practitioners of EMDR:
www.emdrassociation.org.uk.

End of Life Doula UK, www.eol-doula.uk.

End-of-Life Rights Information Line: 0800 999 2434.

The Environment Agency, non-departmental public body:
www.gov.uk. Email: enquiries@environment-agency.gov.uk.
Phone line open Monday to Friday 8 a.m. to 6 p.m.,
0114 282 5312.

Equity Release Council, industry body for the UK equity release
sector, representing qualified financial advisors, solicitors and
others: www.equityreleasecouncil.com. Phone: 0300 012 0239.

Eternal Reefs, funeral director, www.efbox.co.uk. Phone (24/7):
01294 465402.

EverWith Memorial Jewellery: www.everwith.co.uk, 01452 379379.

Family Lives, an organisation offering advice and support for
families: www.familylives.org.uk. Helpline open Monday to
Friday 9 a.m. to 9 p.m., Saturday and Sunday 10 a.m. to 3 p.m.,
0808 800 2222.

Farewill, will-writing service that also offers probate and cremation
services: www.farewill.com, 020 3318 8647.

Flexmort, offers a Mini Mortuary Cooling System for keeping bodies
cool: www.flexmort.com.

Foreign, Commonwealth and Development Office (FOCD):
www.uk.gov/government/organisations, 020 7008 1500.

Forever Together, cremation ashes and remembrance jewellery:
www.forevertogetherjewellery.co.uk. 01942 417315.

Funeral Zone, an online resource for everything to do with funerals:
www.funeralzone.co.uk.

Ginger Bread Advice, a charity offering advice and support for single
parent families: www.gingerbread.org.uk. 020 7428 5400.

GIRES, Gender Identity and Education Society, a charity that aims to
improve substantially the environment in which gender nonconforming people live: www.gires.org.uk. 0132 801 554.
Contact by email on their site.

Government services and information for the UK (mainly England and Wales): www.gov.uk.

Government services and information for Northern Ireland: www.nidirect.gov.uk. Phone line open Monday to Friday 9 a.m. to 5 p.m., 0800 085 2463.

Government services for Scotland: www.gov.scot.

Grief Encounter Child Bereavement Charity: www.griefencounter.org.uk. 0808 802 0111.

Halifax, Cancer Support Team, phone line open 8 a.m. to 8 p.m., seven days a week: 0800 028 2692. Halifax customers only.

Halifax, Specialist Bereavement Team, phone line open 8 a.m. to 8 p.m., seven days a week: 0800 028 1057 or +44 (0) 113 366 0145 from abroad. Halifax customers only.

HM Inspector of Anatomy, information on organ donation: www.organdonation.nhs.uk. 020 7972 4551.

Human Tissue Authority: www.hta.gov.uk, helpline open Monday to Friday 9 a.m. to 5 p.m., 020 7269 1900.

Humanists UK: www.humanism.org.uk. 020 7324 3060.

International Pension Centre: www.gov.uk. 0191 218 7608.

Jigsaw: www.jigsaw4u.org.uk. 020 8687 1384.

Judicial Conduct Investigations Office: www.judicialconduct.judiciary.gov.uk, or www.ojc.judiciary.gov.uk/OJC/complaintlink.do, 020 7073 4719.

KidsHealth Foundation, an American charity providing advice and support on children's health: www.kidshealth.org.

The Law Society of England and Wales: www.lawsociety.org.uk. 020 7320 5650.

The Law Society of Scotland, useful for finding a solicitor in Scotland: www.lawscot.org.uk. 0131 226 7411.

Learn My Way, web-based support for digital learning: www.learnmyway.com.

Life Book, for creating your own autobiography: www.lifebookuk.com. Phone: 0800 160 1118 or 020 3813 9423.

Lifeline 24, home alarm systems: www.lifeline24.co.uk.

Living Well Dying Well: www.lwdwtraining.uk. 01273 474278.

London Probate Department, email: londonprobate@justice.gov.uk.
Phone: enquiries 020 7421 8509, probate helpline: 0300 123
1072, court counter open 10 a.m.
to 4.30 p.m. daily except weekends.

Macmillan Cancer Support: www.macmillan.org.uk. Helpline open
seven days a week 8 a.m. to 8 p.m., 0808 808 00 00.

Maggie's Centres for cancer patients: www.maggiescentres.org, and at
your local main hospital.

Marie Curie: www.mariecurie.org.uk or call free on 0800 090 2309.

The MedicAlert Foundation, home alarm systems:
www.medicalert.org.uk. Phone: 01908 951045.

Middletons, mobility aids. 0800 999 4164.

Mind, infoline for mental health problems: www.mind.org.uk,
0300 123 3393.

Ministry of Justice: www.justice.gov.uk. 0203 334 3555.

Missing People: www.missingpeople.org.uk. You can call the charity
at any time of the day or night on Freefone 116 000.

Motorcycle Funerals: www.motorcyclefunerals.com. 01530 274888 or
0845 3752106.

My Decisions for Advance Statements: www.mydecisions.org.uk.

My Wishes, an app that helps you make your partner's wishes known,
including their will, advance care planning, funeral and bucket
list: www.mywishes.co.uk.

National Association of Funeral Directors: www.nafd.org.uk. Phone
line open Monday to Friday 9 a.m. to 5 p.m., 0121 711 1343.

National Counselling Society: www.nationalcounsellingsociety.org.
01903 200666.

National Debtline: www.nationaldebtline.org. 0808 808 4000.

National Health Service: www.nhs.uk.

The National Institute for Health and Care Excellence (NICE):
www.nice.org.uk. 0300 323 0140.

National Society of Allied and Independent Funeral Directors: www.saif.org.uk. 020 7520 3800.

The Natural Death Centre, independent funeral advice: www.naturaldeath.org.uk. Helpline: 01962 712690.

Nelson's Journey, charity for children in Norfolk up to the age of eighteen who have experienced the death of a parent: www.nelsonsjourney.org.uk. Helpline: 01603 431788.

Office for National Statistics: www.ons.gov.uk.

Office of the Public Guardian, email: customerservices@publicguardian.gov.uk. 0300 456 0300.

One World Memorials: www.oneworldmemorials.com (American).

Organ Donation: www.organdonation.nhs.uk.

Oxfam, charity focused on the alleviation of poverty: www.oxfam.org.uk. 0300 200 133.

Parnell Institute, provides a list of attachment-focused EMDR specialists, www.parnellemdr.com.

PETAL, for people experiencing trauma and loss through murder and culpable homicide in the Hamilton and Glasgow areas of Scotland: www.petalsupport.com. Helpline open Monday to Thursday 9 a.m. to 5 p.m., Friday 9 a.m. to 4 p.m., 01698 324 502.

Red Cross: www.redcross.org.uk. 0344 871 1111.

Royal College of Occupational Therapists: www.rcot.co.uk.

The Samaritans, charity offering support for all kinds of issues: www.samaritans.org. Helpline open 24 hours a day: 08457 909090.

Scattering Ashes: www.scattering-ashes.co.uk. 03192 581012.

Scottish Debt Advisor, a service offering help with debt relief, www.nationaldebtconsultant.co.uk. Phone line open seven days a week, 9 a.m. to 8 p.m., 0808 253 3673, free to all.

Simplicity Cremations: www.simplicitycremations.org.uk. Email: enquiries@simplicitycremations.co.uk. Phone: 0800 484 0514.

Simplicity Funerals: www.simplicity.co.uk. 0330 021 1010.

The Society of Later Life Advisers (SOLLA), email: admin@societyoflaterlifeadvisers.co.uk. 0333 2020 454.

Spare Room: www.spareroom.co.uk. Phone line open Monday to
Friday 9 a.m. to 8.30 p.m., weekends 10 a.m. to 7.30 p.m.,
0161 768 1162.

Sparkle, the national transgender charity: www.sparkle.org.uk

Statista, a commercial statistics firm: www.statista.com.

Step Change, free impartial debt advice: www.stepchange.org.
Helpline open Monday to Friday 8 a.m. to 8 p.m., Saturday
8 a.m. to 4 p.m., 0800 138 1111.

The Suicide Bereavement Support Partnership (SBSP), an umbrella
organisation for suicide support groups: www.uksobs.org.

Support after Murder and Manslaughter (SAMM):
www.samm.org.uk. 0121 472 2912 or 0845 872 3440.

Support after Suicide, does not give individual support but exists to
ensure support is available through various means, research,
signposting, advocacy and campaigning:
www.supportaftersuicide.org.uk.

Survivors of Bereavement by Suicide UK (SOBS): www.uksobs.org.
Helpline open Monday to Friday 9 a.m. to 9 p.m., 0300 111 5065.

Telecare 24, home alarm systems: www.telecare24.co.uk.

Turn2us, a national charity providing practical help to people who are
struggling financially: www.turn2us.org.uk.

UK Council for Psychotherapy: www.psychotherapy.org.uk.
020 7014 9955.

University of the Third Age: www.u3a.org.uk, phone line open
Monday to Friday 9.30 a.m. to 4.30 p.m., 020 8466 6139.

Urology Cancer research and Education (UCARE), an Oxford-based
charity committed to improving the treatment and care of
cancer patients nationally through research and education,
email: ucare@ucare-oxford.org.uk or phone 01865 767777
during office hours.

Victim Support Scotland, phone line open weekdays 8 a.m. to 8 p.m.,
0800 166 1985.

The Wedding Wishing Well Foundation:
> www.weddingwishingwell.org.uk, email:
> info@weddingwishingwell.org.uk. 07875 030393.

When They Get Older, useful information on all matters to do with
> the elderly: www.whentheygetolder.co.uk.

Which?, consumer advice organisation: www.which.co.uk. Phone line
> open Monday to Friday 8.30 a.m. to 6 p.m., Saturday 9 a.m. to
> 1 p.m., 029 2267 0000.

Winston's Wish, a charity supporting children and young people after
> the death of a parent or sibling: www.winstonswish.org.
> Helpline open Monday to Friday 9 a.m. to 5 p.m., 08088 020021.

Yuli Somme, felt shroud maker: www.bellacouche.com. 01647 441405.

Appendix 6
Questions That Might Help You Through the Process

Part One: A Terminal Diagnosis or Life-Threatening Illness – What Can I Do Immediately in Terms of Planning and Care?

Part Two: A Terminal Diagnosis or Life-Threatening Illness – What Can I Do to Plan for the Future?

Part Three: After Death Has Occurred – the Funeral and Immediate Decisions

Part Four: After Death Has Occurred – Registration of the Death, Probate and Looking to the Future

Bibliography

Blaisdell, B., *The Wit and Wisdom of Abraham Lincoln: A Book of Quotations*, Dover Thrift Editions, 2005.

Byrne, Eric, *Games People Play*, Grove Press, 1964.

Cantopher, Tim, *Dying for a Drink*, Sheldon Press, 1996.

Compassion in Dying, *A Guide to Your Rights at the End of Life*, www.compassionindying.org.uk, 0800 999 2434, University Press Information for Patients, Carers and Families, 2011.

Dietrich, A., and McDaniel, W. F., 'Endocannabinoids and Exercise', bmj.com, October 2004.

Doyle, Derek, *Oxford Textbook of Palliative Medicine*, 4th edition, Oxford, 2011.

Gawande, Atul, *Being Mortal: Illness, Medicine, and What Matters in the End*, Profile Books, 2015.

Government Choice of Accommodation Regulations. You can find this document on a search engine, looking for 'The Care and Support and After-care (Choice of Accommodation) Regulations 2014'.

Hardy, Thomas, *The Mayor of Casterbridge*, Smith, Elder and Co., 1886.

Iyer, Rukmini, *The Quick Roasting Tin: 30 Minute One Dish Dinners*, Square Peg, an imprint of Vintage, 2019.

Keogh, Abel, *Dating A Widower, Starting a Relationship With a Man Who's Starting Over*, Ben Lomond Press, 2011.

Kessler, David, *The Sixth Stage of Grief: Finding Meaning*, Simon & Schuster, 2019.

KidsHealth, www.kidshealth.org, 'Helping Your Child Deal with Death', on the website (American).

Kingsley, Philip, *Producing Your Own Will*, Straightforward Guides, 2003.

Klass, D., Silverman, P., and Nickman, S. L., *Continuing Bonds: A New Understanding of Grief*, Routledge, 1996.

Klein, Melanie, *The Psycho-Analysis of Children*, Vintage, 1932.

Kübler-Ross, Elisabeth, *On Death and Dying*, Macmillan, 1969.

Matthews, Jane, *The Carer's Handbook: Essential Information and Support for All Those in a Caring Role*, Robinson, 3rd edition, 2019.

National Institute for Health and Care Excellence, 'End of Life Care for Adults: Service Delivery' (NG142).

Neimeyer, Robert A., et al., 'Grief Therapy and the Reconstruction of Meaning: From Principles to Practice', *Journal of Contemporary Psychotherapy*, 10, 2009.

Office for National Statistics, 'National Survey of Bereaved People (VOICES): England, 2015', www.ons.gov.uk.

Oliver, Jamie, *Get Dead*, Friday Books, 2006.

Parnell, Laurel, *Tapping In: A Step-by-Step Guide to Activating Your Healing Resources Through Bilateral Stimulation*, Sounds True Inc., 2008.

Rowe, Dorothy, *The Successful Self*, HarperCollins, 2010.

The Scottish Government booklet, *What to Do After a Death in Scotland*, is available on the Scottish Government website, www.gov.scot, and is available in registration offices, or you can telephone 0131 244 2193.

Shepherd, Sue, and Gibson, Peter, *The Complete Low FODMAP Diet*, Vermilion, 2014.

Smith, Gordon, *Why Do Bad Things Happen?*, Hay House, 2009.

Stroebe, Margaret, and Schut, Henk, 'The Dual Process Model of Coping with Bereavement: A Decade On', *OMEGA – Journal of Death and Dying*, 61 (4), 2010.

SunLife, 'Cost of Dying Report 2018', www.sunlife.co.uk, 2019.

Tonkin, L., 'Growing Around Grief: Another Way of Looking at Grief and Recovery', *Bereavement Care*, 15 (1), 1996.

Van der Kolk, Bessel, *The Body Keeps the Score*, Penguin Books, 2014.

Walter, Tony, 'A New Model of Grief', *Mortality*, 1 (1), 1996.

Which?, *Making a Will: What to Watch Out For When Reviewing Yours*, Which? Publications, March 2019.

Which? Supplement, *Solutions for Living Independently*, Which? Publications, 2019.

Wienrich, Stephanie (ed.), *The Natural Death Handbook*, Ebury Publishing, 2006.

Worden, William J., *Grief Counselling and Grief Therapy: A Handbook for the Mental Health Practitioner*, Springer Publishing Company, 1991.

Further Reading

Understanding about Death and Dying
Mannix, Kathryn, *With the End in Mind*, William Collins, 2017.
> A thoughtful book by a palliative care doctor with many years of experience, which compassionately explains the process of dying through case studies. It is comforting, but it has been criticised in some quarters for being somewhat rose-tinted. See also her YouTube video.

Hammond, Joe, *A Short History of Falling: Everything I Observed About Love Whilst Dying*, Fourth Estate, 2019.
> A moving description of life with motor neurone disease (MND), when you have two small sons. Particularly strong on the benefits to both parties of asking for help.

Caring for the Living
Gerrard, Nicci, *What Dementia Teaches Us About Love*, Allen Lane, 2019.
> The death of the author's father from dementia and her belief that the disease and its impact on individuals, families and wider society needed light thrown upon it in order to improve the experience and support of those affected.

Planning the Funeral
Callender, R., et al., *The New Natural Death Handbook*, 5th edition, Strange Attractor, 2012. (This can only be obtained from The Natural Death Centre.)

Wynne Willson, J., *Funerals Without God*, 7th edition, British Humanist Association, 2014.

Oliver, Jamie, *Get Dead*, Friday Books, 2006.
> A quirky book about death and dying, containing interesting facts and figures and interviews with those intimately concerned with caring for the dead and those they have left behind.

Grief, Mourning and Starting a New Life

Cavendish, Camilla, *Extra Time*, HarperCollins, 2019.
> An inspirational look at a period of life that hitherto has seen people closing down and is now seen as an opportunity for opening up!

Didion, Joan, *The Year of Magical Thinking*, Alfred A. Knopf, 2005.
> A moving description of the loss of a husband by an accomplished writer.

Fuller, Susan L., *How to Survive Your Grief When Someone You Love Has Died*, self-published, 2007.
> Goes through all the possible responses people have to grief (a long list) and how to recognise and deal with them. I found advice like, 'If I can impart one piece of wisdom to you it is this: let your grief be the guide and follow it where it takes you. In the end your grief will heal you,' and, 'Look for the gifts that grief gives,' so very helpful. The voice feels like that of a kind and knowledgeable friend.

MacDonald, Helen, *H is for Hawk*, Jonathan Cape, 2014.
> A woman finds solace and understanding concerning the death of her father through the training of a hawk.

May, Todd, *Death*, Routledge, 2009.

> A philosopher puts forward a candid and thought-provoking view of how we might live our lives in view of the inescapability of our dying.

Rasmussen, Christina, *How to Let Go of Your Grief and Start Your New Life*, Hay House, 2013.

> The author lost her husband to cancer at age thirty. Her loss and intense grief led her to study how to change one's thought patterns, sending different messages down neural pathways. She explores, also, how to create new habits and behaviours to allow you to inhabit a different life. 'The day I accepted how different I had become because of my grief and realised I was no longer the person I used to be and that I could never go back – a doorway opened.'

Samuel, Julia, *Grief Works*, Penguin, 2017.

> A well-reviewed and critically acclaimed book, which includes many case studies, and is very supportive and inspiring.

Index